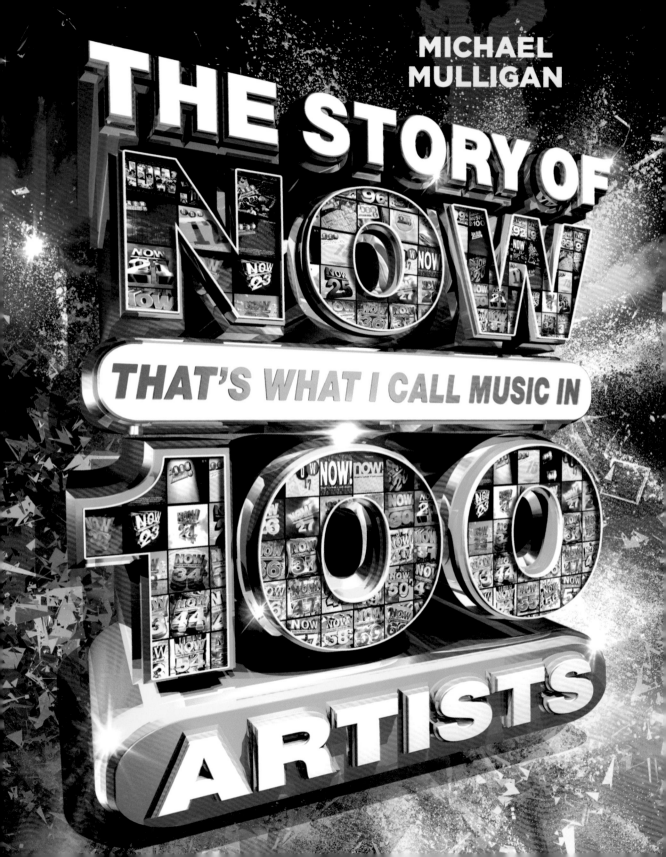

Dedicated to Sarah, with love

CONTENTS

TRAPEZE

INTRODUCTION

Let's rewind to November 1983. Billy Joel was number 1 in the singles chart with 'Uptown Girl', while Duran Duran topped the album chart with *Seven and the Ragged Tiger*. Channel 4 and their Friday evening music showcase *The Tube* were celebrating their first anniversary, ITV launched the comedy-drama *Auf Wiedersehen, Pet*, while the BBC marked the twentieth anniversary of *Doctor Who* with a ninety-minute special entitled *The Five Doctors*.

In the real world Margaret Thatcher was in year four of her eleven-year spell as Prime Minister, the first American cruise missiles arrived at RAF Greenham Common, and Stephen Manderson was born in Hackney, East London – later to grace a few editions of *NOW* as Professor Green.

The Virgin Records label was riding high on a post-punk, post-New Romantic boom, and still reaping the benefit of Mike Oldfield's ten-year-old *Tubular Bells* album. Tired of licensing their biggest hits to third parties who cared more for quantity than quality, Virgin decided to catalogue the last twelve months with 'thirty great tracks including eleven number ones' on a two-record or two-cassette package. And all just in time for the Christmas shopping season.

Of course, TV-advertised compilation albums were nothing new. When the first *NOW* entered the album chart there were fifteen other compilations in the Top 100. The CBS (later Sony) album *Reflections* – a collection of 'original instrumental hits' – spent ninety-two weeks in the chart, significantly longer than the fifty weeks that the first *NOW* hung around.

Telemarketing specialist Ronco topped the charts in early 1983 with *Raiders of the Pop Charts* ('Buy part one and get part two FREE when you buy this album'). It featured seven songs from the Virgin vaults, including the album's only number 1, 'Do You Really Want to Hurt Me' by Culture Club, though customers scanning through *Raiders*' thirty-strong track-listing must have scratched their heads at the non-chart padding provided by The Chaps and Precious Little.

For the first *NOW*, Virgin Records had the good sense to agree a partnership with EMI and include hits from twelve other labels – all killers, no fillers. And, more by accident than design, Virgin founder Richard Branson chanced upon a great brand name when he bought an antique poster advertising Danish bacon, featuring an image of a pig listening to a chicken singing. The caption read 'NOW, That's What I Call Music'.

When the first *NOW* album appeared on the shelves of Woolworths and Our Price on Monday 28 November 1983, Virgin couldn't have

4

known that they were creating a series that would become more iconic with each passing year. Michael Jackson's *Thriller* was the year's bestselling album – *NOW* finished a respectable seventh, despite only being available for the final five weeks.

The answer to why *NOW* has lasted so long lies in the answer to another question – 'Why is pop music so great?'. Regardless of whether you chose Duran Duran over Spandau Ballet, Blur over Oasis or Katy Perry over Lady Gaga, there are only two types of pop music – everything you like and everything you don't. *NOW* has never taken sides. *NOW* has never been judgemental. *NOW* has never been elitist – it is a celebration of pop as in 'popular', in whatever form or guise it should choose to take. The public gets what the public wants.

One of the most pleasant parts of compiling this book has been the amount of times we used the phrase 'and all of their number 1 singles are on *NOW*'. There have been more than 600 number 1 singles on *NOW*. Bob the Builder, Crazy Frog and Psy get equal billing alongside Calvin Harris, Coldplay and Adele. *NOW* is as natural a home for the multi-hit megastar as it is for the one-hit wonder. Each volume is a place for discovery, either by accident or for the curious mind. *NOW* is snapshot of a time and a place, with a track-listing and artwork that will inevitably become tinged by the rosy glow of nostalgia.

So welcome to our *NOW* user guide. This isn't a dry history of NOW; instead we've put the real stars of the series centre stage, picking a hundred heroes from the last thirty-five years. And while we will sing their praises, commend their collaborators, marvel at the moment and pay tribute to the trends, we will take the opportunity to explore the links with the other 2,000-plus artists who have made an appearance

– some obvious links, some rather tenuous, but as they sang on *NOW That's What I Call Disney* (2011), 'It's a small world after all'. Some historical knowledge maybe helpful – ask a responsible adult to explain what a double A-side or a MiniDisc was.

You can, if you wish, look back over any volume and put the songs into different categories – 'love that', 'forgotten all about that', 'not too keen on that' and 'what were they thinking?'. Spare a thought for all the tourists who only ever bought one *NOW* as a memento of their visit to this country. How many look back on their 1991 holiday and marvel that we were all listening to Hale & Pace and MC Nomad?

So, as two of our heroes, Robbie Williams and Kylie Minogue, once said, 'Jump on board, take a ride' (track 14 on *NOW 47*) – and 'read all about it', as the aforementioned Professor Green and Emeli Sandé would have it (track 23 on *NOW 80*, of course). Trivia, particularly pop trivia, may be information of little consequence, but no one ever complained that they knew too much.

PHIL COLLINS

Where better to start than side one, track one of the very first edition, with our honorary King of *NOW*, Phil Collins. With thirteen solo appearances and a further seven with **Genesis**, Phil is among the most decorated artists in *NOW* history, selling 100 million records worldwide as a solo artist and as part of a band. Both of his UK solo number 1 singles are captured for *NOW* posterity – 'You Can't Hurry Love' (*NOW 1*) and 'A Groovy Kind of Love' (*NOW 13*).

'You Can't Hurry Love' was written by legendary Motown songwriters Lamont Dozier and Eddie and Brian Holland, and originally released by The Supremes in 1966, when it peaked at number 3. Vocalist **Diana Ross** made the first of her own three appearances to date on *NOW 21* with 'When You Tell Me That You Love Me'. Collins would make a second Dozier-assisted appearance with 'Two Hearts' (*NOW 14*), which they co-wrote.

Phil's debut solo single 'In the Air Tonight' has been a hit on three separate occasions: reaching number 2 in 1981; a remixed version hitting number 4 in 1988 (*NOW 12*); and back in the charts once more in 2007 when a TV advert featuring a gorilla, a drum kit and a bar of chocolate helped it to number 14, and gave Phil his most recent appearance on *NOW 68*.

Erstwhile bandmates Genesis also loom large in *NOW* history, joining Phil on the very first volume with 'That's All'. They bowed out on *NOW 24* with a live recording of 'Invisible Touch' alongside former old boy **Peter Gabriel**, who also hung up his *NOW* spurs with 'Steam', after four appearances. Genesis guitarist Mike Rutherford, under the flimsy disguise of **Mike and the Mechanics**, carved his own name into *NOW* history on volumes 30 and 33, with 'Over My Shoulder' and 'All I Need Is a Miracle' respectively.

Madness · Culture Club · Kajagoogoo · Duran Duran
UB40 · Phil Collins · Paul Young · Tracey Ullman · Limahl · Genesis
Rod Stewart · Howard Jones · Simple Minds · The Cure · and many more . . .

That's What I Call Music

NOW 1 Did You Know . . .

Released on double vinyl and double cassette on 28 November 1983, the very first edition of *NOW That's What I Call Music* featured thirty songs, eleven of which were number 1 singles. Selling over 1.1 million copies, it spent five weeks at number 1 and topped the Christmas album chart. The original TV ad featured a voiceover from comedian **Tracey Ullman**, who also graced the first two volumes as a recording artist in her own right. Later ads for this first volume replaced her with Cockney DJ Gary Crowley, who did not.

NOW 68 Did You Know . . .

Velvet Underground legend and pop curmudgeon **Lou Reed** made his sole credited *NOW* appearance on volume 68 with 'Tranquilize', alongside **The Killers**. However, it's not the first time Lou had been heard on an edition of *NOW* – the charity cover version of his own 'Perfect Day' credited to **Various Artists** appeared in 1998 on *NOW 39*. The number 1 single sold over a million-and-a-half copies. The Velvet Underground have never appeared on a *NOW*.

13 NOW appearances

'You Can't Hurry Love',
NOW 1, November 1983

'In The Air Tonight',
NOW 68, November 2...

IN OTHER NEWS . . . *NOW 1* (NOVEMBER 1983)

The Colour of Magic by Terry Pratchett was published. The first of forty-one *Discworld* books, the series has sold more than 80 million copies worldwide to date.

The ITV children's series *Danger Mouse* attracted an audience of 21.6 million viewers, a record for a British children's programme. 'Crumbs, DM!'

Influential British graphic artist Barney Bubbles died at the age of 41. He designed record sleeves for the likes of Elvis Costello, Ian Dury and **The Damned**, and later directed promo videos, including **The Specials**' 'Ghost Tow...

80s

NOW 1 Did You Know . . .

Some Men made their only appearance on *NOW 1*. **Men at Work** had four Top 40 hits but enjoyed only a single number 1 with 'Down Under'; they enjoyed it slightly less when, in 2010, the Federal Court of Australia ruled that it borrowed a substantial part of 'Kookaburra', a 1932 song by Marion Sinclair. Elsewhere on *NOW 1* Canadian one-hit wonders **Men Without Hats** had their moment in the sun with their number 6 song 'The Safety Dance'.

NOW 31 Did You Know . . .

NOW 31 kicked off with a Caledonian couple, starting with Clydebank popsters **Wet Wet Wet** making the seventh of nine appearances with the number 7 hit 'Don't Want to Forgive Me Now'. Next up was Edinburgh-born **Edwyn Collins** enjoying his biggest hit to date with the number 4 song 'A Girl Like You'. In 1979 Edwyn had co-founded the influential independent label Postcard Records, launching the career of both his own band Orange Juice and fellow Scots Aztec Camera.

IN OTHER NEWS . . . *NOW 31* (JULY 1995)

US rom-com *Clueless* opened at cinemas. Based loosely on Jane Austen's *Emma*, the (really rather good) soundtrack includes **Supergrass** hit 'Alright' (*NOW 31*). The 2014 video for 'Fancy' by **Iggy Azalea** featuring **Charli XCX** (*NOW 88*) was a homage to *Clueless*.

Amazon.com sold its first book: Douglas Hofstadter's *Fluid Concepts and Creative Analogies: Computer Models of the Fundamental Mechanisms of Thought*.

'Boom Boom Boom' by The Outhere Brothers (*NOW 31*) was number 1 for the whole month . . .

10
NOW appearances

'Is There Something I Should Know?',
NOW 1, November 1983

'White Lines (Don't Do It)',
Duran Duran featuring Melle Mel and Grandmaster Flash and The Furious Five,
NOW 31, July 1995

DURAN DURAN

History will always show that **Phil Collins** was track 1, side 1 of *NOW 1*, but Messrs Le Bon, Rhodes, Taylor, Taylor and Taylor were only two minutes and fifty-three seconds behind him, with their first number 1, 'Is There Something I Should Know?'. As if to compensate for this, the good folk at *NOW* would allow the beau Brummies top billing for three of their subsequent appearances, with 'The Reflex' (*NOW 3*), 'A View to a Kill' (*NOW 5*) and 'Notorious' (*NOW 8*) all being allowed to open proceedings.

It has always been considered a 'big thing' to record a James Bond film theme, but until **Sam Smith**'s 'Writing's on the Wall' (*NOW 92*) broke the duck in 2015, none of the previous twenty-three efforts had been able to claim the number 1 slot. Both 'View to a Kill' and **Adele**'s 2012 theme to *Skyfall* had to settle for number 2, with the Duranies frustrated by **Paul Hardcastle**'s '19' and Adele's path blocked by **Swedish House Mafia**'s 'Don't You Worry Child' (*NOW 83*).

In 1985 the band took a hiatus, but the gnomes of *NOW* were still kept busy with two offshoot projects. Taylors John and Andy partnered with **Robert Palmer** and **Chic** drummer Tony Thompson to form **The Power Station**. Their cover of the T. Rex song 'Get It On (Bang a Gong)' was a number 22 hit and appeared on *NOW 5*. Meanwhile, Roger Taylor, along with Simon Le Bon and Nick Rhodes, formed **Arcadia**; their single 'Election Day' reached number 7 and was featured on *NOW 6*.

In 1995 Duran Duran went 'all New York' on us, releasing two singles synonymous with the Big Apple. In addition to releasing a cover of **Lou Reed**'s 'Perfect Day', the band served up a version of the anti-drugs rap anthem 'White Lines (Don't Do It)' (*NOW 31*), and even roped in original performers **Melle Mel**, Grandmaster Flash and The Furious Five to help out. The original version appeared on *NOW 3* and was a number 7 hit, while the Duran Duran cover reached number 17 and was the last *NOW* appearance to date for all concerned.

80s

NOW 1 Did You Know . . .

Demonstrating that pop moved pretty fast in 1983, the first *NOW* includes **Kajagoogoo**'s biggest hit 'Too Shy', the debut single from the now former Kajagoogoo singer **Limahl** 'Only For Love' and the first post-Limahl Kajagoogoo single 'Big Apple'. Only Limahl would be back on future volumes – his 'The Never Ending Story' can be found on *NOW 4*.

NOW 56 Did You Know . . .

Los Angeles rap trio 213 never had a hit, but the individual members did, including **Nate Dogg**, who partnered with **50 Cent** for '21 Questions', a number 6 single and his only *NOW* appearance. **Warren G**'s two NOW appearances are 'Smokin' Me Out' (*NOW 37*) and 'Prince Igor' (*NOW 39*), which borrows a melody from an 1888 composition by Alexander Borodin. The trio was completed by **Snoop Dogg**, whose five *NOW* appearances – all collaborations – include the number 1 'California Gurls' (*NOW 76*), with **Katy Perry**.

IN OTHER NEWS . . . *NOW 56* (NOVEMBER 2003)

Channel 4 broadcast the last episode of *Brookside*. The popular, and sometimes controversial, Liverpool-based soap opera ran for twenty-one years.

Singer Bobby Hatfield died aged 63. As one half of **The Righteous Brothers** he had a number 1 in 1990 with 'Unchained Melody' (*NOW 18*), after the twenty-five-year-old song was used in the film *Ghost*.

Arnold Schwarzenegger was sworn in as Governor of California. He had announced his decision to run for office back in August on *The Tonight Show with Jay Leno*.

13
NOW appearances
'Red Red Wine',
NOW 1, November 1983
'Swing Low',
NOW 56, November 2003

UB40

Our dear friends UB40 have a long and illustrious history with *NOW*, featuring thirteen times in the first twenty years, including all three of their number 1 singles. Seven of these appearances are documented on the first ten *NOW*s, including two entries – 'Red Red Wine' and 'Please Don't Make Me Cry' – on the inaugural edition.

Of their thirteen appearances, nine have been cover versions and four have been recorded in collaboration with other artists. Serial collaborator **Chrissie Hynde** has made as many appearances alongside UB40 as she has with her own band **The Pretenders**, including the 1985 number 1 'I Got You Babe' (*NOW 6*) and a cover version of **Dusty Springfield**'s 'Breakfast in Bed' (*NOW 13*). Following her death in March 1999, Dusty made her own solitary *NOW* appearance on *NOW 42*, with 'You Don't Have to Say You Love Me'.

'I'll Be Your Baby Tonight', credited to **Robert Palmer** featuring UB40 on *NOW 18*, is one of only a few associated appearances for Bob Dylan. Never appearing as an artist in his own right, Dylan originally recorded this song in 1967. In a delightful turn of *NOW* synchronicity, a few years later Dylan would record his own version of 'Can't Help Falling in Love', a worldwide smash for UB40 in 2003 that kicked off *NOW 26*. Keeping up?

UB40's anti-apartheid anthem 'Sing Our Own Song' (*NOW 7*) featured a list of illustrious backing vocalists, among them British singer-songwriter **Jaki Graham**. Graham herself has four *NOW* appearances to her name, all of them consecutive (*NOW 5* to *NOW 8*). 'Mated' – her *NOW 6* entry with **David Grant** – was written by maverick rock wunderkind Todd Rundgren, who sadly plays no further part in this story.

80s

NOW 1 Did You Know . . .

Although **Malcolm McLaren** will be remembered for his management 'skills' – Sex Pistols, Adam and the Ants, Bow Wow Wow – he had six Top 40 hits of his own, including the number 3 'Double Dutch' (*NOW 1*). In 1999 it returned to the charts when Dope Smugglaz took their version, 'Double Double Dutch', to number 15. Malcolm's second appearance was 'Madam Butterfly' (*NOW 4*), Puccini's entire 1904 opera condensed into a six-minute dance track.

NOW 43 Did You Know . . .

Dutch trance outfit **Alice Deejay** made the first of three appearances with the 1999 number 2 'Better Off Alone' (actually credited to **DJ Jurgen** presents Alice Deejay for this one release). It was the first of five Top 40 hits in an eighteen-month spell that included 'Back in My Life' (*NOW 44*) and 'Will I Ever' (*NOW 46*). In 2012 **David Guetta** sampled 'Better Off Alone' for his number 6 single 'Play Hard' (*NOW 85*), featuring **Ne-Yo** and **Akon**.

IN OTHER NEWS . . . *NOW 1* (NOVEMBER 1983)

Michael Jackson released his single 'Thriller'. Promoted with an innovative fourteen-minute video, it peaked at number 10, though it would chart again, reaching number 12 shortly after his death in 2009.

ITV broadcast the first episode of the sitcom *Up the Elephant and Round the Castle*, starring Jim Davidson and Anita Dobson, and with theme music by Keith Emerson of Emerson, Lake and Palmer.

American rapper Nayvadius Wilburn was born in Atlanta, Georgia. As **Future** he made his first *NOW* appearance with **Ariana Grande** on 'Everyday' (*NOW 96*).

6
NOW appearances

'Karma Chameleon', *NOW 1*, November 1983

'Your Kisses Are Charity', *NOW 43*, July 1999

CULTURE CLUB

Ambition, androgyny, big hats and even bigger tunes, Culture Club were a cornerstone of the very first edition of *NOW* with not one, but two entries: 'Karma Chameleon', a number 1 single in thirty countries, and 'Victims', a Christmas number 3, held at bay by **Slade**'s 'My Oh My' and the **Flying Pickets**' 'Only You' (*NOW 3*). As with their 1983 number 2 'Church of the Poison Mind', 'Victims' featured singer Helen Terry, who had one solo Top 40 hit with 'Love Lies Lost' in 1984 before moving into TV production. Since 2001 she has been executive producer of *The BRIT Awards*.

Boy George appeared once under his own name with 'Everything I Own' (*NOW 9*), and once with **Jesus Loves You** and 'Bow Down Mister' (*NOW 19*). The latter included vocals from legendary Indian singer Asha Bhosle, star of a thousand Bollywood movies, heroine of **Cornershop**'s 1998 number 1 'Brimful of Asha' (*NOW 39*) and recognised by *The Guinness Book of Records* as the most recorded artist in music history. And while we're playing 'Spot the Collaborator', that's Claire Torry of 'Dark Side of the Moon' fame joining Culture Club on the 1984 number 2 'The War Song' (*NOW 4*).

Released by **E-Zee Possee** featuring **MC Kinky,** the acid-house anthem 'Everything Starts with an E' (*NOW 17*) features lyrics written by Boy George credited to his 'Angela Dust' persona. Banned by the BBC, the single started life as an instrumental by one-time Haysi Fantayzee frontman **Jeremy Healy**, who would return six years later with 'Stamp!' (*NOW 35*) by Jeremy Healy and **Amos**. MC Kinky, aka Caron Geary, would pop up as ragamuffin toaster on **Erasure**'s only number 1, 'Take a Chance on Me' (*NOW 22*).

Culture Club split in 1986 but were 'back back back' in 1998 with the number 4 'I Just Wanna Be Loved' (*NOW 41*), and one last Top 40 hit the following year, 'Your Kisses Are Charity' (*NOW 43*). Pre-Culture Club, drummer Jon Moss auditioned for The Clash, toured with **The Damned** and The Stranglers, and appeared on Adam and the Ants' 1981 single 'Cartrouble'. Jon's first band, London, enjoyed fleeting success but split after one album. Their singer, Riff Regan, pursued a career as scriptwriter for both Frankie Howerd and sitcom *Birds of a Feather*.

80s

NOW 1 Did You Know . . .

Since volume 1, *NOW* has been the natural home of the One Hit Wonder. So it proved with music photographer Lynn Goldsmith, who – under the pseudonym **Will Powers** – scored a number 17 hit with 'Kissing With Confidence'. The song was co-written by **Steve Winwood**, who appeared on *NOW 8* with 'Higher Love', and **Nile Rodgers**. So far Nile's only appearance as a credited artist was on *NOW 94*, with 'Give Me Your Love' by **Sigala** featuring **John Newman** and Nile Rodgers.

NOW 44 Did You Know . . .

A cover of 'Tragedy' by the **Bee Gees** means **Steps** had as many songs on *NOW* written by Barry, Robin and Maurice Gibb as the Bee Gees managed themselves. The Brothers Gibb have a more impressive showing as songwriters: another ten acts, including **Jimmy Somerville**, **Kim Wilde** and **Boyzone**, have covered a Bee Gees song and seen it appear on a volume of *NOW*.

IN OTHER NEWS . . . *NOW 44* (NOVEMBER 1999)

A 22-year-old University of Oregon student, Jeffrey Levy, became the first person in the US to be prosecuted for illegally downloading music and films from the internet.

The English writer and actor Quentin Crisp died at the age of 90. Crisp was the subject of the **Sting** song 'Englishman in New York', which featured on *NOW 18*.

After thirty-two years BBC Television retired the original screen saver, their famous Test Card F. You might know it better as 'small girl playing noughts

14
NOW appearances
'Let's Stay Together',
NOW 1, November 1983
'When the Heartache Is Over',
NOW 44, November 1999

TINA TURNER

Remarkably, 'Let's Stay Together' was Tina Turner's first solo UK hit single, peaking at number 6 in late 1983. It was the first of thirty Top 40 singles for Tina in the UK, and was produced by Martyn Ware and Ian Craig Marsh's British Electric Foundation. Ware and Marsh are better known for their **Heaven 17** incarnation, appearing separately on the first *NOW* with their number 2 hit 'Temptation'. It was kept off the top spot by Spandau Ballet's 'True'.

Grammy-award winning 'What's Love Got to Do with It' on *NOW 3* was written by British songwriters Terry Britten and Graham Lyle. They struck gold for Tina again on *NOW 6* with 'We Don't Need Another Hero (Thunderdome)'. Former England rugby captain Lawrence Dallaglio appeared on the single as a schoolboy singing backing vocals with the Kings House Choir.

Closing off the second side of *NOW 4*, the number 26 hit 'Private Dancer' was written by Mark Knopfler but never used by his group Dire Straits. Despite sales of over a hundred-million albums and five Top 40 hits between 1985 and 1986 alone, Dire Straits remain one of the biggest bands of all time not to appear on a *NOW* release. However, Mark does have one additional *NOW* credit, as 'Relax' by **Deetah** (*NOW 41*) samples 'Why Worry' from Dire Straits' 1985 album *Brothers in Arms*.

With fourteen *NOW* entries spanning the first *NOW* to *NOW 44*, Ms Turner is by some distance the most garlanded 'Tina' in *NOW* history. 'It's Only Love' – a duet on *NOW 6* with **Bryan Adams** – ensured that the Canadian rocker could also lay claim to being the most chronicled 'Bryan', although he has little chance of claiming the 'Adams' crown if William Adams, aka **will.i.am**, and his twenty-plus credits stakes

80s

NOW 1 Did You Know . . .

Howard Jones's career got off to a flyer when he made his chart and *NOW* debut with the 1983 number 3 'New Song', swiftly followed by his biggest hit 'What Is Love?', which was only denied the top spot by **Paul McCartney** and 'Pipes of Peace' (both *NOW 2*). Howard's last appearance was 'Life in One Day' (*NOW 5*), with backing vocals from the Afrodiziak trio, who can also be heard on **Madness**' 'Michael Caine' (*NOW 2*) and 'Nelson Mandela' (*NOW 3*) by **The Special AKA**.

NOW 32 Did You Know . . .

'Gangsta's Paradise' provided **Coolio** with his only number 1 in October 1995. Featuring guest vocals from one **L.V.** (short for Large Variety, apparently), it sampled Stevie Wonder's 1976 song 'Pastime Paradise'. In Australia it spent fourteen weeks at number 1, a record that stood for twenty-two years until broken by **Ed Sheeran**'s 'The Shape of You'. Coolio's only other *NOW* appearance was 'C U When U Get There' (*NOW 37*), which used music from Johann Pachelbel's seventeenth-century 'Canon In D Major', also the source for **The Farm**'s 1990 number 4 'All Together Now'.

IN OTHER NEWS . . . NOW 32 (NOVEMBER 1995)

ITV broadcast six episodes of *The Beatles Anthology* documentary series. The following month a 'new' single, 'Free As a Bird', charted at number 2, behind **Michael Jackson**'s 'Earth Song'.

The seventeenth James Bond film, *GoldenEye*, opened in cinemas. It was the first of four films starring Pierce Brosnan in the lead role.

Alan Hull, singer and guitarist with the folk-rock band Lindisfarne, died, aged 50. In 1990 they had a number 2 hit with 'Fog on the Tyne', featuring footballer Paul Gascoigne.

6

NOW appearances

'(Keep Feeling) Fascination',
NOW 1, November 1983

'Don't You Want Me',
NOW 32, November 1995

THE HUMAN LEAGUE

Twenty-four months after the seismic success of their *Dare* album, Philip Oakey led The Human League to *NOW* glory across two quite distinct periods. Phase one began with their number 2 single '(Keep Feeling) Fascination', blocked in a quest for their second chart topper by Spandau Ballet's 'True'. Although we mourn the lack of Spandau appearances, main man Gary Kemp has two writing credits, as 'True' was sampled for **P.M. Dawn**'s 1991 number 3 'Set Adrift on Memory's Bliss' (*NOW 20*) and **Nelly**'s 2005 number 6 'N Dey Say' (*NOW 61*).

In the three years between '(Keep Feeling) Fascination' and 'Human' (*NOW 8*), songwriter Jo Callis – formerly of Scottish new-wave band The Rezillos – had departed and the League drafted in powerhouse production duo Jimmy Jam and Terry Lewis. Jam and Lewis's most prolific partnership was with **Janet Jackson**, who made her own debut with 'What Have You Done for Me Lately?', one track ahead of 'Human' on *NOW 8*. Another Jam and Lewis song, 'Love Is All That Matters' (*NOW 13*), stalled at number 41 and marked the start of a seven-year gap before our next sighting of The Human League.

Phase two began with the 1995 number 6 'Tell Me When' (*NOW 30*), their best chart position since their first appearance thirteen years earlier. Along with 'One Man in My Heart' (*NOW 31*), it was produced by Ian Stanley, previously a member of **Tears for Fears** and co-writer of their 1984 number 4 'Shout'. A re-release of the global smash 'Don't You Want Me' (*NOW 32*) – 1.6 million UK sales and counting – is the last entry for the band to date, although **The Farm** had carved their name on the *NOW* tablet with their own inimitable interpretation on *NOW 23*.

A fertile breeding ground for the post-punk synth sound, Sheffield not only spawned The Human League, but also **ABC** (a solitary entry in the canon – 'When Smokey Sings' on *NOW 10*) and **Heaven 17**, consisting of Human League founding members Martyn Ware and Ian Craig Marsh, alongside old pal Glenn Gregory. Their *NOW* career consists of a succinct three-song catalogue, topped and tailed by two different versions of 'Temptation' (*NOW 1* and *NOW 23*), with distinctive guest vocals from Carol Kenyon, who can also be heard on **Robbie Nevil**'s only appearance, 'C'est la Vie' (*NOW 9*).

SIMPLE MINDS

Simple Minds began their music career as short-lived punk outfit Johnny and the Self-Abusers. After one unsuccessful single the band morphed into Simple Minds, taking their name from the lyrics to **David Bowie**'s song 'The Jean Genie'. Their first appearance on *NOW 1* coincided with a move away from early art-rock efforts to the anthemic sound typified by their number 13 hit 'Waterfront'. Their big break came when their 1985 single 'Don't You (Forget About Me)' (*NOW 5*) was used in the film *The Breakfast Club*, resulting in a US number 1.

'Don't You (Forget About Me)' is the only one of Simple Minds' eight *NOW* appearances not written by the band. That honour goes to Steve Schiff and Keith Forsey. In the eighties the latter was the 'go-to guy' for soundtrack hits, gifting the world gems like **Limahl**'s 'The Never Ending Story' (*NOW 4*), along with 'Flashdance … What a Feeling' for Irene Cara, and 'The Heat Is On' for Glenn Frey (from *Beverly Hills Cop*).

Clocking in at six minutes and thirty-nine seconds, 'Belfast Child' (*NOW 14*) is one of the longest-ever number 1 singles, and one of the longest songs on *NOW*. However, it can't lay claim to either title: the longest number 1 is 'All Around the World' by **Oasis** (nine minutes and thirty-eight seconds) while the longest song on *NOW* is **Don McLean**'s number 2 hit 'American Pie' (eight minutes and twenty-seven seconds) on *NOW 20*. And to round it all off, the longest number 1 on *NOW* is **Meat Loaf**'s 'I'd Do Anything for Love (But I Won't Do That)' (seven minutes and fifty-eight seconds) on *NOW 26*.

Suggesting that it is one big happy family at *NOW*, in 1984 singer Jim Kerr was married to **Chrissie Hynde** of **The Pretenders** (three *NOW* appearances as a solo artist plus two with her band). He later married actress Patsy Kensit, who at some time or other was married to **Liam Gallagher** (one solo *NOW* appearance and thirteen with Oasis), Dan Donovan of **Dreadzone** (one *NOW* appearance) and former Haysi Fantayzee frontman turned DJ **Jeremy Healy** (one *NOW* appearance).

80s

NOW 1 Did You Know . . .

Get ready to dance around your handbags to 'Give It Up', the only *NOW* appearance and only number 1 single by **KC and the Sunshine Band**. However, our friendship with Harry Wayne Casey and his crew didn't end there; in 1992 **KWS** scored their only number 1 with a cover of 'Please Don't Go' (*NOW 22*), while the 1998 number 2 from **Bamboo**, 'Bamboogie' (*NOW 39*), sampled the Florida outfit's 1975 number 21 'Get Down Tonight'.

NOW 30 Did You Know . . .

Sting's first *NOW* appearance came courtesy of 'An Englishman in New York' on *NOW 18*. His second and so far final *NOW* appearance came on volume 30, when he teamed up with English reggae singer **Pato Banton** for 'The Cowboy Song'. Both Sting singles peaked at number 15. Pato managed three further *NOW* appearances: 'Baby Come Back' (*NOW 29*) featuring **UB40** siblings **Ali and Robin Campbell**, 'Bubbling Hot' (*NOW 30*) and 'Groovin'' (*NOW 34*).

8
NOW appearances
'Waterfront',
NOW 1, November 1983
'She's a River',
NOW 30, April 1995

IN OTHER NEWS . . . *NOW 30* (APRIL 1995)

Channel 4 broadcast the American sitcom *Friends* and the hospital drama *ER* for the first time in the UK.

Chris Evans took over the BBC Radio 1 *Breakfast Show* from Steve Wright. And in (probably) related news . . .

Wake Up!, the fourth album by **The Boo Radleys**, entered the album chart at number 1. The lead single 'Wake Up Boo!' peaked at number 9 and is included on *NOW 30*, their only appearance to date.

80s

DOUBLE CD, CASSETTE & MINIDISC

NOW 1 Did You Know . . .

New Edition had four Top 40 hits between 1983 and 1997 but never matched their number 1 debut 'Candy Girl', co-written by Maurice Starr, also responsible for both New Kids on the Block number 1s. In 1985 the band parted company with **Bobby Brown**, but he recovered to make four more *NOW* appearances, have fifteen Top 40 hits and marry **Whitney Houston**. Three of those that Bobby left behind managed one Top 40 hit as Bell Biv DeVoe, as did fifth member Ralph Tresvant, as a solo artist.

NOW 43 Did You Know . . .

R&B trio **Fierce** made their first appearance with 'Dayz Like That', a 1999 number 11. The song was co-written by Michelle Escoffery, who had greater success when she wrote 'Just a Little' (*NOW 52*) and gave **Liberty X** their only number 1. She also had a hit as an artist, singing on 'Think About Me', the fifth Top 40 single for **Artful Dodger**. Fierce made their second and final appearance with 'Sweet Love 2K' (*NOW 45*), a re-working of Anita Baker's only Top 40 hit, in 1986.

IN OTHER NEWS . . . *NOW 43* (JULY 1999)

Garbage headlined a concert in Edinburgh to mark the opening of the new, devolved Scottish Parliament.

Spice Girls singer Victoria Adams married footballer David Beckham at Luttrellstown Castle, near Dublin, Ireland.

Actor Bill Owen died, aged 85. For twenty-seven years he played Compo in the BBC comedy *Last of the Summer Wine*, though in the sixties he had success writing songs for **Cliff Richard** and Engelbert Humperdinck.

7
NOW appearances

'The Sun and the Rain',
NOW 1, November 1983

'Lovestruck',
NOW 43, July 1999

MADNESS

The seven talented members of **Madness** all wrote at least one of their appearances, with pianist Mike 'Barso' Barson writing their first, 'The Sun and the Rain' (*NOW 1*), and their last, 'Lovestruck' (*NOW 43*), the latter with saxophonist Lee 'Kix' Thompson, who also wrote 'Uncle Sam' (*NOW 6*) with guitarist Chris 'Chrissy Boy' Foreman. Master-of-ceremonies and trumpet-player Cathal 'Chas Smash' Smyth wrote 'Michael Caine' (*NOW 2*) with drummer Dan 'Woody' Woodgate, while singer Graham '**Suggs**' MacPherson and bass player Mark 'Bedders' Bedford conclude our nickname-laden statistic with 'One Better Day' (*NOW 3*).

No nickname for Labi Siffre, but he provided the band with their tenth Top 40 hit, 'It Must Be Love'.

A number 14 hit for Labi in 1971, Madness' version reached number 4 in 1981 and number 6 in 1992, resulting in its appearance on *NOW 21*. **Tracey Ullman** made her second appearance on *NOW 2* with 'My Guy', a gender re-arrangement of Madness' 1980 number 3 'My Girl', while Dan Woodgate can be found behind the drums on both **Voice of the Beehive** appearances, 'Don't Call Me Baby' (*NOW 12*) and 'I Think I Love You' (*NOW 20*).

Throughout the eighties, Camden's finest spent a total of 214 weeks in the singles chart, a record they share with our old friends **UB40**. That Suggs and co achieved their tally by 1986 – when the band first split – makes it even more impressive. Suggs also made two solo appearances, both cover

versions, with The Beatles' 'I'm Only Sleeping' (*NOW 32*) and Simon and Garfunkel's 'Cecilia' (*NOW 34*), the latter featuring **Louchie Lou** and **Michie One**, who made their own debut on *NOW 25* with 'Shout (It Out)'.

Madness – minus Suggs – accompanied **Feargal Sharkey** on his Cathal-penned solo debut 'Listen to Your Father' (*NOW 4*), also the first single released on the band's own Zarjazz label. Feargal appeared once more, with the Maria McKee-written number 1 'A Good Heart' (*NOW 6*). In the early nineties both Suggs and Cathal provided backing vocals for perpetual axe-grinder and three-time *NOW* entrant **Morrissey**, who graciously wrote his 1992 Top 40 single 'You're the One for Me, Fatty' in tribute to Cathal.

80s

NOW 2 **Did You Know . . .**

Only two volumes old and the die was cast. There were already six acts making their second appearance on the fledgling *NOW* series, while 'hot property de jour' **Culture Club** were notching up their third. After just two appearances we said 'goodbye' to Kajagoogoo and Tracey Ullman, and twenty-one artists were destined to be filed under the 'one-*NOW* wonder category. Fifteen number 1 singles had been included and we had our first eight cover versions.

NOW 54 **Did You Know . . .**

Of the forty-two songs on *NOW 54*, eight had their roots in reality TV shows. **Kym Marsh**, **Darius** and **Liberty X** all emerged from ITV's *Popstars*, **Girls Aloud** and **One True Voice** from the follow-up series *Popstars: The Rivals*, while **David Sneddon**, **Sinéad Quinn** and **Ainslie Henderson** were all graduates of the BBC show *Fame Academy*.

IN OTHER NEWS . . . *NOW 2* (MARCH 1984)

Andrew Lloyd Webber's 'rock musical' *Starlight Express* opened at the Victoria Apollo Theatre in London. It ran for over 7,400 performances, eventually closing in January 2002.

Arnold Ridley, the veteran British actor, died at the age of 88. He was best known for playing Private Godfrey in the sitcom *Dad's Army*.

The romantic comedy *Romancing The Stone* opened in cinemas. Starring Michael Douglas, Kathleen Turner and Danny DeVito, it was one of the Top 10 biggest films of 1984, although the theme song by **Eddy Grant** could only make it to number 52.

13
NOW appearances
'Radio Ga Ga',
NOW 2, March 1984
'Flash', by Queen and Vanguard
NOW 54, April 2003

QUEEN

300-million record sales worldwide, the biggest-selling album of all time in the UK (*Greatest Hits* – six million and counting) and thirteen regal entries in the *NOW* canon, Queen also hold the distinction of all four members having written a hit single featured on *NOW*: Roger Taylor ('Radio Ga Ga', *NOW 2*), John Deacon ('I Want to Break Free', *NOW 3*), **Freddie Mercury** ('Bohemian Rhapsody' *NOW 21*), and **Brian May** ('Too Much Love Will Kill You', *NOW 33*).

Cumulatively, the Queen family contribute twenty tracks over the years – on top of the thirteen Queen inclusions there are four additional entries from Freddie Mercury and three from Brian May. May's last appearance – and the last Queen-related appearance to date – was in support of be-hatted pop ragamuffin **Dappy** on his 2012 hit 'Rockstar' (*NOW 81*).

Freddie Mercury had the second of nine solo Top 40 hits with 'Barcelona' (*NOW 10*), a duet with Spanish soprano **Montserrat Caballé**. 'Barcelona' would not be Queen's first brush with opera on *NOW*. The opening melody of 'It's a Hard Life' (*NOW 4*) is based on Ruggero Leoncavallo's aria 'Vesti la giubba' from the opera *Pagliacci*. In 2000, the English tenor Russell Watson recorded a version of 'Barcelona' for his debut album; his duet partner of choice was Shaun Ryder of **Happy Mondays**.

Queen's most recent appearance, 'Flash' (*NOW 54*), reached number 15 in March 2003 and was a remix of Queen's 1980 number 10 single by German duo **Vanguard**. In 2013, Brian May released a new version of this song entitled 'Save The Badger Badger Badger'. Both songs include a contribution from larger-than-life actor Brian Blessed but 'Badger' would only make number 79.

80s

NIK KERSHAW

'A young man who's had nothing but hits' – not our words, but those of the venerable Radio 1 rock-jock Tommy Vance as he introduced Nicholas David Kershaw to the Live Aid stage. And in July 1985 that was hard to dispute – six Top 40 singles, two Top 10 albums within the space of nine months, and three-quarters of the way through a taut but admirable four-song run across the first six *NOW* releases. With sixty-two weeks in the Top 40 singles chart between 1984 and 1985, Kershaw was the biggest-selling solo artist in the UK.

'Wouldn't It Be Good' (*NOW 2*) was the first of four Kershaw singles to feature a video directed by legendary British graphic designer Storm Thorgerson, who, as part of the Hipgnosis collective, conceived some of the most iconic album sleeves of all time, from **Genesis** to **Paul McCartney** and Led Zeppelin to **Muse**. A schoolboy contemporary of Pink Floyd, he was responsible for all but three of the band's album sleeves, including the ubiquitous *Dark Side of the Moon* design. Pink Floyd have yet to appear on *NOW*

A featured artist on *NOW*s 2, 3 and 4, and a cover star on two of those, Nik Kershaw's final appearance and last Top 40 hit to date can be found in the shape of 'When a Heart Beats' (*NOW 6*). On the same edition, Kershaw can be heard on 'Nikita' by **Elton John** – his highest charting single for nine years – providing both guitar and backing vocals alongside **George Michael**. Despite a second **Wham!** appearance with 'Edge of Heaven' (*NOW 7*), it would be *NOW 22* and another collaboration with Elton before George's first credited contribution.

The second act of Nik's career brought perhaps his most famous hit – the monster smash 'The One and Only', which he wrote for Chesney Hawkes. Number 1 in nine countries and a Top 10 hit in the US, it was taken from the Hawkes-starring film, *Buddy's Song*, and dislodged 'The Stonk' (*NOW 19*) by **Hale and Pace** and **The Stonkers** at the top before it was dethroned by another movie hit, 'Shoop Shoop Song (It's in His Kiss)' by **Cher**. Both the film themes spent five weeks at number 1 and, shame on us, neither were chronicled by *NOW*

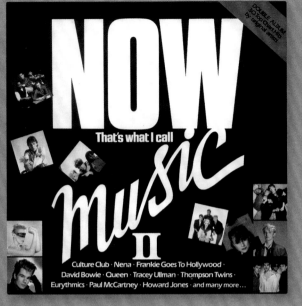

80s

NOW 2 Did You Know . . .

For Thin Lizzy *NOW* came a little too late in the day, but two of the band's guitarists made solo appearances, beginning with **Snowy White** and his only Top 40 hit 'Bird of Paradise'. **Gary Moore** paired up with Thin Lizzy frontman **Phil Lynott** for his first appearance, the 1985 number 5 'Out in the Fields' (*NOW 5*), the second of an impressive eleven Top 40 hits that also included 'Empty Rooms' (*NOW 6*) and 'Over the Hills and Far Away' (*NOW 9*).

NOW 6 Did You Know . . .

While **Ultravox** never managed a number 1 single, singer **Midge Ure** had his moment of glory in 1985 when 'If I Was' displaced **David Bowie** and **Mick Jagger**'s 'frolicsome' version of 'Dancing in the Streets' at number 1. 'If I Was' featured **Level 42**'s Mark King on bass-playing duties, and along with 'Call of the Wild' (*NOW 7*) was one of Midge's two *NOW* appearances. In 1981 Midge collaborated with Phil Lynott on 'Yellow Pearl', which would serve as the *Top of the Pops* theme tune until 1986, when it was replaced by **Paul Hardcastle**'s 'The Wizard' (*NOW 8*).

IN OTHER NEWS . . . *NOW 6* (NOVEMBER 1985)

American actor Phil Silvers died, aged 74. He was best known for playing Master Sergeant Ernie Bilko, the inspiration for the cartoon series *Top Cat*.

BBC TV broadcast the first episode of the crime drama *Edge of Darkness*. The soundtrack by **Eric Clapton** and Michael Kamen won the 1986 BAFTA Award for Best Music.

The Prince and Princess of Wales visited the USA where, at a reception hosted by President Ronald Reagan, Diana took to the dancefloor with **John Travolta**.

4
NOW appearances
'Wouldn't It Be Good',
NOW 2, March 1984

'When a Heart Beats',
NOW 6, November 1985

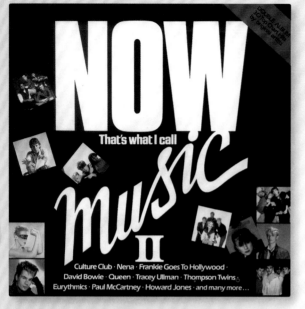

80s

NOW 2 Did You Know . . .

Making the first of just four *NOW* appearances was **David Bowie** with 'Modern Love'. Making his only *NOW* appearance was **Thomas Dolby** with his number 17 hit 'Hyperactive!'. In July 1985, when David Bowie needed to assemble a band at short notice to perform for an estimated 1.5 billion people watching Live Aid, he asked Thomas Dolby to put that band together. Among the four songs they performed that day were 'Modern Love' and 'Heroes' (*NOW 93*).

NOW 46 Did You Know . . .

'Don't Be Stupid (You Know I Love You)' was the last of four appearances for **Shania Twain**, a short but sweet run that began with wedding-reception favourite 'You're Still the One' (*NOW 39*) and continued with her number 3 hit 'That Don't Impress Me Much' (*NOW 44*). Our favourite has to be 'Man! I Feel Like a Woman!' (*NOW 45*); seemingly the only song title in the history of *NOW* to include TWO exclamation marks!! Honourable mention to **Snap!** 'Exterminate!' (*NOW 24*), who split the topical punctuation across artist and title.

IN OTHER NEWS . . . *NOW 46* (JULY 2000)

In Bow, East London, five men and five women were the first UK contestants to enter the *Big Brother* house.

In the US a judge ordered file-sharing site Napster to halt the trading of copyrighted music between its users.

X-Men opened in cinemas. In common with most Marvel Comics films it includes a cameo role for Stan Lee, one of the original comic-book writers of *X-Men*, *Spider-Man*, *Hulk* and *Black Panther*.

4

NOW appearances

'Relax',
NOW 2, March 1984

'The Power of Love',
NOW 46, July 2000

FRANKIE GOES TO HOLLYWOOD

Frankie Goes to Hollywood managed four appearances on *NOW* – with only three singles. Their debut 'Relax' (*NOW 2* and *NOW 26* – it went back into the Top 10 when re-released in 1993) spent five weeks at number 1. When the follow-up 'Two Tribes' (*NOW 3*) charted at number 1 in June 1984, 'Relax' climbed back up the chart from number 31 to number 2. For two weeks in July 1984 Frankie were in the rare position of having both the number 1 and number 2 slots, a feat that has so far only been matched six times in UK Singles chart history.

'Two Tribes' spent an impressive nine weeks at number 1, but there are a few in the *NOW* history books that have hung on longer. **Wet Wet Wet**'s 'Love Is All Around' (*NOW 28*) spent fifteen weeks at the top, as did 'One Dance' (*NOW 95*) by **Drake** featuring **WizKid** and **Kyla**. **Queen**'s 'Bohemian Rhapsody' (*NOW 21*) can boast fourteen weeks at number 1 courtesy of nine weeks in 1975–76 and five weeks in 1991–92. 'Umbrella' (*NOW 67*) by **Rihanna** featuring **Jay-Z**,

and more recently 'Despacito' (*NOW 97*) by Luis Fonsi and **Daddy Yankee** featuring **Justin Bieber**, both managed ten weeks at the top.

Frankie's third single, 'The Power of Love' (*NOW 46*), was also their third number 1, matching a record previously set by fellow Merseysiders Gerry and the Pacemakers back in 1963. Frankie even recorded a version of The Pacemakers' number 8 hit 'Ferry Cross the Mersey' for their debut album *Welcome to the Pleasuredome*. 'The Power of Love' didn't make it onto *NOW* first time around, but joined the club in 2000 when it re-charted at number 6.

In 1989 singer **Holly Johnson** appeared alongside other Liverpool musicians, including **Paul McCartney**, **The Christians** and the song's writer **Gerry Marsden**, on a new recording of 'Ferry Cross the Mersey' (*NOW 15*), released in support of the Hillsborough Disaster Fund. Holly's only other appearance was also on *NOW 15* with his number 4 single 'Americanos'.

'AROUND THE WORLD',
East 17 (*NOW 29*)

United Kingdom

'Belfast Child', **Simple Minds** (*NOW 14*)

'Ferry Cross the Mersey', **Gerry Marsden/Paul McCartney/Holly Johnson/The Christians** (*NOW 15*)

'Strawberry Fields Forever', **Candy Flip** (*NOW 17*)

'Glory Box', **Portishead** (*NOW 30*)

'Little Britain', **Dreadzone** (*NOW 33*)

'Waterloo Sunset', **Cathy Dennis** (*NOW 36*)

'O.T.B. (On the Beach)', **York** (*NOW 46*)

'Drifting Away', **Lange feat. Skye** (*NOW 51*)

'Solsbury Hill', **Erasure** (*NOW 54*)

'Chelsea Dagger', **The Fratellis** (*NOW 65*)

'London Bridge', **Fergie** (*NOW 65*)

'Beautiful Girls', **Sean Kingston** (*NOW 68*)

'Hey Now', **London Grammar** (*NOW 87*)

'A Bridge Over You', **The Lewisham & Greenwich NHS Choir** (*NOW 93*)

'Barking', **Ramz** (*NOW 99*)

Europe

'Take My Breath Away', **Berlin** (*NOW 9*)

'The Final Countdown', **Europe** (*NOW 9*)

'Barcelona', **Freddie Mercury & Montserrat Caballé** (*NOW 10*)

'Make It on My Own', **Alison Limerick** (*NOW 21*)

'Vienna', **Ultravox** (*NOW 24*)

'One', **Mica Paris** (*NOW 30*)

'He's on the Phone', **St Etienne** (*NOW 33*)

'Rotterdam', **Beautiful South** (*NOW 35*)

'What Do You Want from Me?', **Monaco** (*NOW 36*)

'We're Going to Ibiza', **Vengaboys** (*NOW 44*)

'Painkiller', **Turin Brakes** (*NOW 54*)

'From Paris to Berlin', **Infernal** (*NOW 64*)

'Destination Calabria', **Alex Gaudino feat. Crystal Waters** (*NOW 67*)

'Miami 2 Ibiza', **Swedish House Mafia vs Tinie Tempah** (*NOW 77*)

'Pompeii', **Bastille** (*NOW 84*)

'Budapest', **George Ezra** (*NOW 88*)

'I Took a Pill in Ibiza', **Mike Posner** (*NOW 93*)

'Paris', **The Chainsmokers** (*NOW 96*)

'Galway Girl', **Ed Sheeran** (*NOW 98*)

'Feel It Still', **Portugal. The Man** (*NOW 99*)

United States of America

'Relax', **Frankie Goes to Hollywood** (*NOW 2*)

'This Is Not America', **David Bowie & Pat Metheny Group** (*NOW 5*)

'Miami Vice Theme', **Jan Hammer** (*NOW 6*)

'Amityville (The House on the Hill)', **Lovebug Starski** (*NOW 7*)

'French Kissin' in the USA', **Deborah Harry** (*NOW 8*)

'Manhattan Skyline', **A-ha** (*NOW 9*)

'Fairytale of New York', **The Pogues & Kirsty MacColl** (*NOW 10*)

'An Englishman in New York', **Sting** (*NOW 18*)

'Walking in Memphis', **Marc Cohn** (*NOW 20*)

'America (What Time Is Love)', **The KLF** (*NOW 21*)

'Something Good', **Utah Saints** (*NOW 22*)

'Oh Carolina', **Shaggy** (*NOW 24*)

'Tennessee (The Mix)', **Arrested Development** (*NOW 24*)

'I Believe', **Marcella Detroit** (*NOW 28*)

'Say What You Want', **Texas** (*NOW 36*)

'Drinking In LA', **Bran Van 3000** (*NOW 44*)

'Sweet Dreams My LA Ex', **Rachel Stevens** (*NOW 56*)

'Dakota', **Stereophonics** (*NOW 60*)

'(Is This the Way to) Amarilo', **Tony Christie** (*NOW 60*)

'Beverly Hills', **Weezer** (*NOW 61*)

'America', **Razorlight** (*NOW 65*)

'Put Your Hands Up for Detroit', **Fedde Le Grand** (*NOW 65*)

'Waking Up in Vegas', **Katy Perry** (*NOW 73*)

'California Gurls', **Katy Perry feat. Snoop Dogg** (*NOW 76*)

'Hollywood', **Michael Bublé** (*NOW 77*)

'LA Love (La La)', **Fergie** (*NOW 90*)

'Malibu', **Miley Cyrus** (*NOW 97*)

Rest of the World

'Wishful Thinking', **China Crisis** (*NOW 2*)

'China in Your Hand', **T'Pau** (*NOW 10*)

'Kingston Town', **UB40** (*NOW 17*)

'This Is How We Do It', **Montell Jordan** (*NOW 31*)

'Ecuador', **Sash! feat. Rodriguez** (*NOW 37*)

'Inkanyezi Nezazi', **Ladysmith Black Mambazo** (*NOW 42*)

'Uncle John from Jamaica', **Vengaboys** (*NOW 46*)

'Diamonds from Sierra Leone', **Kanye West** (*NOW 62*)

'Left My Heart in Tokyo', **Mini Viva** (*NOW 74*)

'Everybody Hurts', **Helping Haiti** (*NOW 75*)

'Princess of China', **Coldplay & Rihanna** (*NOW 82*)

'Gangnam Style', **Psy** (*NOW 83*)

'Havana', **Camilla Cabello feat. Young Thug** (*NOW 98*)

UK locations: 15
European locations: 18
US locations: 24
Rest of World locations: 12

NOW 2 Did You Know . . .

German singer **Nena** (real name Gabriele Kerner) spent three weeks at number 1 in March 1984 with '99 Red Balloons', and while this is her only appearance, she is spared the 'one-hit wonder' tag as history will show her follow-up 'Just a Dream' made number 70 later that year. Staying with our German theme, this was also our only sighting of **Joe Fagin**. 'That's Livin' Alright' was the theme from the ITV comedy series *Auf Wiedersehen, Pet*, and starred **Jimmy Nail**, who we will meet on *NOW 5*.

NOW 67 Did You Know . . .

'Sheila' was the second appearance by South London troubadour **Jamie T**, and marks the only *NOW* credit for the late poet laureate Sir John Betjeman, whose 1958 work 'The Cockney Amorist' was sampled. The video featured actor Bob Hoskins lip-synching the song's lyrics. Jamie's biggest hit, and only other appearance, was 'Calm Down Dearest' (*NOW 66*), which reached number 9 in 2007, though he has four other Top 40 singles to his name, including the 2009 number 23 'Chaka Demus'.

N OTHER NEWS . . . *NOW 67* (JULY 2007)

Wembley Stadium hosted the London Live Earth concert, an event staged to increase awareness of environmental issues. Headline acts include **Genesis**, **Razorlight** and **Snow Patrol**.

Comedian, actor and television presenter Mike Reid died, aged 67. Best known for playing Frank Butcher in *EastEnders*, in 1975 he had a number 10 single with his version of 'The Ugly Duckling'.

BBC Two screened the first episode of the American science-fiction series *Heroes*.

7

NOW appearances

'Pipes of Peace',
NOW 2, March 1984

'Dance Tonight',
NOW 67, July 2007

PAUL McCARTNEY

It's March 1984, *NOW That's What I Call Music Volume 2* (or *Volume II*, if you're being precise), and for Sir James Paul McCartney opportunity knocks! Kicking off the first of seven credited appearances (although others abound as part of charitable collectives), 'Pipes of Peace' was the first solo number 1 single under his own name – 1982's 'Ebony and Ivory' was a duet with Stevie Wonder and 1978's two-million selling 'Mull of Kintyre' is credited to Wings. 'Pipes of Peace' was the second of four Top 3 singles that Paul scored from 1983 to 84.

NOW 4 opened with a 'Special Dance Mix' of the number 2 hit 'No More Lonely Nights', taken from the much-maligned *Give My Regards to Broad Street* project. The soundtrack still reached number 1 in the album charts, only to be usurped by 1984's all-conquering **Frankie Goes to Hollywood**. Upon its theatrical release, *Broad Street* was accompanied by the *Rupert the Bear* animated short, which gifted the world the number 3 Frog Chorus single 'We All Stand Together'. After thirty-four years, it still remains Sir Paul's last solo single to hit such lofty heights.

Significantly, *NOW 4* was the first of the series to be released on the then new-fangled CD format. Reduced to a snug fifteen tracks, this version acted as a round-up of previous editions, with four tracks culled from *NOW 3* and **Queen**'s 'Radio Ga Ga' from *NOW 2*. With no McCartney on it, the single CD album's arrival was heralded with **Duran Duran**'s 'The Reflex'. It would be another two years before *NOW 8* became the next CD release, though a year-end retrospective, *NOW '86*, was released in October of that year – not be confused with *NOW 86*, released twenty-seven years later.

McCartney is one of only two Beatles to make a credited *NOW* appearance, although it wasn't until *NOW 45* that **John Lennon** scored his only entry with a re-released 'Imagine'. However, the annals of *NOW* are paved with Lennon–McCartney songwriting gold, most notably **Wet Wet Wet**, whose nine appearances include 'With a Little Help from My Friends' (*NOW 12*) and 'Yesterday' (*NOW 38*), while 'Strawberry Fields Forever' (*NOW 17*) gave **Candy Flip** a brief moment in the sun, and **Suggs** made one of two solo appearances with a jaunty skank through 'I'm Only Sleeping' on *NOW 32*.

80s

NOW 3 Did You Know . . .

'This is it: the Pig One'. *NOW 3* was announced with a TV advert featuring an 'oh so eighties' sunglasses-wearing pig, voiced by acclaimed British actor (and former wrestler) Brian Glover. It was also the first volume to feature the classic eighties red, blue and green circles logo. The pig only lasted two more volumes, but the logo adorned another fourteen.

NOW 34 Did You Know . . .

Ireland's premier Drum & Bass duo – **U2**'s very own **Larry Mullen** and **Adam Clayton** – weighed in with their interpretation of Lalo Schifrin's seminal 'Theme From Mission: Impossible', a number 7 hit single. Only nine months earlier, the other 50 per cent of U2 – Paul 'Bono' Hewson and David 'The Edge' Evans – had made their own contribution to film, having penned the James Bond theme song 'GoldenEye' for **Tina Turner**.

IN OTHER NEWS . . . *NOW 34* (AUGUST 1996)

Oasis played two consecutive nights in the grounds of Knebworth House, in Hertfordshire. An estimated 2.5 million people applied for 250,000 tickets. 'Nice one', 'top one' and, indeed, 'sorted'.

Zoë Ball presented Channel 4's *The Big Breakfast* for the last time, moving to the BBC Saturday morning show *Live & Kicking*. As The Singing Corner, regular *L&K* contributors Trevor and Simon would score a 1990 number 68 smash with 'Jennifer Juniper'.

Films opening in August 1996 included *The Crow: City of Angels*. It included roles for two acclaimed singers, Iggy Pop and Ian Dury. Scant consolation for both, who have yet to appear on a numbered *NOW* album.

6
NOW appearances
'Locomotion',
NOW 3, July 1984
'Walking on the Milky Way',
NOW 34, August 1996

OMD (ORCHESTRAL MANOEUVRES IN THE DARK)

'OMG it's OMD!' said nobody in 1984, because the phrase had yet to be coined, but you join us on *NOW 3* where 'Locomotion' kicked off the electro-pop pioneers' compact six-song run spanning twelve years and thirty-one *NOW*s. 'Locomotion' was the seventh of eighteen Top 40 hits for the Wirral-based synth wranglers, all of them original compositions, though, as the title suggests, their fifth appearance, 'Dream of Me (Based on Love's Theme)' (*NOW 25*), sampled Barry White's 1973 single.

Forever associated with Liverpool's notorious Eric's Club, OMD have the most *NOW* entries of any of their contemporaneous Merseyside muckers: **Frankie Goes to Hollywood** come close with four, **Dead or Alive** and Bill Drummond's **KLF** register twice, and it's one a piece for **Pete Wylie** and Ian Broudie's **Lightning Seeds**. Julian Cope and Echo and the Bunnymen remain, as yet, unchronicled by *NOW*.

Before signing to Virgin Records and their DinDisc subsidiary, OMD released 'Electricity' as a one-off single on Tony Wilson's legendary Factory Records. Despite their rich musical legacy, Factory only score two entries in the *NOW* canon – **Happy Mondays**' 'Step On' (*NOW 17*) and **New Order**'s 'Regret' (*NOW 25*). A second and final entry for New Order – 'True Faith '94' – can be found on *NOW 29*, but it was released on London Records after the Factory label's collapse.

And so, from Eric's to Factory to **Atomic Kitten** in two easy, if slightly incongruous, steps. During a lull in their OMD activities, Andy McCluskey and Stuart Kershaw founded the Kitten as an outlet for their poppier sensibilities. The duo co-wrote the majority of Atomic Kitten's debut album *Right Now* and three of the group's eleven *NOW* entries – 'See Ya' (*NOW 45*), 'I Want Your Love' (*NOW 46*) and the million-selling 'Whole Again' (*NOW 48*). 'Whole Again' remains Andy McCluskey's only UK number 1 single to date.

BANANARAMA

80s

Presenting Keren, Sara and Siobhan, the biggest female group in the world! Ever! In *The Guinness Book of Records* as the most successful female group of all time, with more hit singles than any other girl band. They first appeared with the number 3 'Robert De Niro's Waiting' on *NOW 3*, which, as previously mentioned, also saw the first of three appearances by the Pig, wearing a different pair of sunglasses on each sleeve, and, on *NOW 4*, some new-fangled Walkman headphones.

Bananarama's biggest global hit came in 1986 with 'Venus' (*NOW 7*), and also marked the beginning of their long relationship with producers Stock, Aitken and Waterman. The song was originally a hit for Dutch band Shocking Blue, reaching number 1 in the US in 1970, a feat repeated by Bananarama sixteen years later. For their debut single, Nirvana also plundered the Shocking Blue catalogue for a cover of their 1969 track 'Love Buzz'. Nirvana – like the Foo Fighters after them – are yet to appear on a numbered *NOW*.

Despite twenty-five Top 40 hits, Bananarama never made number 1, though they had two more number 3 singles, starting with 'Love in the First Degree' (*NOW 10*), their biggest seller in the UK. In 1988 it was nominated for Best British Single at the BRIT Awards but lost out to another Stock, Aitken and Waterman production, 'Never Gonna Give You Up' by **Rick Astley**. By the time of their third number 3, the 1989 Comic Relief single 'Help!' (*NOW 14*), featuring the near mythical Lananeeneenoonoo,

Siobhan Fahey had departed for **Shakespears Sister**, with Jacquie O'Sullivan drafted in as replacement.

Bananarama had their first two hits in 1982, both in partnership with Fun Boy Three. Terry Hall of Fun Boy Three has been a frequent chart visitor, singing on seven Top 40 singles with The Specials – including the 1981 number 1 'Ghost Town' – plus further hits with The Colour Field and with Vegas, and earning writing credits on two of **The Lightning Seeds**' Top 40 singles. Despite all that, his only *NOW* credit is as co-writer of **Akon**'s 2005 number 5 'Belly Dancer (Bananza)' (*NOW 62*), which samples the 1981 Fun Boy Three debut single 'The Lunatics (Have Taken Over the Asylum)'.

80s

NOW 3 Did You Know . . .

Former singer with the band Japan, **David Sylvian** made his only appearance with the 1984 number 17 'Red Guitar'. The year before he had his biggest 'solo' hit in collaboration with Ryuichi Sakamoto, previously of Japanese synth pioneers Yellow Magic Orchestra. 'Forbidden Colours' was taken from the soundtrack to the film *Merry Christmas, Mr Lawrence*, starring **David Bowie**. In 2000, one-hit wonders **Watergate** made their only appearance with a 'Forbidden Colours' remix, retitled 'Heart of Asia' (*NOW 45*).

NOW 15 Did You Know . . .

Fine Young Cannibals made the fourth of five appearances with 'Good Thing'. One of five Top 40 hits, it featured Jools Holland on piano, and gave them their second number 1 in the US. The first was 'She Drives Me Crazy' (*NOW 14*), though it got no higher than number 5 in the UK. David Steele and Andy Cox – the non-singing members of FYC, and both previously in The Beat – also made one appearance as **Two Men, a Drum Machine and a Trumpet** with 'I'm Tired of Getting Pushed Around' (*NOW 11*).

IN OTHER NEWS . . . *NOW 3* (JULY 1984)

Purple Rain opened in cinemas, with **Prince** making his acting debut as 'The Kid'. The following March it won an Oscar for Best Original Song Score.

The actor James Mason died, aged 75. In 1947 he starred in *Odd Man Out*, the first ever winner of a BAFTA Award for Best British Film.

Singer Frankie Valli married Randy Clohessy. 'Beggin'', Frankie's 1967 single with The Four Seasons, was covered by **MadCon** on *NOW 71*.

8
NOW appearances
'Robert De Niro's Waiting', *NOW 3*, July 1984
'Cruel Summer '89', *NOW 15*, August 1989

80s

NOW 4 Did You Know . . .

NOW 4 includes the first of only two credited appearances by **Michael Jackson**. 'Farewell My Summer Love', an early seventies recording, was remixed and released by his former label Motown to capitalise on the huge success of 'Thriller'. Elsewhere on this volume, Michael provides (uncredited) vocals for 'Somebody's Watching Me' by **Rockwell**. Rockwell was born Kennedy William Gordy, and is the son of Motown founder Berry Gordy Jr. Berry's many claims to fame include being co-writer of 'Reet Petite', a number 1 hit for **Jackie Wilson** on *NOW 9*.

NOW 73 Did You Know . . .

On *NOW 73* we said a fond 'adieu' to **Sophie Ellis-Bextor**, after an impressive run of nine *NOW* appearances. Originally a member of indie also-rans theaudience, Sophie's *NOW* credits began on volume 46 with Italian DJ **Spiller** and the number 1 'Groovejet (If This Ain't Love)'. This would be Sophie's only chart topper, though her first two solo hits, 'Take Me Home' (*NOW 50*) – a cover of a 1979 **Cher** single – and 'Murder on the Dancefloor' (*NOW 51*), would both fall just shy at number 2.

11
NOW appearances
'Passengers',
NOW 4, November 1984
'Tiny Dancer (Hold Me Closer)',
Ironik featuring Chipmunk
and Elton John,
NOW 73, November 2009

IN OTHER NEWS . . . *NOW 73* (JULY 2009)

American businessman Allen Klein died, aged 77. In the course of a colourful career he managed both The Beatles and **Rolling Stones**, along with soul singer Sam Cooke and producer Phil Spector.

The British science fiction film *Moon* opened in cinemas. It stars Sam Rockwell and was the feature debut of director Duncan Jones, son of **David Bowie**.

Paul McCartney performed the first concert to be staged at Citi Field baseball stadium in New York, and was joined onstage by Billy Joel. In 2008 Billy had played the last concert to be staged at Shea Stadium, and was joined onstage by Paul McCartney.

ELTON JOHN

When Elton made his *NOW* debut, his chart career already spanned twelve years and boasted thirty-three Top 40 hits, including the first of seven number 1s. Subsequent chart toppers include 'Sacrifice' (*NOW 18*), 'Are You Ready for Love' (*NOW 56*) and 'Ghetto Gospel' (*NOW 61*) by **2Pac** featuring Elton John. Elton's *NOW* number 1 quartet is completed with 'Don't Let the Sun Go Down on Me' (*NOW 22*), a song he and **George Michael** first performed together at Live Aid in 1985.

Elton's last appearance to date, on *NOW 73*, comes courtesy of two British R&B acts, **Ironik** and **Chipmunk**. 'Tiny Dancer (Hold Me Closer)' samples Elton's 1972 song 'Tiny Dancer'. Never officially released as a single in the UK, 'Tiny Dancer' was a Top 40 hit in the US, Australia and Canada. Chipmunk also appears on *NOW 73* with 'Diamond Rings', featuring fellow *NOW* debutant **Emeli Sandé**. These were the first of seven appearances for Chipmunk, while Emeli has so far notched up an impressive twelve.

Other artists who have felt the benefit of Elton's talent include **Scissor Sisters**, whose only number 1 to date, 'I Don't Feel Like Dancin'' (*NOW 65*) was co-written by Elton, who also plays piano on the recording. **Ellie Goulding**'s version of 'Your Song' (*NOW 78*) gave her a number 2 hit, and the same song helped **Aloe Blacc** to number 1 when he sampled it for his hit 'The Man' (*NOW 88*).

Sir Elton is included in a rather elite clique among *NOW* alumni. Having been knighted in 1998, he is part of a list that also includes Sir Barry Gibb (2018), Sir **Mick Jagger** (2002), Sir **Tom Jones** (2006), Sir **Paul McCartney** (1997), Sir **Cliff Richard** (1995) and Sir **Rod Stewart** (2016). We also offer a humble bow to Sir Van Morrison (2016), included on this list by dint of his writing contribution to 'Sweet Little Mystery' by **Wet Wet Wet** (*NOW 10*).

80s

NOW 4 Did You Know . . .

Featuring one of two appearances by The Undertones' former singer **Feargal Sharkey**, 'Listen to Your Father', a number 23 hit, was written by one Carl Smyth, aka Chas Smash of top pop combo **Madness**, who notched up seven *NOW* listings of their very own. Although the Feargal-fronted Undertones split shortly before the inaugural *NOW*, their debut single 'Teenage Kicks' was covered (briefly) by **One Direction** and is included on *NOW 84*.

NOW 53 Did You Know . . .

There's something of a food and drink motif going on here. While Status Quo brought 'Jam Side Down', **Romeo** featuring **Christina Milian** decided 'It's All Gravy', Spanish girl-group **Las Ketchup** served up 'The Ketchup Song (Aserejé)', and hedging their bets on beverages were Belgians **Milk Inc.** with 'Walk on Water'. **Supergrass** were good enough to say – or rather sing – 'Grace', though this particular song was named after the daughter of **Squeeze** songwriter Chris Difford. Squeeze have only the one *NOW* appearance to date, with 'Hourglass' on *NOW 10*.

IN OTHER NEWS . . . *NOW 53* (NOVEMBER 2002)

At the cinema this month, *Die Another Day*, the twentieth James Bond film and the fourth and final 007 mission for Pierce Brosnan.

Also on the big screen, *Harry Potter and the Chamber of Secrets* was released, the second of eight films in the Potter portfolio.

Lonnie Donegan, the King of Skiffle, died this month, aged 71. Before The Beatles, when the charts were still in black and white, Lonnie notched up twenty-eight Top 40 Hits.

6
NOW appearances
'The Wanderer',
NOW 4, November 1984

'Jam Side Down',
NOW 53, November 2002

STATUS QUO

Status Quo had already enjoyed twenty-nine Top 40 hits before their first *NOW* appearance on volume 4. To date they have bothered the Top 40 chart compilers on fifty-seven occasions, hanging around for a combined 331 weeks – that's almost six-and-a-half years! Perhaps surprisingly they managed only one number 1 single – 'Down Down' in 1974 – though three further hits halted at number 2. Two of these found their way onto *NOW* – 'In the Army Now' (*NOW 8*) and 'The Anniversary Waltz (Part One)' (*NOW 18*).

One of Status Quo's *NOW* appearances was a collaboration with **The Beach Boys**, on a version of the latter's 1964 hit 'Fun, Fun, Fun'. The Quo's other single collaborators include folk singer Maddy Prior, the Corps of Army Choir and – dare we say 'bizarrely'? – German trance-music outfit **Scooter**. Scooter's five appearances on *NOW* include four in a row from *NOW 52* to *NOW 55*.

Following in the footsteps of **Tears for Fears**, who in 1986 re-recorded their hit 'Everybody Wants to Rule the World' as 'Everybody Wants to Run the World', in 1988 Status Quo re-recorded 'Rocking All Over the World' as 'Running All Over the World'. Both athletic-themed versions were released in support of the Sport Aid campaign, raising funds for famine relief in Africa.

Originally calling themselves The Scorpions, our favourite denizens of the double denim also tried their luck as The Spectres, Traffic and Traffic Jam before rebranding as The Status Quo and landing their first Top 10 hit, 'Pictures of Matchstick Men', in 1968. Contrary to popular opinion, Status Quo were not the first band onstage at Live Aid in 1985. That honour actually went to the Band of the Coldstream Guards.

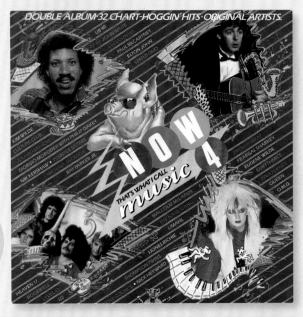

80s

NOW 4 Did You Know . . .

Italian producer and songwriter **Giorgio Moroder** has five *NOW* credits, two of them on volume 4, including his only *NOW* appearance as an artist: 'Together in Electric Dreams' by **Philip Oakey** and Giorgio Moroder was a number 3 hit, taken from the film *Electric Dreams*, while 'The Never Ending Story' by **Limahl** opened the film of that name; a third Moroder soundtrack connection is Oscar-winning number 1 'Take My Breath Away' by **Berlin** (*NOW 9*), from *Top Gun*. The Moroder files are completed by **Donna Summer**'s 'I Feel Love' (*NOW 32*), a reissue of the 1977 number 1, and **Martine McCutcheon**'s cover of 'On the Radio' (*NOW 48*).

NOW 99 Did You Know . . .

Making her second and third *NOW* appearances is the succinctly named **Mabel**. Her first, 'Finders Keepers' by Mabel featuring **Kojo Funds** (*NOW 98*), was co-written with her step-brother **Marlon Roudette**, as was her second appearance, 'Fine Line' by Mabel and **Not3s** (*NOW 99*). Not3s X Mabel switched top billing for her third listing, 'My Lover' (also *NOW 99*). Marlon's previous band, **Mattafix**, popped up on *NOW 62* with 'Big City Life', while his solo debut was the number 7 hit 'When the Beat Drops Out' on *NOW 90*.

20
NOW appearances

'Pride (in the Name of Love)'
NOW 4, November 1984

'You're the Best Thing About'
NOW 99, March 2018

IN OTHER NEWS . . . *NOW 4* (NOVEMBER 1984)

In the US Ronald Reagan won a second term as President, winning forty-nine of fifty states. At 73 years old he was the oldest person to be sworn in for a second term.

Actress Scarlett Johansson was born in New York City. She also enjoys a slightly lower profile as a recording artist, and while she has yet to appear on any volume of *NOW*, she does feature in the video for **Justin Timberlake**'s 'What Goes Around . . . Comes Around' (*NOW 66*).

On 25 November 1984, Bob Geldof and **Midge Ure** assembled the musicians who would become Band Aid at SARM West Studios, in Notting Hill, London. At the time of release it was the bestselling single ever in the UK, though it has since been surpassed by **Elton John**'s 'Candle in the Wind 1997'.

U2

U2 had already had two Top 40 hits when they made their *NOW* debut with 'Pride (in the Name of Love)' on *NOW 4*. Six of U2's number 1s have appeared on *NOW*, starting with 'The Fly' on *NOW 20*, and most recently with 'Sometimes You Can't Make It on Your Own' on *NOW 61*. Two of U2's appearances were written for film soundtracks: 'Elevation (Tomb Raider Mix)' (*NOW 49*) comes – unsurprisingly – from the 2001 film *Lara Croft: Tomb Raider,* while 'Hold Me, Thrill Me, Kiss Me, Kill Me' (*NOW 32*) was written for *Batman Forever* (1995). The latter also included 'Kiss from a Rose' by **Seal** (*NOW 31*).

In addition to two of the band's soundtrack spin-offs – 'Theme from *Mission: Impossible*' by

Larry Mullen and **Adam Clayton** (*NOW 34*) and **Tina Turner**'s 'GoldenEye' (*NOW 32*), written by Bono and The Edge – U2 can also lay claim to two cover versions on *NOW*. **Mica Paris**'s version of 'One' (*NOW 30*) didn't do quite as well as U2's original number 7 placing, peaking at number 29. However, the **Pet Shop Boys** use of 'Where the Streets Have No Name' in a medley with **Frankie Valli**'s 'Can't Take My Eyes Off You' (*NOW 20*) matched the U2 song, with both reaching number 4.

U2 currently have the largest spread of *NOW* appearances for any living artist – ninety-five volumes between their debut on *NOW 4* and their most recent showing on *NOW 99*. Their eighth appearance, 'Sweetest Thing' (*NOW 41*), was originally the

B-side of 'Where the Streets Have No Name'. Needing a 'new' song to promote their 1998 'best of' collection, they chose to re-record 'Sweetest Thing' and were rewarded with a number 3 single. The promo video features an appearance from that other great Irish boyband and *NOW* favourites, **Boyzone**.

U2 only rocked up at the studio to record nineteen of their twenty *NOW* entries. The odd one out is the 2004 number 1 'Take Me to the Clouds Above' by **LMC** vs. U2 (*NOW 57*), which samples 'With or Without You', U2's 1987 number 4 hit. LMC appeared in the Top 40 one more time with 'You Get What You Give', a cover of the **New Radicals** song that appeared on *NOW 43*.

Between 1981 and 1996, Kim, of the positively Von Trapp-ian Wilde family, landed twenty Top 40 hits, ten of them co-written by brother Ricky with father Marty, including Kim's *NOW* debut 'The Second Time' (*NOW 4*), a number 29 single in October 1984. Between 1958 and '62, Marty had eleven Top 40 hits of his own, and thirteen years before Kim's first hit 'Kids in America' reached number 2, Wilde Senior had chart success with rock behemoths **Status Quo**, co-writing their second of over fifty Top 40 singles, 'Ice in the Sun'.

Kim's cover of Holland, Dozier and Holland's 'You Keep Me Hangin' On' (*NOW 8*) provided her biggest hit in both the UK and the US. Originally recorded by The Supremes, it reached number 1 on the *Billboard* Hot 100 in 1966. Twenty-one years later, Kim's hi-NRG re-interpretation ensured the song was a US number 1 for a second time, while in the UK it equalled the number 2 of 'Kids in America'. The Supremes vocalist **Diana Ross** made the first of three appearances in 1991 with the Christmas number 2 'When You Tell Me That You Love Me' (*NOW 21*).

In 1988 Kim supported **Michael Jackson** on the European leg of his *Bad* tour and made two more Top 40 appearances with 'You Came' (*NOW 13*) and 'Four Letter Word' (*NOW 14*). Kim's final appearance was 'If I Can't Have You' (*NOW 25*), originally a number 4 hit for Yvonne Elliman in 1978. Written by **Bee Gees** for the *Saturday Night Fever* soundtrack, the brothers Gibb released their own version as the B-side of their single 'Stayin' Alive'.

In 1987 two separate acts charted under the moniker **Mel and Kim**. The first were the Appleby siblings, who had a number 1 with 'Respectable', and scored two *NOW* entries with 'Showing Out (Get Fresh at the Weekend)' (*NOW 8*) and 'That's the Way It Is' (*NOW 11*); Kim (Appleby, that is) would return as a solo artist on *NOW 18* and *19* with songs written with former Bros drummer Craig Logan. The second, Mel (Smith) and Kim (Wilde), scored a number 3 hit for Comic Relief with 'Rockin' Around the Christmas Tree', with a video featuring a fresh-faced cameo from triple-*NOW* entrants (volumes *9*, *10* and *16*), **Curiosity Killed the Cat**.

KIM WILDE

NOW 4 Did You Know . . .

The 1984 number 3 'Doctor Doctor' was the third and final appearance for Anglo-New Zealand trio **Thompson Twins**. Their first, 'Hold Me Now' (*NOW 2*), made number 4 in December 1983, and went one better in the US where it was their biggest hit. In the UK their best showing was 'You Take Me Up' (*NOW 3*), stuck at number 2 behind **Lionel Richie**'s only appearance, 'Hello' (*NOW 4*), which spent six weeks at the top. In 1985 Thompson Twins played the Philadelphia leg of Live Aid, joined onstage by Madonna and **Nile Rodgers** for a rendition of The Beatles' 'Revolution'.

NOW 25 Did You Know . . .

San Francisco group **4 Non Blondes** made their only appearance with their sole Top 40 hit, 'What's Up?', which spent two weeks at number 2 in 1993, behind **Take That**'s first chart topper, 'Pray' (*NOW 26*). 'What's Up?' returned to the Top 10 and *NOW 28* in 1994, providing a number 7 for one-hit wonder **DJ Miko**. 4 Non Blondes' Linda Perry went on to a successful career writing for others, giving us **Gwen Stefani**'s 'What You Waiting For?' (*NOW 60*) and 'Candyman' (*NOW 67*) by **Christina Aguilera**.

IN OTHER NEWS . . . *NOW 25* (AUGUST 1993)

On the 29th of the month, **One Direction**'s **Liam Payne** was born.

At Pinewood Studios, Bruce Dickinson played his last gig with **Iron Maiden** (until he re-joined the band in 1999).

Lyricist Bernie Taupin, best known for his work with **Elton John**,

5
NOW appearances

'The Second Time', *NOW 4*, November 1984

'If I Can't Have You', *NOW 25*, August 1993

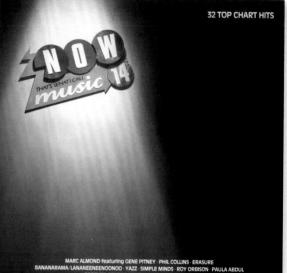

80s

NOW 4 Did You Know . . .

With two appearances, including 'Too Late for Goodbyes', **Julian Lennon** boasts twice as many *NOW* appearances as father **John Lennon**. **Miley Cyrus** also has the edge over her dad, racking up four appearances so far to **Billy Ray Cyrus**'s one. A greater disparity is between **Lily Allen**, with nine appearances, and the one by father Keith Allen courtesy of his **Fat Les** membership. All should be cordial in the Wilson household, as Brian Wilson's **Beach Boys** have two *NOW* appearances, as do his daughters Wendy and Carnie, two thirds of trio **Wilson Philips**.

NOW 14 Did You Know . . .

The Smiths managed just the one *NOW* appearance with 'What Difference Does It Make?' on volume 2, and having graced us with his first three solo singles – all Top 10 hits – 'The Last of the Famous International Playboys' on *NOW 14* afforded us a last glimpse of their former front man **Morrissey**. However, he can also claim one 'behind the scenes' credit courtesy of **Mark Ronson** featuring **Daniel Merriweather**, whose 'Stop Me' (*NOW 67*) fused The Smiths' 'Stop Me If You Think You've Heard This One Before' with The Supremes' 1966 number 8 'You Keep Me Hanging On'.

6
NOW appearances
'Hot Water',
NOW 4, November 1984

'Tracie',
NOW 14, March 1989

IN OTHER NEWS . . . *NOW 14* (MARCH 1989)

On 2 March, halfway through an episode of ITV police drama *The Bill*, Pepsi aired a two-minute advert that launched Madonna's latest single 'Like a Prayer'.

At the sixty-first Academy Awards, *Rain Man* won four Oscars, including Best Actor for Dustin Hoffman.

Having hit the top spot the previous December with 'Especially for You', his duet with **Kylie Minogue**, **Jason Donovan** scored the first of three solo number 1s with 'Too Many Broken Hearts'.

LEVEL 42

The Isle of Wight has hosted some of the largest musical gatherings ever seen in the UK, but Level 42 might be that island's only link thus far to *NOW*. Between 1983 and 1994, Level 42 managed twenty Top 40 hits, peaking with 'Lessons in Love' (*NOW 7*), which had to settle for three weeks at number 3, and suffer the ignominy of watching *Spitting Image*'s 'The Chicken Song' hold onto the top slot.

Fronted by slap-bass maestro and singer Mark King, the band's run of *NOW* appearances started with 1984's 'Hot Water' (*NOW 4*) and finished with 'Tracie' (*NOW 14*) in 1989. When Level 42's label, Polydor Records, took out an insurance policy to cover the band in 1987, they announced that they had insured the plank spanker's thumb for a whopping £3 million. Said thumb had a brief moment at number 1 when Mark played bass on **Midge Ure**'s 1985 single 'If I Was' (*NOW 6*).

Although he was never officially a member of the band, keyboard player Wally Badarou co-wrote four of Level 42's six *NOW* appearances. Wally's keyboard skills first graced the charts when he played on the 1979 number 2 'Pop Muzik' by M. Much in demand as a session musician, Wally can be heard on hits by Foreigner, **Grace Jones**, **Joe Cocker**, Talking Heads and **Robert Palmer**, though his only success as a solo artist came with 'Police Officer', which reached number 48 in 1985.

Another artist who said 'Hello' for the first and only time on volume 4 was former Commodores frontman **Lionel Richie**. Although the number 1 hit was his only *NOW* appearance as a performer, he was also responsible for writing **Faith No More**'s number 3 hit 'Easy' (*NOW 24*). The same song was sampled by **Cam'Ron** featuring **Juelz Santana**, **Freekey Zekey** and **Toya** for the 2003 number 8 hit 'Hey Ma' (*NOW 54*).

SIMPLY RED

Mick Hucknall's first group was Manchester punk outfit The Frantic Elevators, who folded in 1983, but not before they recorded an early version of Simply Red's 'Holding Back the Years', the first of their two US number 1 singles; it was re-recorded and captured on *NOW 7* in 1986. The same punk scene produced Factory Record's arty Durutti Column, who share a number of former members with Simply Red, most notably Tim Kellet, who had chart-topping success with Olive in 1997 ('You're Not Alone').

'The Right Thing' on *NOW 9* heralded a four-year absence for Simply Red, though that particular volume is more newsworthy as the last *NOW* to be issued as a single CD. It was two discs all the way from there. In 1991 Simply Red's fourth album, *Stars*, was released, still one of the Top 20 all-time bestselling albums in the UK and home to five Top 40 singles, three of them captured by *NOW*: 'Something's Got Me Started' (*NOW 20*), 'Stars' (*NOW 21*) and 'For Your Babies' (*NOW 23*).

Although Simply Red have thirty-two Top 40 hits, their only number 1 to date is 'Fairground' (*NOW 32*), which spent four weeks at the top in October 1995. The distinctive drum sound was sampled from 'Give It Up' (*NOW 26*) by Dutch duo **The Goodmen**, aka DJs René ter Horst and Gaston Steenkist, who in turn sampled 'Fanfarra' by **Sérgio Mendes**. Sérgio made his only artist appearance with **Black Eyed Peas** on 'Mas Que Nada' (*NOW 64*), while René and Gaston resurfaced in 2001 as **Chocolate Puma** with the number 6 'I Wanna Be You' (*NOW 48*).

In 2008, Mick appeared on the BBC's *Celebrity Mastermind*, answering questions on the life and career of Henri Matisse. *Coronation Street* actress Sally Lindsay won the competition, with eighteen points from her specialist subject, *Carry On* films. Sally can also boast one chart topper, reaching number 1 in 1980 with St Winifred's School Choir and 'There's No One Quite Like Grandma'. The song knocked **John Lennon**'s posthumous single '(Just Like) Starting Over' off pole position, but was in turn dethroned by his 'Imagine' two weeks later.

80s

THIRTY TOP 30 HITS– DOUBLE ALBUM

80s

NOW 5 Did You Know . . .

Stephen 'Tin Tin' Duffy made his only appearance with the number 14 hit 'Icing on the Cake'. In the seventies, while a student at Birmingham Polytechnic, he formed **Duran Duran** with John Taylor and Nick Rhodes. He had another Top 40 hit in 1996 with 'Hanging Around' by Me Me Me, a one-off project that also included Alex James of **Blur** and Justin Welch of Elastica. In 2004 he began writing with **Robbie Williams** and scored another four credits on *NOW*, including the 2004 number 1 'Radio' (*NOW 59*).

NOW 33 Did You Know . . .

Saint Etienne first made the Top 40 in 1990 with a cover of Neil Young's 1970 single 'Only Love Can Break Your Heart'. They made their only *NOW* appearance with their biggest hit, the 1995 number 11 'He's on the Phone', which also featured uncredited (on *NOW*, at least) French DJ Étienne Daho. Saint Etienne singer **Sarah Cracknell** made a second appearance in 2009 with 'The Journey Continues', a number 11 single in the company of DJ **Mark Brown**.

IN OTHER NEWS . . . *NOW 5* (AUGUST 1985)

Michael Jackson bought ATV Music for $47 million, and with it the publishing rights to the majority of The Beatles' songs.

Madonna married actor Sean Penn in Malibu, California, on her twenty-seventh birthday.

ITV launched the soap opera *Albion Market*. It lasted a hundred episodes and finished one year after it began. Singer Helen Shapiro, who had a number 1 in 1961 with 'Walking Back to Happiness', appeared in four episodes.

9
NOW appearances
'Money's Too Tight (to Mention)',
NOW 5, August 1985

'Never Never Love',
NOW 33, March 1996

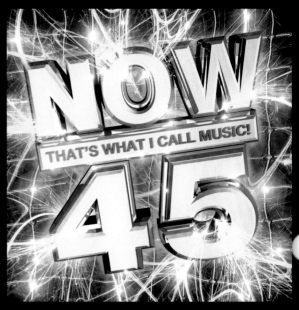

90s

NOW 6 Did You Know . . .

NOW 6 marks the last appearance by **Eurythmics**, going out on a high with their only number 1 single, 'There Must Be an Angel (Playing with My Heart)'. The single, written by **Annie Lennox** and David A. Stewart, features a harmonica solo by Stevie Wonder. This was the second time in less than a year that Stevie featured on a number 1 single, having previously played harmonica on 'I Feel for You' by Chaka Khan.

NOW 45 Did You Know . . .

In an eighteen-month spell starting September 1998, **Honeyz** had five Top 10 hits and *NOW* captured them all. Their debut and biggest hit was the number 4 smoocher 'Finally Found' (*NOW 41*). Spotting a winning formula, they followed up with three more ballads before finally lifting the tempo with 'Won't Take It Lying Down' (*NOW 45*). The group split in 2002 before opportunity knocked in 2005 with the ITV programme *Hit Me, Baby, One More Time*, then another 'one more time' with *The Big Reunion* in 2012.

4

NOW appearances

'It's Only Love',
Tina Turner with Bryan Adams,
NOW 6, November 1985

'Don't Give Up',
Chicane Featuring Bryan Adams,
NOW 45, April 2000

IN OTHER NEWS . . . *NOW 45* (APRIL 2000)

HRH the Duke of Kent and **Mick Jagger** opened The Mick Jagger Centre, at Dartford Grammar School, in Kent. The facility includes two theatres, rehearsal rooms and a recording studio.

Press reports stated that export of Sony's new PlayStation 2 games console would be controlled by the Trade Ministry of Japan, amid concerns it could be used for military purposes.

In a Channel 4 poll to choose the nation's favourite TV advert, the 1999 Guinness 'Surfer' advert, featuring music by **Leftfield**, came out on top.

BRYAN ADAMS

Bryan Adams made his first *NOW* appearance on volume 6 with 'It's Only Love', a duet with **Tina Turner**, marking the fourth of fourteen appearances for the woman born Anna Mae Bullock. Bryan had to wait more than ten years for his next *NOW* appearance with 'The Only Thing that Looks Good on Me Is You' (*NOW 34*), though ever the busy little Canuck, he did rack up another nine Top 40 singles in the interim, including the still record-breaking, sixteen weeks at number 1 '(Everything I Do) I Do It for You'.

As with his first appearance, Bryan's last showing on *NOW* was another collaboration, though perhaps unexpectedly this one saw him teaming up with English trance act **Chicane**. Chicane had previously worked with Clannad singer **Máire Brennan** (*NOW 43*) and would enjoy a further hit with **Tom Jones** (*NOW 64*), but 'Don't Give Up', their partnership with Bryan, gave them their only number 1.

90s

In 1992 house outfit **Rage** scored a number 3 hit with a cover of Bryan's 'Run to You' (*NOW 23*). In 2002 Bryan got his name on another number 1 dance single, courtesy of Spanish/German/Dutch trio **DJ Sammy & Yanou** featuring **Do**, who covered the 1984 song 'Heaven' (*NOW 53*). DJ Sammy would try a similar trick on *NOW 54*, though his cover of **Don Henley**'s 'The Boys Of Summer' had to settle for number 2, kept off the top slot by **Christina Aguilera**'s 'Beautiful'.

Bryan's total to date of two number 1s has been equalled by fellow Canadians **Céline Dion** and **Nelly Furtado**. Toronto born **Drake** can look at three, so far, including 'One Dance', featuring **WizKid** and **Kyla**; it managed a 'Bryan-threatening' fifteen weeks at number 1, but was eventually removed from the summit by another Canadian. All hail the mighty **Justin Bieber** who, in a period of just eighteen months, managed to rack up his first six chart-toppers.

30 TOP CHART HITS

QUEEN · FEARGAL SHARKEY · PHIL COLLINS & MARILYN MARTIN · ELTON JOHN · LEVEL 42 · ARCADIA · EURYTHMICS · UB40 · MADNESS · NIK KERSHAW · SIMPLE MINDS · MIDGE URE · MARILLION · TINA TURNER · KATE BUSH · PLUS MANY MORE

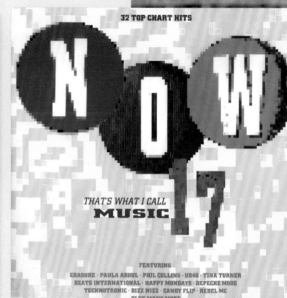

32 TOP CHART HITS

THAT'S WHAT I CALL **MUSIC** 17

FEATURING

ERASURE · PAULA ABDUL · PHIL COLLINS · UB40 · TINA TURNER · BEATS INTERNATIONAL · HAPPY MONDAYS · DEPECHE MODE · TECHNOTRONIC · BIZZ NIZZ · CANDY FLIP · REBEL MC · PLUS MANY MORE

80s

NOW 6 Did You Know . . .

Rocking the funky codpiece and making the first of two appearances were American soul outfit **Cameo**. Their seven Top 40 entries included the number 15 'Single Life' (*NOW 6*) and the number 3 hit 'Word Up' (*NOW 8*). In 1999 'Word Up' was covered by former Spice Girl **Melanie B**, giving her the second of five Top 40 hits and an appearance on *NOW 43*. It would have another lease of life in 2014 when **Little Mix** took their version to number 6 and made their fourth of fifteen appearances so far on *NOW 87*.

NOW 17 Did You Know . . .

After four *NOW* appearances we said goodbye to **D-Mob**, aka house music producer Dancin' Danny D. His run began on *NOW 13* with 'We Call It Acieed' by D-Mob and **Gary Haisman**, followed by 'It's Time To Get Funky' by D-Mob & **LRS** (*NOW 15*), 'C'mon and Get My Love' by D-Mob and **Cathy Dennis** and finally 'Put Your Hands Together' by D-Mob and **Nuff Juice** (*NOW 17*). Of his four collaborators, only Cathy Dennis would grace *NOW* again as a performer, with her Top 20 hits 'Too Many Walls' (*NOW 20*) and 'Waterloo Sunset' (*NOW 36*).

IN OTHER NEWS . . . *NOW 6* (NOVEMBER 1985)

Rocky IV opened at cinemas. The soundtrack includes 'Living in America' by **James Brown**, which peaked at number 5, his highest ever UK chart position.

Cilla Black presented the first episode of *Blind Date*, a role she would perform for the next eighteen years. Voiceover announcements came from 'Our Graham' Skidmore, who would later perform the same function for **Vic Reeves** and **Bob Mortimer**'s *Shooting Stars*.

*NOW That's What I Call Music: The Christmas Album** was released. It spent two weeks at number 1, knocking *NOW 6* off the top spot.

*Or *The Christmas Tape*, if you bought it on cassette

5
NOW appearances
'She's So Beautiful',
NOW 6, November 1985

'Stronger than That',
NOW 17, April 1990

CLIFF RICHARD

Look away now, all you young pretenders. By the time he made his first appearance on *NOW 6*, Cliff had already racked up ten number 1 singles with another four to follow. To date he has spent a total of 46 weeks at number 1, and a jaw-dropping 970 weeks – that's eighteen-and-a-half years! – in the Top 40. Cliff's top-spot tally includes three Christmas number 1s (one of them with The Shadows), a feat that has only been bettered by The Beatles.

Cliff's fourth *NOW* appearance, 'I Just Don't Have the Heart' (*NOW 16*), was written and produced by the hugely successful team of Mike Stock, Matt Aitken and Pete Waterman. Two of Cliff's other *NOW* hits – 'My Pretty One' (*NOW 10*) and 'Stronger than That' (*NOW 17*) – were penned and produced by the slightly lower profile but hugely talented Alan Tarney. Elsewhere on *NOW* you'll find his name next to production credits for **A-Ha**'s 'Hunting High and Low' (*NOW 7*) and **Pulp**'s 'Disco 2000' (*NOW 33*).

Ever the trendsetter, Cliff and the Young Ones released the first official Comic Relief single back in 1986. A re-recording of his 1962 number 1 'The Young Ones' was the first of thirteen number 1s so far for Comic Relief, and it is a rare occurrence of an artist taking the same song to number 1 on two completely separate occasions. The only song on *NOW* that can boast that claim is **Queen**'s 'Bohemian Rhapsody' (*NOW 21*), which was the Christmas number 1 in 1975 and 1991.

Cliff is one of fourteen artists to have both represented the UK at the Eurovision Song Contest (twice in his case) and appeared on *NOW*. However, only four of the UK songs entered made the *NOW* history books. The lucky ones are 'Love City Groove' by **Love City Groove** (*NOW 31*), 'Ooh Ah . . . Just a Little Bit' by **Gina G** (*NOW 34*), 'Where Are You' by Imaani (*NOW 40*) and, most recently, 'Say It Again' by **Precious** (*NOW 43*).

80s

NOW IN THIRTY-FIVE NUMBERS

1 Song by ABBA

1 **'Christmas' Song**
'Merry Christmas Mr Lawrence (Heart of Asia)' *(NOW 45)* by Watergate

2 **Songs that have appeared in 3 different versions**: 'A Little Respect' (Erasure, Björn Again and Wheatus) and 'Axel F' (Harold Faltermeyer, Crazy Frog and Clock)

4 **Volumes featuring The Pig** *(NOW 3, 4, 5 and 100)*

4 **The first edition of *NOW* to appear on CD**

4 **The last *NOW* to feature artists on the cover**

4 **Number of 'Bands' on *NOW***: KC & the Sunshine Band, The Gap Band, Steve Miller Band, and Gary Barlow & the Commonwealth Band

5 **Foreign-language number 1s**: Los Lobos, 'La Bamba' *(NOW 10)*; Enigma, 'Sadness Part 1' *(NOW 19)*; Las Ketchup, 'Asereje (The Ketchup Song)' *(NOW 53)*; Yolanda B Cool & DCup, 'We No Speak Americano' *(NOW 76)*; Psy, 'Gangnam Style' *(NOW 83)*

6 **Volumes on MiniDisc** *(43 to 48)*

6 **Side 1, song 1s** for Queen

9 **Most number 1s on *NOW*** for Spice Girls

10 **Number 1** singles by *The X Factor winners*

13 **Most appearances on consecutive volumes** for Girls Aloud *(NOW 54, 'Sound of the Underground', to NOW 66, 'I Think We're Alone Now')*

15 **Most number 1 hits** on one volume *(NOW 88)*

All stats based on *NOW* volumes 1 to 99

20 Last *NOW* volume issued with companion VHS video

21 First *NOW* volume with TV advert by DJ Mark Goodier

22 Christmas number 1s in the first 34 years

23 Other national and regional *NOW* brands around the world

30 Fewest songs on any volume (*NOW 1, 2, 3, 5, 6, 9* and *10*)

35 Years since *NOW 1* on 28 November 1983

35 Last *NOW* volume released on vinyl

39 Robbie Williams appearances (solo, Take That and charity projects)

46 Most songs on any volume (*NOW 76, 87, 92* and *98*)

62 First *NOW* volume available to download

64 Last *NOW* volume issued on cassette tape

67 Number of songs to credit Max Martin as writer

86 Longest gap between appearances (David Bowie, *NOW 7* to *NOW 93*)

90 Appearances by 26 different X Factor artists

95 Largest spread of appearances (U2: 20 songs, volumes 4 to 99)

97 The *NOW* volume with the most 'featurings', at 21

595 Highest price in pounds for a copy of *NOW 8* on CD*

602 Number 1 singles

1,199 One-*NOW* Wonders (artists who have so far only appeared once)

2,089 Different artists so far

76,000,000 UK sales so far (as of April 2018)

* Source: Discogs.com

PET SHOP BOYS

Lennon and McCartney, Jagger and Richards, Neil and Chris: all the best musical national treasures arrive in pairs, and with twenty-two Top 10 hits, four number 1 singles and fifty-million record sales, our favourite pokerfaced art-pop doyens are clearly no exception. And their *NOW* career is as colourful as their couture – five original compositions, five cover versions and one collaboration with the reigning crown prince of *NOW*, **Robbie Williams**.

The Pets were three Top 40 hits into their career before 'Opportunities (Let's Make Lots of Money)' gifted them their debut appearance on *NOW 7*. This of course means their first number 1 hit, 'West End Girls', was cruelly denied. But fear not! Generously trousered hip-pop 'nawty boys' **East 17** righted a wrong on *NOW 25* with their own inimitable take of the iconic track. It was the third of ten entries for Tony, Brian and the other two. In 2003 **Mis-Teeq** had their final pre-split hit with the 'West End Girls'-sampling number 13 'Style'.

Pet Shop Boys scored their third number 1 with the 1987 Christmas chart topper 'Always on My Mind' (*NOW 11*), originally a number 9 for Elvis Presley in 1972. **UB40** would follow suit, getting their third number 1 with a cover of '(I Can't Help) Falling in Love' (*NOW 26*). We should gloss over the twenty seconds of 'Jailhouse Rock' in **Jive Bunny and The Mastermixers'** 'Swing the Mood' (*NOW 15*), and someone needs to have a quiet word with **Scouting for Girls** about 'Elvis Ain't Dead' (*NOW 69*).

The video for 'She's Madonna' (*NOW 66*) was directed by Swede Johan Renck, recently back in the spotlight for directing **David Bowie**'s final videos for 'Blackstar' and 'Lazarus'. Johan's illustrious directorial career is pre-dated by a slightly more fleeting one in pop when, as **Stakka Bo**, he scored his only UK Top 40 hit and solitary *NOW* appearance with 'Here We Go' (*NOW 26*). Coincidentally, the same volume also featured 'Go West' by Pet Shop Boys and **Go West** performing 'The Tracks of My Tears'. Very Pet Shop Boys.

NOW 7 Did You Know . . .

Doctor and the Medics made their first appearance with the number 1 single 'Spirit in the Sky', previously a number 1 in 1970 for one-hit wonder Norman Greenbaum, and a number 1 again in 2003 for Gareth Gates featuring The Kumars. Doctor and the Medics made one more appearance, on *NOW 8*, with a cover of **ABBA**'s 1974 number 1 'Waterloo'. Their version featured Roy Wood of Wizzard – not to be confused with 'The Wizard' (also *NOW 8*), one of two appearances for **Paul Hardcastle**.

NOW 72 Did You Know . . .

Making both her first and second appearance was **Alesha Dixon**, with 'The Boy Does Nothing' and her biggest hit 'Breathe Slow', a number 3 in February 2009. Alesha would make three more appearances, including 'To Love Again' (*NOW 74*), co-written by **Gary Barlow**. Prior to her solo success Alesha made two *NOW* appearances with R&B trio Mis-Teeq, and was briefly married to MC Harvey of **So Solid Crew**, who had a number 1 with their 2001 chart debut '21 Seconds' (*NOW 50*).

IN OTHER NEWS . . . *NOW 7* (AUGUST 1986)

She's Gotta Have It, Spike Lee's first feature-length film, opened at cinemas. The cast includes graffiti-artist-cum-rapper Fab Five Freddy, immortalised in Blondie's 1981 number 5 'Rapture'.

EastEnders actress Anita Dobson had a number 4 single with 'Anyone Can Fall in Love', a vocal version of the soap opera's theme tune.

BBC TV screened the first episode of Alan Bleasdale's First World War drama *The Monocled Mutineer,* starring Paul McGann, and with a brief appearance by Clare Grogan of Altered Images.

11
NOW appearances

'Opportunities
(Let's Make Lots of Money)',
NOW 7, August 1986

'Love etc.',
NOW 72, April 2009

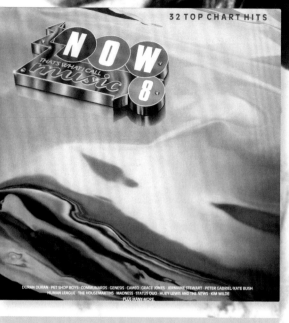

32 TOP CHART HITS

DURAN DURAN · PET SHOP BOYS · COMMUNARDS · GENESIS · CAMEO · GRACE JONES · JERMAINE STEWART · PETER GABRIEL/KATE BUSH
HUMAN LEAGUE · THE HOUSEMARTINS · MADNESS · STATUS QUO · HUEY LEWIS AND THE NEWS · KIM WILDE
PLUS MANY MORE

90s

NOW 8 Did You Know . . .

Making his only appearance to date was 'The Bard of Barking', **Billy Bragg**. 'Greetings to the New Brunette' featured additional guitar from **The Smiths'** Johnny Marr, and backing vocals by **Kirsty MacColl**. In 1988 Billy would enjoy a number 1 single when, along with pianist Cara Tivey, he recorded a version of The Beatles' 'She's Leaving Home', his contribution to a Childline charity project. Released as a double A-side single, the flip was 'With a Little Help from My Friends' by **Wet Wet Wet**, which appeared on *NOW 12*.

NOW 53 Did You Know . . .

Entering into *NOW* folklore on volume 53 was mononymous marvel **Darius**. He rose to fame via *Popstars* in 2001, and a year later resurfaced on *Pop Idol*, alongside **Will Young**, Gareth Gates, **Zoe Birkett** and **Rik Waller**. His legacy begins with the number 1 hit 'Colourblind', and continues with a further four Top 10 smashes. In 2003 Darius appeared in the Channel 4 programme *Hollyoaks*, performing his only non-Top 20 and non-*NOW* hit, 'Girl in the Moon'. There's a lesson in that somewhere . . .

IN OTHER NEWS . . . *NOW 8* (NOVEMBER 1986)

John Farnham released *Whispering Jack*, the biggest-selling album in Australia by an Australian artist. It spawned his only UK Top 40 single, 'You're the Voice'.

Sid and Nancy opened at cinemas. The tragic story of Sex Pistol Sid Vicious and his girlfriend Nancy Spungen, it stars Gary Oldman and Chloe Webb in the title roles. In 2018 Gary Oldman would win Best Actor at both the Golden Globes and Academy Awards for his portrayal of Winston Churchill in *Darkest Hour*.

The BBC TV drama series *The Singing Detective*, written by Dennis Potter and starring Michael Gambon, was shown for the first time. Its soundtrack album of pre-Second World War songs reached number 10 in the Album Chart.

JANET JACKSON

Janet Jackson first tasted success in 1986 when she began working with Grammy-award winning writers and producers Jimmy Jam and Terry Lewis. She has since scored thirty-eight Top 40 hits and nine appearances on *NOW*. Her 1998 number 6 hit 'Got 'til It's Gone' (*NOW 38*) sampled Joni Mitchell's 1970 number 11 'Big Yellow Taxi'; a cover version of the same song would provide **Counting Crows** featuring **Vanessa Carlton** with their only appearance to date on *NOW 54*.

Despite chalking up seventeen Top 10 hits Janet has yet to score a UK number 1, though she has come close on two occasions. 'The Best Things in Life Are Free', a 1992 duet with Luther Vandross, was kept off the top by **Snap!**'s 'Rhythm Is a Dancer' (*NOW 22*), while the 1993 ballad 'That's the Way Love Goes' (*NOW 26*) had to queue up behind the 'Five Live' EP that included 'Somebody to Love' by **George Michael** and **Queen** (*NOW 25*).

Janet's duet with Luther Vandross re-charted in 1995, when it was re-released to coincide with a new Greatest Hits collection, and the same year she reached number 3 with 'Scream', a duet with brother **Michael Jackson**. Other collaborators have included **Busta Rhymes**, **Nelly** and **Beenie Man**, the latter on the 2002 number 9 'Feel It Boy' (*NOW 53*). Often overlooked – can't imagine why – is 'Two to the Power', a 1984 duet with Cliff Richard that peaked at number 83.

Jimmy Jam and Terry Lewis's first success as writers and producers came with 'Just Be Good to Me' by The S.O.S. Band. The 1984 number 13 has since been adapted as 'Dub Be Good to Me' by **Beats International** featuring **Lindy Layton** (*NOW 17*), and 'Just Be Good to Green' by **Professor Green** featuring **Lily Allen** (*NOW 76*). We also have Jam and Lewis to thank for, among many others, 'Human' by **The Human League**, 'I Didn't Mean to Turn You On' by **Robert Palmer** (both *NOW 8*) and 'No More Drama' by **Mary J. Blige** (*NOW 52*).

90s

9
NOW appearances

'What Have You Done for Me Lately', *NOW 8*, November 1986

'Feel It Boy', Beenie Boy featuring Janet Jackson, *NOW 53*, November 2002

30 TOP CHART HITS

BEN E. KING · BOY GEORGE · CURIOSITY KILLED THE CAT · SIMPLY RED · A-HA · FREDDIE MERCURY
5 STAR · MENTAL AS ANYTHING · GENESIS · UB40 · BON JOVI · WESTWORLD · JACKIE WILSON
PLUS MANY MORE

80s

THAT'S WHAT I CALL MUSIC!

NOW 9 Did You Know . . .

The Housemartins make their third of four *NOW* appearances with 'Caravan of Love', a cover of a song by Isley Jasper Isley. 'Caravan of Love' gave The Housemartins their only number 1 single, and although it didn't appear on either of the band's studio albums, it did grace their greatest hits collection, *Now That's What I Call Quite Good*. Catchy title. 'Caravan of Love' is one of two a-cappella number 1s to feature on *NOW*, the other being 'Only You' by **The Flying Pickets** (*NOW 2*). Written, of course, by Vince Clarke, later of Erasure.

NOW 54 Did You Know . . .

Two ex-members of **Destiny's Child** both made their *NOW* debut on volume 54. 'Dilemma' by **Kelly Rowland** was the first of five appearances, and the first of two number 1s. The other, 'When Love Takes Over', appeared on *NOW 73*, and saw Kelly featuring on a **David Guetta** tune. Also stepping up to the plate is **Beyoncé** with ''03 Bonnie & Clyde', a first vocal collaboration with her then-boyfriend **Jay-Z**. It also marked the first of her eight *NOW* appearances to date, all of which have charted in the Top 5.

IN OTHER NEWS . . . *NOW 9* (MARCH 1987)

Lethal Weapon, starring Mel Gibson and Danny Glover, opened at cinemas. Glover's wife in this film and its three sequels is played by singer Darlene Love, who had a US number 1 single in 1962 with 'He's a Rebel'.

The Justified Ancients of Mu Mu released their debut single, 'All You Need Is Love'. They would wait another year for their only *NOW* appearance with 'It's Grim Up North (Part 1)' on volume 20, though chief 'Ancients' Jimmy Cauty and Bill Drummond enjoyed four other appearances as **The KLF** and **The Timelords**. Speaking of Timelords . . .

Patrick Troughton, best known as the second *Doctor Who* (1966–69), died at a comic convention at Columbus, Georgia. He was 67.

13

NOW appearances

'Sometimes',
NOW 9, March 1987

'Solsbury Hill',
NOW 54, April 2003

ERASURE

Synth pop duo Andy Bell and Vince Clarke can boast twelve of their thirteen *NOW* appearances being Top 10 hits, with only 'I Love Saturday' (*NOW 29*) stalling in the Top 20. This illustrious CV belies the fact that their first three singles failed to break the Top 50, despite Clarke having previously written Top 10 hits for **Depeche Mode**, Yazoo and a short-lived collaboration with **Feargal Sharkey**, The Assembly.

Eleven of Erasure's thirteen *NOW* appearances have been originals; the two covers being 'Take a Chance on Me' (*NOW 22*), one of four **ABBA** songs they recorded for the *ABBA-esque* EP in 1992. It gave the band their only number 1 single to date, and matched the chart peak of the Swedish quartet's original. The second was a cover of **Peter Gabriel**'s 1977 hit 'Solsbury Hill'. Peaking at number 13, three places higher than Peter's

version, its appearance on *NOW 54* marks Erasure's last showing to date.

Prior to his success in Erasure, Vince Clarke had been a founding member of Depeche Mode, penning their early hits 'New Life' and 'Just Can't Get Enough'. The latter song made an appearance on *NOW 72*, when covered by **The Saturdays** and released as the official Comic Relief song of 2009.

Erasure can also lay claim to providing **Dollar** with their only *NOW* appearance, when pop-star-turned-burger-van-salesman David Van Day and his sometime partner Thereza Bazar chose to cover 'Oh L'Amour' (*NOW 11*). Dollar's version reached number 11, considerably higher than the Erasure version, which failed to break the Top 40.

80s

BON JOVI

Bon Jovi's first foray into *NOW* territory came with the number 4 hit, 'Livin' on a Prayer', the first of eighteen singles by the band to make the Top 10. However, Bon Jovi have yet to reach number 1; the closest they have got so far is the 1994 number 2 'Always', but it was kept firmly in its place by **Whigfield**'s 'Saturday Night', and then by **Pato Banton**'s 'Baby Come Back' (both *NOW 29*).

'Livin' on a Prayer' was co-written by **Jon Bon Jovi** and guitarist Richie Sambora with prolific and successful songwriter Desmond Child, whose other *NOW* credits include **Robbie Williams**'s 'Old Before I Die' (*NOW 37*) and Katy Perry's 'Waking Up In Vegas' (*NOW 73*). The band's third appearance, 'It's My Life' (*NOW 47*), was written with Max Martin; his even more extensive *NOW* credits include **Britney Spears**'s 'Oops! . . . I Did It Again' (*NOW 46*) and **Ellie Goulding**'s 'Love Me Like You Do' (*NOW 91*).

Away from his band, Jon Bon Jovi has one solo appearance on *NOW* with the number 13 hit 'Janie, Don't Take Your Love to Town' (*NOW 38*). His first taste of solo success came in 1990 with 'Blaze of Glory', from the soundtrack to the Western *Young Guns II*. The film briefly included Jon in an uncredited role, though a few years on, his 'that's definitely him' acting parts included the role of handyman and love interest in *Ally McBeal*.

In 2010 Jon Bon Jovi was among the artists to appear on the number 1 single 'Everybody Hurts' by **Helping Haiti** (*NOW 75*), a charity project raising funds for victims of the 2010 Haiti earthquake. Other artists involved included **Leona Lewis**, **Rod Stewart**, **Mariah Carey**, **Michael Bublé**, **Kylie Minogue**, **Robbie Williams** and members of **Take That** and **Westlife**. **R.E.M.**'s original version of 'Everybody Hurts' appeared on *NOW 25* in 1993, when it reached number 7.

90s

30 TOP CHART HITS

BEN E. KING·BOY GEORGE·CURIOSITY KILLED THE CAT·SIMPLY RED·A-HA·FREDDIE MERCURY
5 STAR·MENTAL AS ANYTHING·GENESIS·UB40·BON JOVI·WESTWORLD·JACKIE WILSON
PLUS MANY MORE

90s

NOW 9 Did You Know . . .

'Down to Earth' was the first of three appearances for **Curiosity Killed the Cat**. Debut single 'Misfit' (*NOW 10*) had barely crept into the Top 100 when first released in 1986, but eventually peaked at number 7 in July 1987, its success undoubtedly helped by a video directed by Andy Warhol. The band's third appearance, 'Name and Number' (*NOW 16*), was sampled by **De La Soul** for their 1991 number 10 'Ring Ring Ring (Ha Ha Hey)', and by **Little Mix** featuring **Missy Elliott** for their 2013 number 16 'How Ya Doin'?'.

NOW 64 Did You Know . . .

Starting with dialogue sampled from Roger Corman's 1966 film *The Wild Angels*, **Primal Scream**'s 'Loaded' (*NOW 17*) was the pick of a slew of indie/dance crossover tracks released in the late eighties and early nineties. Their second appearance, with 'Rocks' (*NOW 27*), saw the band embrace their inner Rolling Stones, their efforts rewarded with a number 7 hit. Their third and final appearance came with 'Country Girl' (*NOW 64*), at which time the frequently changing line-up included former Stone Roses bass player Gary 'Mani' Mounfield.

5
NOW appearances
'Livin' on a Prayer',
NOW 9, March 1987
'Who Says You Can't Go Home',
NOW 64, July 2006

IN OTHER NEWS . . . *NOW 64* (JULY 2006)

Roger 'Syd' Barrett died, aged 60. A founding member of Pink Floyd, he wrote their first two singles, 'Arnold Layne' and 'See Emily Play', and played on their first two albums.

BBC TV broadcast the last weekly edition of *Top of the Pops*. The number 1 single was 'Hips Don't Lie' by **Shakira** featuring **Wyclef Jean** (*NOW 65*).

In California, singer **Avril Lavigne** married fellow Canuck Deryck Whibley, singer of **Sum 41**.

30 TOP CHART HITS

80s

M/A/R/R/S · PET SHOP BOYS · T'PAU · WET WET WET · THE COMMUNARDS · ERASURE · BILLY IDOL
KISS · HEART · CURIOSITY KILLED THE CAT · BANANARAMA · JOHNNY HATES JAZZ · LOS LOBOS
WHITESNAKE · NINA SIMONE · FREDDIE MERCURY AND MONTSERRAT CABALLÉ
PLUS MANY MORE

NOW 10 Did You Know . . .

Lining up all the 'ones' are **M/A/R/R/S** – a one-hit wonder, with one *NOW* appearance and a cracking number 1 single. A one-off collaboration between members of indie outfits Colourbox and A.R. Kane, the tune features a plethora of samples lifted from seventies and eighties funk artists, including **James Brown**, Trouble Funk, **Kool and the Gang** and Eric B. & Rakim. The single was actually a double A-side with 'Antina (The First Time I See She Dance)'; bonus points if you can whistle, or even remember, that particular ditty.

NOW 38 Did You Know . . .

NOW 38 gave us the first of two appearances from Cheshire dance act **Dario G**, both of them Top 10 hits. Their debut single 'Sunchyme' was based around a sample from 'Life in a Northern Town', a number 15 hit for Dream Academy in 1985. In 1994, Dream Academy's Nick Laird-Clowes contributed lyrics to two songs on Pink Floyd's album *The Division Bell*. Dario G's second appearance was 'Dream to Me' (*NOW 48*), this time featuring a sample from **The Cranberries**' 1994 single 'Dreams'.

IN OTHER NEWS . . . *NOW 10* (NOVEMBER 1987)

Actress Karen Gillan was born in Inverness. In the 2008 comedy series *The Kevin Bishop Show*, Karen's character roles included Mary Poppins and **Katy Perry**.

Ventriloquist Jimmy Tamley won TV talent show *New Faces of 87*. In second place was squeaky-voiced funny man Joe Pasquale.

On 22 November two Chicago television stations had their signal hacked. On both occasions the hackers broadcast an image of the Channel 4 TV host **Max Headroom**.

9
NOW appearances

'Sweet Little Mystery',
NOW 10, November 1987

'Yesterday',
NOW 38, November 1997

WET WET WET

Wet Wet Wet's nine appearances began on *NOW 10* with their number 5 hit 'Sweet Little Mystery', the second of their thirteen Top 10 singles. The Scottish band shared writing credits with Irish troubadour Van Morrison and English folk singer John Martyn. Second appearance, 'Angel Eyes (Home and Away)' (*NOW 11*), was co-written by **Squeeze** lyricist Chris Difford, while appearances three and nine – 'With a Little Help from My Friends' (*NOW 12*) and 'Yesterday' (*NOW 38*) – were covers of songs written by **John Lennon** and **Paul McCartney** for The Beatles.

'With a Little Help from My Friends' (*NOW 12*) was the first of three number 1s and the first of three occasions that the band forced **Kylie Minogue** to settle for a number 2 spot. 'With a Little Help . . .' kept 'Got to Be Certain' at bay; 'Goodnight Girl' blocked the way for 'Give Me Just a Little More Time' (both *NOW 21*). In 1994 Kylie's 'Confide in Me' (*NOW 29*) was one of six different singles that stalled at number 2 during The Wets' fifteen-week run at the top with 'Love Is All Around' (*NOW 28*).

The band's biggest hit, 'Love Is All Around' (*NOW 28*), was originally written by Reg Presley of The Troggs, and it gave that band a number 5 hit in 1967. The Wets' version was recorded for the 1994 Richard Curtis film *Four Weddings and a Funeral*. According to singer **Marti Pellow**, Curtis had offered them the option of covering this song, Barry Manilow's 'Can't Smile Without You' or **Gloria Gaynor**'s 'I Will Survive' (*NOW 25*). Gloria's original version was included on the resulting soundtrack album.

Wet Wet Wet enlisted the assistance of veteran songwriters Terry Britten and Graham Lyle for appearance number eight, 'If I Never See You Again' (*NOW 37*). Elsewhere on *NOW* the pair had written two of **Tina Turner**'s hits – 'What's Love Got to Do with It' (*NOW 3*) and 'We Don't Need Another Hero (Thunderdome)' (*NOW 16*). Britten also had a hand in penning 'Heaven Help' for **Lenny Kravitz** (*NOW 26*) and 'Jam Side Down' for **Status Quo** (*NOW 53*).

80s

NOW 11 Did You Know . . .

Reflecting the latest craze among the groovy youth, *NOW 11* featured four house music tracks in a row, all of them Top 10 hits: 'Doctorin' the House' by **Coldcut** featuring **Yazz and The Plastic Population**, 'House Arrest' by **Krush**, 'The Jack that House Built' by **Jack N Chill** and 'Rock Da House' by **The Beatmasters** featuring **The Cookie Crew**. Of these, only Yazz and The Plastic Population would return, with the number 1 hit 'The Only Way Is Up' (*NOW 13*).

NOW 35 Did You Know . . .

NOW 35 was our last glimpse of English dance combo **Clock**, who 'clocked up' three appearances, all of them cover versions. 'Axel F' (*NOW 30*) was originally a number 2 hit for Harold Faltermeyer on *NOW 5*, taken from the 1984 film *Beverly Hills Cop*. In 2005 a version by **Crazy Frog** (*NOW 61*) went one better, spending four weeks at number 1. Clock's second appearance, 'Woomph! There It Is' (*NOW 31*), was their version of a 1993 number 34 by Tag Team, while 'Oh, What a Night' (*NOW 35*) reworked The Four Seasons' 1976 number 1 'December, 1963 (Oh, What a Night)'.

IN OTHER NEWS . . . *NOW 11* (MARCH 1988)

Beetlejuice, Tim Burton's second film as director, was released. The soundtrack includes two calypso songs by Harry Belafonte, 'The Banana Boat Song' and 'Jump in the Line (Shake Senora)'.

The once-familiar green one pound note, first printed in 1797, was replaced by the one pound coin and was no longer legal tender.

Andy Gibb, youngest brother of **Bee Gees** Barry, Maurice and Robyn, died in hospital at the age of 30. His one Top 10 hit, 'An Everlasting

9

NOW appearances

'Heaven Is a Place on Earth', *NOW 11*, March 1988

'Always Breaking My Heart', *NOW 35*, November 1996

BELINDA CARLISLE

Belinda first tasted chart success with all-female five-piece The Go-Go's, who scored a number 1 album in the US but only managed one Top 40 single in the UK. In January 1988 'Heaven Is a Place on Earth' (*NOW 11*) not only gave her a first solo hit, but also her only number 1 when it displaced the Christmas chart-topper **Pet Shop Boys**' 'Always on My Mind' (also *NOW 11*). Oscar-winning actress Diane Keaton directed the promotional video for 'Heaven . . .'.

Six of Belinda's nine *NOW* appearances and eleven of her Top 40 hits, including 'Heaven Is a Place on Earth' and 'Leave a Light On' (*NOW 16*), were written by Rick Nowels. You'll find his name listed on lots of other *NOW* entries, including the number 1 singles 'Life Is a Rollercoaster' by **Ronan Keating** and 'I Turn to You' by **Melanie C**, both on *NOW 47*. 'Leave a Light On' features a slide-guitar solo from former Beatle George Harrison.

Belinda's last *NOW* appearance to date came on volume 35 with the number 8 hit 'Always Breaking My Heart', written for her by Per Gessle of Swedish duo **Roxette**. Guitarist Per and singer Marie Fredriksson managed six Top 10 hits between 1989 and 1993, including 'The Look' (*NOW 15*) and 'It Must Have Been Love' (*NOW 17*).

In 1982 The Go-Go's scraped into the singles chart with 'Our Lips Are Sealed', co-written by the band's guitarist **Jane Wiedlin** with Terry Hall, then of The Specials. Although The Go-Go's version could get no higher than number 47, Terry released his own version with his next band Fun Boy Three, and notched up their fourth Top 10 hit when the single peaked at number 7 in May 1983. In 1989 Jane played Joan of Arc in the film *Bill & Ted's Excellent Adventure*.

KYLIE MINOGUE

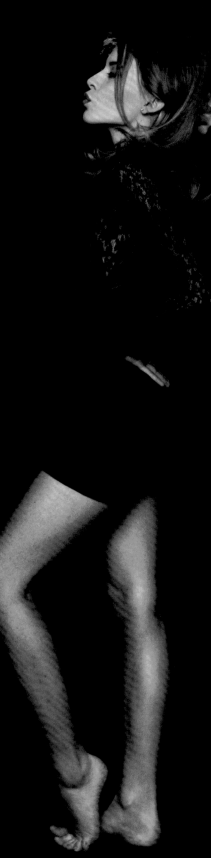

Kylie wasn't the first TV star to forge a career as a pop star and grace *NOW* – step forward **Jimmy Nail** with 'Love Don't Live Here Anymore' (*NOW 5*) – but with fifty-one Top 40 singles, including seven number 1s, duets with **Jason Donovan**, Nick Cave AND **Robbie Williams**, and twenty-four *NOW* appearances, Kylie is the fourth-most decorated *NOW* veteran of all time (tied with **David Guetta**), and the only solo artist to appear in four different decades. To quote her song, 'Wow' (*NOW 69*).

What we shall refer to as the 'soap phase' brought Kylie her first four appearances, including the mischievous – 'did she say funk?' – 'Step Back in Time' (*NOW 18*). After an absence of six years, her fifth number 1, 'Spinning Around' (*NOW 46*), marked the start of her second, 'imperial phase'. The single was co-written by **Paula Abdul** (four appearances, commencing with 'Straight Up' on *NOW 14*) and originally intended for her own musical career. In 2014 Kylie donated those gold lamé hot pants from the video to the Melbourne Performing Arts Collection, thereby preserving the posterior for posterity.

Kylie has never been short of musical courtiers, most famously Rob Davis from Glam rockers Mud, who co-wrote the enormo-hit 'Can't Get You Out of My Head' (*NOW 50*) with **Cathy Dennis**. Karen Poole, ex-**Alisha's Attic**, chipped in with 'Chocolate' (*NOW 22*), while Jake Shears and Babydaddy of **Scissor Sisters** contributed 'I Believe in You' (*NOW 60*). Long-time fans **Manic Street Preachers** helped Kylie embrace her inner indie on 'Some Kind of Bliss', her first UK single to miss the Top 20, a state of affairs that bassist Nicky Wire has publicly apologised for.

And so to the 'golden years', and with 'Dancing' (*NOW 99*), Kylie registered her first appearance since 'Get Outta My Way' (*NOW 77*) in 2010. Taken from her sixth number 1 album, *Golden*, much was made of Kylie's re-invention as a country-disco diva, something she herself described as 'like Dolly Parton standing on a dance floor'. Her choice of collaborators did nothing to dispel this, as she decamped to Nashville in 2017 to work with songwriter Steve McEwan (Faith Hill, Keith Urban, Kenny Chesney) and Nathan Chapman, Grammy Award-winning producer of **Taylor Swift**'s 'Love Story' (*NOW 72*).

30 TOP CHART HITS

PET SHOP BOYS · WET WET WET · T'PAU · MEL & KIM · MORRISSEY
BELINDA CARLISLE · KYLIE MINOGUE · BILLY OCEAN · BOMB THE BASS · JERMAINE STEWART
BANANARAMA · EDDY GRANT · EDDIE COCHRAN · WHITESNAKE · JOHNNY HATES JAZZ · ELTON JOHN · THE MISSION
PLUS MANY MORE

90s

NOW 11 Did You Know . . .

Eddie Cochran's 'C'mon Everybody' made number 6 when it was first released in 1958 then peaked at number 14 thirty years later after it soundtracked a TV advert for Levi's jeans. The advertising campaign started in 1985 when actor **Nick Kamen** disrobed to the sound of Marvin Gaye's 'I Heard It Through the Grapevine'. While Marvin never appeared on *NOW*, Nick popped up once with a cover of another Motown classic, 'Loving You Is Sweeter than Ever' (*NOW 9*).

NOW 99 Did You Know . . .

Norwegian singer and songwriter **Ina Wroldsen** made her second appearance, with **Jax Jones**, on the number 7 single 'Breathe'. Her first appearance as an artist came a year earlier when she provided vocals on 'Places' (*NOW 96*), the sixth Top 40 single for French DJ **Martin Solveig**. However, she has another fourteen credits as a songwriter, including number 1 hits for **Clean Bandit** ('Symphony', featuring **Zara Larsson**, on *NOW 97*), **Jess Glynne** ('Hold My Hand' on *NOW 90*) and **James Arthur** ('Impossible' on *NOW 84*).

IN OTHER NEWS . . . *NOW 99* (MARCH 2018)

Scientist and author Professor Stephen Hawking died, aged 76. In 1994 he added his vocal talents to the Pink Floyd album *The Division Bell*.

A new ten-pound note was issued, with an image of author Jane Austen replacing naturalist Charles Darwin.

At the thirty-first Annual Nickelodeon Kids' Choice Awards **Fifth Harmony** won Favourite Music Group, while **Shawn Mendes** and **Demi Lovato** won in the Favourite Male and Female Artist categories.

24
NOW appearances
'I Should Be So Lucky',
NOW 11, March 1988
'Dancing',
NOW 99, March 2018

80s

NOW 13 Did You Know . . .

'Girl You Know It's True' (*NOW 13*) and 'Girl I'm Gonna Miss You' (*NOW 16*) were the only two 'appearances' for German R&B duo **Milli Vanilli**. As we know, appearances can be deceptive, and so it proved when it was revealed that the public faces of the band, Fab Morvan and Rob Pilatus, didn't actually sing on any of their hits. In February 1990 they won the Grammy award for Best New Artist. Four days later, for the first time in the event's thirty-three-year history, the award was revoked.

NOW 72 Did You Know . . .

Another Welsh warbler marking their most recent appearance on *NOW 72* was **Duffy**. In 2008 she announced her arrival with the number 1 album *Rockferry*, and a number 1 single, 'Mercy' (*NOW 69*). She followed this up with three more Top 40 hits, 'Warwick Avenue' (*NOW 70*), 'Stepping Stone' (*NOW 71*) and 'Rain on Your Parade' (*NOW 72*). At the BRITs the following February, she went home with the awards for Best Album, Best Female Solo Artist and Best Breakthrough Act. Since then there have been no more visits to the Top 40 or *NOW*; come back soon, Duffy.

IN OTHER NEWS . . . *NOW 13* (NOVEMBER 1988)

Actress Emma Stone was born. Her TV break came in 2004 when she won the role of Laurie Partridge in the VH1 talent show *In Search of the Partridge Family*.

Cliff Richard released 'Mistletoe and Wine'; the bestselling single of 1988, it was originally written for the musical *Scraps*, an adaptation of Hans Christian Andersen's *The Little Match Girl*.

The Bill Murray film *Scrooged* opened at cinemas. The soundtrack includes 'Put a Little Love in Your Heart' by **Annie Lennox** and Al Green, a number 28 single that Christmas.

7
NOW appearances

'Kiss', The Art of Noise featuring Tom Jones, *NOW 13*, November 1988

'Islands in the Stream', Vanessa Jenkins, Bryn West and Tom Jones featuring Robin Gibb, *NOW 72*, April 2009

TOM JONES

Sir Tom Jones can look back on a distinguished career that has so far produced thirty solo Top 40 hits – yet all of his *NOW* appearances, all Top 40 hits too, have been collaborations or duets. His *NOW* résumé begins with 'Kiss' (*NOW 13*) by **The Art of Noise** featuring Tom Jones. This cover of the 1986 **Prince** single peaked at number 5, the highest chart position for The Art of Noise and one place higher than the Prince original had managed.

An all-Welsh partnership, 'Mama Told Me Not to Come' by Tom Jones and the **Stereophonics** (*NOW 45*) was written by acclaimed American songwriter Randy Newman, and reached number 4 in 2000. Randy was also responsible for 'You Can Keep Your Hat On', a song that Tom recorded for the 1997 film *The Full Monty*. Surprisingly 'Hat' has never been a UK hit single despite versions by **Joe Cocker** and American rock band Three Dog Night – who, incidentally, had a 1970 number 3 hit with 'Mama Told Me Not to Come'.

Tom's last *NOW* appearance to date was 'Islands In The Stream' (*NOW 72*), with Vanessa Jenkins, Bryn West and **Robin Gibb**. This cover of the 1983 number 7 hit for Kenny Rogers and Dolly Parton was written by the **Bee Gees**' Robin Gibb, along with his brothers Barry and Maurice. It gave Tom his first number 1 single for forty-three years and, at a youthful 68 years old, the accolade of oldest living person to score a number 1 single.

Tom Jones also 'appears' on the number 4 hit 'The Ballad of Tom Jones' (*NOW 39*) by **Space** with **Cerys** of Catatonia, though unlike Milli Vanilli there was no subterfuge. In 1999 Tom and Cerys actually got to sing together and scored a number 17 hit with 'Baby, It's Cold Outside', a song that had originally appeared in the 1949 romantic comedy *Neptune's Daughter*.

80s

32 TOP CHART HITS

MARC ALMOND featuring GENE PITNEY · PHIL COLLINS · ERASURE
BANANARAMA/LANANEENEENOONOO · YAZZ · SIMPLE MINDS · ROY ORBISON · PAULA ABDUL
BROTHER BEYOND · S'XPRESS · KIM WILDE · INXS
PLUS MANY MORE

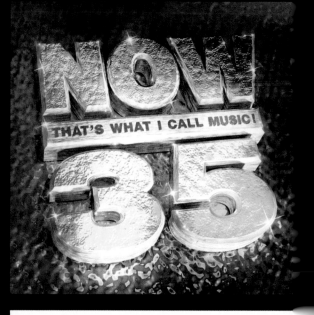

NOW 14 Did You Know . . .

Paula Abdul was a cheerleader for the Los Angeles Lakers basketball team when she was approached by The Jacksons to choreograph the video for their 1984 single 'Torture'. Dancer became singer in 1988 when she scored the first of seven Top 40 hits, and four *NOW* appearances, with 'Straight Up' (*NOW 14*). Her biggest hit was the 1990 number 2 'Opposites Attract' (*NOW 17*), officially credited to Paula Abdul with The Wild Pair. The video, in which Paula dances with cartoon character MC Skat Kat, won the 1991 Grammy Award for Best Short Form Video.

NOW 35 Did You Know . . .

Before **Crowded House** could tick off their first *NOW* appearance, **Paul Young**'s version of their song 'Don't Dream It's Over' (*NOW 20*) gave him the last of his three. The 1991 Crowded House album *Woodface* yielded their only Top 10 hit, 'Weather with You' (*NOW 21*), and two further Top 40 entries, 'Four Seasons in One Day' (*NOW 22*) and 'It's Only Natural' (*NOW 23*). 'Don't Dream It's Over' (*NOW 35*) was reissued in 1996 to promote a new Greatest Hits collection, and gave the band a number 25 single and their most recent *NOW* appearance.

IN OTHER NEWS . . . *NOW 14* (MARCH 1989)

American singer **Colby O'Donis** was born. He has two appearances on *NOW*, alongside **Lady Gaga** (*NOW 72*) and **Akon** (*NOW 73*), but his musical career began at the age of ten when he sang 'Mouse in the House' for the film *Stuart Little*.

The Louvre Pyramid opened in Paris. Both the pyramid and the interior of the Louvre Museum are locations for the 2006 film *The Da Vinci Code*.

American photographer Robert Mapplethorpe died. His images grace the cover of Patti Smith's *Horses*, Paul Simon's *Negotiations and Love Songs*

7
NOW appearances

'Buffalo Stance',
NOW 14, March 1989

'Woman',
NOW 35, November 1996

NENEH CHERRY

80s

'Buffalo Stance' began life as the B-Side of 1987 single 'Looking Good Diving' by duo Morgan-McVey. Neneh's number 3 hit version contains a mention of the Bristol Sound System, The Wild Bunch, a team that included Grant Marshall and Robert Del Naja of **Massive Attack**. Also receiving a name check is **Bomb the Bass**, aka DJ Tim Simenon. The song includes samples of 'Buffalo Gals' by **Malcolm McLaren** and '(Hey You) The Rock Steady Crew' (*NOW 1*) by **Rock Steady Crew**.

In 1990 Neneh recorded a version of 'I've Got You Under My Skin' (*NOW 18*) for *Red Hot + Blue*, a collection of Cole Porter songs released to raise funds for AIDS research. Neneh's single reached number 25, while **Deborah Harry** and Iggy Pop's duet 'Well, Did You Evah!' peaked at number 42. Other contributors to the album included **Kirsty MacColl** and **The Pogues**, Aztec Camera and **Erasure**. A 1992 follow-up album, *Red Hot + Dance*, included three new songs by **George Michael**, one of them the number 4 single 'Too Funky' (*NOW 23*).

In 1994 Neneh paired up with Senegalese singer **Youssou N'Dour** for another number 3 hit, '7 Seconds' (*NOW 29*). While Neneh sang all her parts in English, Youssou switched between English, French and West African language Wolof. At the 2005 Live 8 benefit concert at London's Hyde Park, Youssou shared vocals on a version of '7 Seconds' with **Dido**. Youssou first graced the charts in 1989 when he sang with **Peter Gabriel** on the single 'Shaking the Tree'.

Neneh scored her only number 1 to date when she teamed up with **Cher**, **Chrissie Hynde** and **Eric Clapton** for the 1995 Comic Relief single 'Love Can Build a Bridge' (*NOW 30*), a cover of a 1990 song by country music duo The Judds. The single was produced by Peter Asher who, as one half of Peter and Gordon, scored a 1964 number 1 with 'World Without Love', a song written by **John Lennon** and **Paul McCartney** but never recorded by The Beatles.

THE BEAUTIFUL SOUTH

The Beautiful South were formed by the former singer and drummer with **The Housemartins**, Paul Heaton and Dave Hemingway, and scored a number 2 hit at the first attempt with 'A Song for Whoever' (*NOW 15*). With the exception of 'Everybody's Talkin'' (*NOW 28*) all the band's *NOW* appearances were written by Paul Heaton, along with guitarist Dave Rotheray. 'Everybody's Talkin'' was written by Fred Neil, and had been a number 23 hit for Nilsson in 1969, when it featured in the film *Midnight Cowboy*.

The band's next three appearances, 'You Keep It All In' (*NOW 16*), 'A Little Time' (*NOW 18*) – their only number 1 – and 'Bell Bottomed Tear' (*NOW 22*), all featured Briana Corrigan as a third vocalist. By the time of their fifth appearance, 'Good As Gold (Stupid As Mud)' (*NOW 27*), Briana had left and the band had recruited Jacqui Abbott. Jacqui sang on the band's other six *NOW* appearances but also left, in 2000, to be replaced by Alison Wheeler.

'A Little Time' features piano by Pete Wingfield. A genuine one-hit wonder, Pete had a number 7 in 1975 with 'Eighteen with a Bullet'. Elsewhere on *NOW* you can hear him play keyboards on 'Respect Yourself' (*NOW 4*) by **The Kane Gang** and 'I'm Gonna Be (500 Miles)' (*NOW 13*) by **The Proclaimers**. The Beautiful South's penultimate *NOW* appearance, 'Perfect 10' (*NOW 41*), features additional guitar from their Go! Discs label-mate **Paul Weller**.

In 1998 another former Housemartin, **Norman Cook**, joined Heaton and Hemingway on The Beautiful South album *Quench* as 'Rhythm Consultant'. Norman also made his post-Housemartins *NOW* debut on volume 15 with 'Blame It on the Bassline', his only Top 40 single under his own name. The fourth member of the 'classic' Housemartins line-up, Stan Cullimore, is now a travel journalist and writer of children's TV programmes.

90s

NOW 15 Did You Know . . .

Jive Bunny and the Mastermixers make their only *NOW* appearance with the number 1 hit 'Swing the Mood'. After five weeks at the top it was toppled by Black Box, with 'Ride on Time', who would hold on at the peak for six weeks, only to be beaten by . . . Jive Bunny and the Mastermixers, with their second single, 'That's What I Like'. 'Swing the Mood' is a medley of fourteen 'golden oldies', topped and tailed by Glenn Miller's 1940 instrumental 'In the Mood', and credits twenty-eight different songwriters.

NOW 42 Did You Know . . .

Instrumental number 1 hits used to be commonplace, though most of the credit for that lies with The Shadows, who scored five of them between 1960 and 1963. *NOW* managed to feature the only three instrumental number 1s since it started in 1983, beginning with 'Doop' by **Doop** (*NOW 27*), 'Flat Beat' by **Mr Oizo** (*NOW 42*) and 'Animals' by **Martin Garrix** (*NOW 86*). The 'Flat Beat' video starred a yellow puppet called Flat Eric; both he and the tune had featured previously in a TV advert for Levi's Sta-Prest jeans.

IN OTHER NEWS . . . NOW 42 (MARCH 1999)

Singer **Dusty Springfield** died, aged 59. In a chart career spanning thirty-two years she scored twenty Top 40 hits, including one number 1 in 1966 with 'You Don't Have to Say You Love Me'.

At the 71st Academy Awards, Roberto Benigni won the Best Actor Oscar for *Life is Beautiful*. He was the first person to win the award for a film he also directed since Laurence Olivier in *Hamlet* in 1948.

Lawyers representing **Oasis** agreed to pay former drummer Tony McCarroll £550,000 after he sued the band over unpaid royalties.

11
NOW appearances
'Song for Whoever', *NOW 15*, August 1989
'How Long's a Tear Take to Dry?', *NOW 42*, March 1999

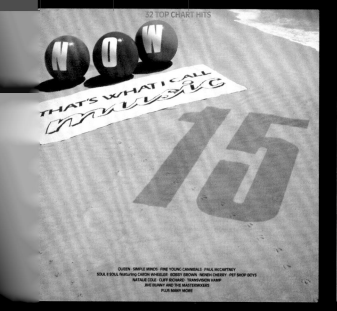

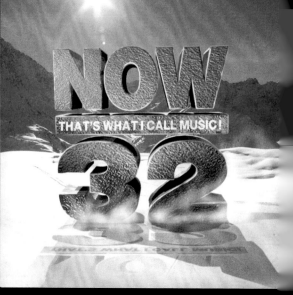

NOW 15 Did You Know . . .

'Every Little Step' was the first of four appearances and one of five Top 10 singles for **Bobby Brown**. From 1992 to 2006 he was married to **Whitney Houston**. His biggest hit came in 1994 with the number 3 single 'Two Can Play That Game' (*NOW 30*). Bobby was previously a member of **New Edition**, who made one *NOW* appearance with 'Candy Girl' (*NOW 1*). In 1989 he appeared in the film *Ghostbusters II*, playing the doorman at the mayor's residence.

NOW 32 Did You Know . . .

Jimmy Nail had his first hit with 'Love Don't Live Here Anymore' (*NOW 5*), a cover of the 1978 number 2 from **Rose Royce**. His sole number 1 came with 'Ain't No Doubt' (*NOW 22*), featuring additional vocals by Sylvia Mason-James. In 2000 Sylvia sang backing vocals on **Robbie Williams**'s 'Rock DJ' and 'Kids', his duet with **Kylie Minogue** (both *NOW 47*). Jimmy's final *NOW* appearance was the 1995 number 18 'Big River' (*NOW 32*).

IN OTHER NEWS . . . NOW 15 (AUGUST 1989)

Actress Hayden Panettiere was born, best known for playing cheerleader Claire Bennet in *Heroes* and Juliette Barnes in *Nashville*. In 2012 her single 'Telescope', from *Nashville* season one, reached number 26 in the Country Music Chart.

Harry Corbett OBE, the creator of Sooty, died, aged 71. His maternal uncle was Harry Ramsden, founder of the fish and chip restaurant chain that bears his name.

The **Rolling Stones** started their *Steel Wheels* tour at the now demolished Veterans Stadium in Philadelphia. It was their last tour to include original bassist

6
NOW appearances
'Back to Life
(However Do You Want Me)',
NOW 15, August 1989

'I Care' *NOW 32*.

SOUL II SOUL

Soul II Soul's six *NOW* appearances featured six different lead singers, starting with **Caron Wheeler** on 'Back to Life (However Do You Want Me)' (*NOW 15*). Caron was previously a member of vocal trio Afrodiziak and appeared on hits by Elvis Costello, **Heaven 17**, **Madness** and **The Special AKA**, including the latter's 'Nelson Mandela' (*NOW 3*). 'Missing You' (*NOW 18*) featured **Kym Mazelle**, who had scored a 1989 number 7 hit with 'Wait', a duet with Dr Robert of **The Blow Monkeys**.

For 'Joy' (*NOW 22*), Soul II Soul switched to a male singer in the shape of Jamaican Richie Stephens. In 1993 Richie released two singles on the Motown label, though both failed to chart. *NOW* appearance number 4 was 'Wish' (*NOW 26*), this time featuring a lead vocal from Melissa Bell, mother of 2008 *X Factor* winner **Alexandra Burke**.

Caron Wheeler briefly re-joined the band in 1995 and, while she provided lead vocals for three songs for the next album, *Volume V*, she left again before it was finished. Lead vocals on 'Love Enuff' (*NOW 31*) came from the powerful lungs of Penny Ford, previously singer with **Snap!** on their number 1 hit 'The Power'. Soul II Soul's final appearance to date was 'I Care' (*NOW 32*), with a lead vocal from Charlotte Kelly.

'I Care' was written by Walter Morrison, originally singer and keyboard player in seventies funk outfit The Ohio Players. In 1978, Walter, along with George Clinton and Garry Shider, wrote the anthemic 'One Nation Under a Groove' for Funkadelic. The drum sound from Soul II Soul's 1989 number 5 single 'Keep On Movin'' was sampled for 'Tom's Diner' (*NOW 18*), a number 2 hit in 1990 for **DNA** featuring Suzanne Vega.

90s

THIRTY-FIVE YEARS, THIRTY-FIVE SONGS FROM THIRTY-FIVE FILMS

1 **Eurythmics**, 'Sexcrime (Nineteen Eighty-Four)' (*NOW 4*) from *1984* (1984)

2 **Simple Minds**, 'Don't You (Forget About Me)' (*NOW 5*) from *The Breakfast Club* (1985)

3 **Tina Turner**, 'We Don't Need Another Hero' (*NOW 6*) from *Mad Max Beyond Thunderdome* (1985)

4 **Billy Ocean**, 'When the Going Gets Tough . . .' (*NOW 7*) from *The Jewel of the Nile* (1985)

5 **Berlin**, 'Take My Breath Away' (*NOW 9*) from *Top Gun* (1986)

6 **Phil Collins**, 'Two Hearts' (*NOW 14*) from *Buster* (1988)

7 **Bobby Brown**, 'On Our Own' (*NOW 16*) from *Ghostbusters II* (1989)

8 **Roxette**, 'It Must Have Been Love' (*NOW 18*) from *Pretty Woman* (1990)

9 **Righteous Brothers**, 'Unchained Melody' (*NOW 18*) from *Ghost* (1990)

10 **Bill Medley & Jennifer Warnes**, '(I've Had) The Time of My Life' (*NOW 19*) from *Dirty Dancing* (1987)

11 **Queen**, 'Bohemian Rhapsody' (*NOW 21*) from *Wayne's World* (1992)

12 **Annie Lennox**, 'Love Song for a Vampire' (*NOW 24*) from *Bram Stoker's Dracula* (1992)

13 **UB40**, 'I Can't Help Falling in Love' (*NOW 26*) from *Sliver* (1993)

14 **Wet Wet Wet**, 'Love Is All Around' (*NOW 28*) from *Four Weddings and a Funeral* (1994)

15 **Lisa Loeb & Nine Stories**, 'Stay (I Missed You)' (*NOW 29*) from *Reality Bites* (1994)

16 **Louis Armstrong**, 'We Have All the Time in the World' (*NOW 29*) from *On Her Majesty's Secret Service* (1969)

17 **Seal**, 'Kiss from a Rose' (*NOW 31*) from *Batman Forever* (1995)

18 **Coolio feat. LV**, 'Gangsta's Paradise' (*NOW 32*) from *Dangerous Minds* (1995)

19 **Underworld**, 'Born Slippy' (*NOW 34*) from *Trainspotting* (1996)

20 **Cardigans**, 'Lovefool' (*NOW 37*) from *William Shakespeare's Romeo + Juliet* (1996)

21 **R Kelly**, 'I Believe I Can Fly' (*NOW 37*) from *Space Jam* (1996)

22 **Ronan Keating**, 'When You Say Nothing At All' (*NOW 44*) from *Notting Hill* (1999)

23 **Aaliyah**, 'Try Again' (NOW 46) from *Romeo Must Die* (2000)

24 **All Saints**, 'Pure Shores' (*NOW 47*) from *The Beach* (2000)

25 **Melanie C**, 'I Turn to You' (*NOW 47*) from *Bend It Like Beckham* (2002)

26 **Gabrielle**, 'Out of Reach' (*NOW 49*) from *Bridget Jones's Diary* (2001)

27 **Chad Kroeger feat. Josey Scott**, 'Hero' (*NOW 53*) from *Spider-Man* (2002)

28 **Michael Andrews feat. Gary Jules**, 'Mad World' (*NOW 56*) from *Donnie Darko* (2001)

29 **will.i.am**, 'Bang Bang' (*NOW 86*) from *The Great Gatsby* (2013)

30 **Pharrell**, 'Happy' (*NOW 87*) from *Despicable Me 2* (2013)

31 **Idina Menzel**, 'Let It Go (*NOW 88*) from *Frozen*

32 **Ellie Goulding**, 'Love Me Like You Do' (*NOW 91*) from *Fifty Shades of Grey* (2015)

33 **Sam Smith**, 'Writing's on the Wall' (*NOW 92*) from *Spectre* (2015)

34 **Justin Timberlake**, 'Can't Stop the Feeling!' (*NOW 94*) from *Trolls* (2016)

35 **P!nk**, 'Just Like Fire' (*NOW 94*) from *Alice Through the Looking Glass* (2016)

JIMMY SOMERVILLE

The achievements of Jimmy Somerville are unique within the *NOW* canon. Across the first twenty volumes, Jimmy appeared ten times as a primary performer with three separate acts: twice with **Bronski Beat**, five times with **The Communards** and on four occasions as a solo artist. On top of this, Jimmy also provided backing vocals on **Banderas'** 'This Is Your Life' (*NOW 19*) and popped up with one final solo appearance on *NOW 31*, with a cover version of Susan Cadogan's 1975 number 4 'Hurts So Good'.

The Communards' 'Don't Leave Me This Way' – originally a 1977 hit for Harold Melvin and the Blue Notes – was the biggest-selling single of 1986. It appeared on *NOW 8* alongside two of that year's other bestsellers, 'I Want to Wake Up with You' by **Boris Gardner** and 'Every Loser Wins' by **Nick Berry**. Older fans of *EastEnders* will wallow in misty-eyed nostalgia at the memory of Nick Berry/Simon Wicks's heartfelt power ballad, whereas younger viewers may be moved to tears to learn that the storyline involved Ian Beale playing drums in a band originally known as Dog Market.

Jimmy's debut hit as a solo artist – 1989's 'Comment Te Dire Adieu' (*NOW 16*) – was actually credited as a duet with former Mo-dette **June Miles-Kingston**. A staple of the post-punk and new wave scene, June can most famously be heard providing backing vocals on the Fun Boy Three's final single 'Our Lips Are Sealed', a Top 10 hit in the Spring of 1983. Originally recorded by Françoise Hardy in 1968, 'Comment Te Dire Adieu' remains the only *NOW* writing credit for the legendary Serge Gainsbourg.

Both 'Comment Te Dire Adieu' and 'Read My Lips' (*NOW 17*) were early productions by Belgian-born Pascal Gabriel. However, his *NOW* story dates back to the late eighties, with a pair of trailblazing co-writing credits – 'Beat Dis' by **Bomb the Bass** (*NOW 11*) and 'Theme from S'Express' (*NOW 12*). Pascal also produced 'I Believe' (*NOW 19*) for self-confessed West Country lunatics **EMF**, the second of nine Top 40 hits and the first of two *NOW* entries, which included a cover of The Monkees' 'I'm a Believer' (*NOW 31*), alongside comedians **Reeves** and **Mortimer**.

DEBUT APPEARANCE: *NOW 16*

MOST RECENT APPEARANCE: *NOW 31*

32 TOP CHART HITS

TEARS FOR FEARS · WET WET WET · ERASURE · BELINDA CARLISLE
THE BEAUTIFUL SOUTH · TINA TURNER · QUEEN · LIVING IN A BOX
MILLI VANILLI · ADEVA · BOBBY BROWN · RICHARD MARX
PLUS MANY MORE

80s

NOW 16 Did You Know . . .

Making their debut with 'You're History' were **Shakespears Sister**, a name inspired by a 1985 single by **The Smiths** and comprising ex-**Bananarama** member Siobhan Fahey and American Marcella Detroit, who as Marcella Levy had co-written **Eric Clapton**'s 1977 hit 'Lay Down Sally'. Their biggest hit, 'Stay' (*NOW 21*), was written by the pair with David A. Stewart of **Eurythmics**, and spent eight weeks at number 1 in 1992. They made their final appearance later the same year with 'I Don't Care' (*NOW 22*), the fourth of six Top 40 hits.

NOW 31 Did You Know . . .

German singer **Billie Ray Martin** made her only solo appearance with the number 6 single 'Your Loving Arms', produced by electronic dance outfit **The Grid**, who included former Soft Cell keyboard player Dave Ball in their ranks and made one appearance of their own with the 1994 number 3 'Swamp Thing' (*NOW 28*). Billie Ray was also singer on **S'Express**' second appearance 'Hey Music Lover' (*NOW 14*), and co-wrote and sang on 'Talking with Myself' (*NOW 17*), the only appearance for **Electribe 101**.

IN OTHER NEWS . . . *NOW 16* (NOVEMBER 1989)

After twenty-eight years, checkpoints were opened on the Berlin Wall allowing free movement between East and West Germany.

At the cinema, Walt Disney musical animation *The Little Mermaid* opened, one of the ten biggest films of the year.

Nine days before Armistice Day, BBC One broadcast 'Goodbyeee', the final episode of *Blackadder Goes Forth*.

4

NOW appearances

'Comment Te Dire Adieu', Jimmy Somerville featuring June Miles-Kingston, *NOW 16*, November 1989

'Hurts So Good'

NOW 17 Did You Know . . .

Depeche Mode have fourteen Top 10 singles but have never enjoyed a number 1. The first of three *NOW* appearances, 'Enjoy the Silence' (*NOW 17*) came nine years after their first Top 10 hit, 'I Just Can't Get Enough'. A cover of the latter was the closest they got to the top spot when **The Saturdays** took it to number 2 in 2009 (*NOW 72*). A list of the good and the great who have covered 'Enjoy the Silence' includes **Tori Amos**, **Keane** and **Susan Boyle**.

NOW 53 Did You Know . . .

To date **Eminem** has only two *NOW* appearances, both of them number 1s and part of the tally of nine number 1 singles he has amassed. The video for 'Without Me' (*NOW 53*) sees Eminem dressed as a masked crime fighter, and the song includes a nod to Neal Hefti's 1966 *Batman* TV theme. His second appearance, 'Smack That' (*NOW 66*) by **Akon** featuring Eminem, is also one of Akon's three number 1s, all of which appear on *NOW*, the others being 'Lonely' (*NOW 61*) and 'Sexy Chick' (*NOW 74*) by **David Guetta** featuring Akon.

N OTHER NEWS . . . *NOW 17* (APRIL 1990)

wo months after his release from prison, Nelson Mandela attended his own tribute concert at Wembley Stadium. Artists performing ncluded **Aswad**, Tracy Chapman, **Peter Gabriel**, Terence Trent D'Arby and Neil Young.

John Waters's film *Cry-Baby*, starring Johnny Depp in the title role, opened in cinemas. Like Waters's previous film, *Hairspray*, it would be adapted for the stage as a musical.

wo giants of jazz died: the singer Sarah Vaughan, aged 66, and saxophonist Dexter Gordon, aged 67.

5

NOW appearances

'Killer', Adamski featuring Seal, *NOW 17*, April 1990

'My Vision', Jakatta featuring Seal, *NOW 53*, November 2002

SEAL

'Officially' Seal doesn't have any number 1 singles, but as he both co-wrote and sang on **Adamski**'s 1990 chart topper 'Killer' (*NOW 17*), we will give him the benefit of the doubt. Seal tried again with 'Killer' in 1991 when he released a 'solo' version, though this could do no better than number 8. 'Killer' did manage to get back to number 1 for three weeks in 1993 when **George Michael**'s version appeared on his *Five Live* EP.

Seal's second *NOW* appearance, 'Crazy', spent one week at number 2, frustrated by **Enigma**'s 'Sadness (Part I)' (both *NOW 19*). He also had two goes at the chart with his next appearance, 'Prayer for the Dying' (*NOW 28*); it peaked at number 14 in May 1994, and was re-released the following year, when it only managed to get to number 51.

In 1997 Seal recorded a version of 'Fly like an Eagle' by **Steve Miller Band**, and 'sampled' himself, adding some lyrics from his hit 'Crazy' to the end of the song. Steve Miller Band's only appearance to date is 'The Joker' (*NOW 18*). It topped the US chart when first released in 1974 but waited sixteen years to repeat the feat in the UK, after it was featured in a TV commercial for Levi's jeans.

Speaking of 'The Joker' . . . Seal's fourth *NOW* appearance, 'Kiss from a Rose' (*NOW 31*), reached number 20 when first released in 1994, but peaked at number 4 the following year when it was included in the film *Batman Forever*. And continuing the film motif, Seal's collaboration with **Jakatta**, 'My Vision' (*NOW 53*), is his most recent appearance and features a sample from Thomas Newman's score for the 1994 film *The Shawshank Redemption*.

90s

90s

NOW 20 Did You Know . . .

Prince made just two appearances on *NOW*, both featuring his band **The New Power Generation**. 'Gett Off' (*NOW 20*) reached number 4, and quotes **James Brown**'s 1969 single 'Mother Popcorn'. Second appearance 'Thunder' (*NOW 22*) was issued as a picture disc, showing the band line-up augmented by Prince's future wife, Mayte Garcia. The NPG had their own number 15 hit in 1995 with 'The Good Life', while their singer and keyboard player **Rosie Gaines** reached number 4 in 1997 with 'Closer than Close' (*NOW 37*).

NOW 30 Did You Know . . .

We have Simon Cowell to thank for boyband **Ultimate Kaos** and their two appearances, 'Some Girls' (*NOW 29*) and 'Hoochie Booty' (*NOW 30*). Under their original name, Chaos, the band had a 1992 number 55 single with a cover of **Michael Jackson**'s 'Farewell My Summer Love' (*NOW 4*). In 2003 Ultimate Kaos singer Haydon Eshun appeared in the reality TV series *Reborn in the USA*, finishing fourth in the competition that was won by ex-Spandau Ballet singer Tony Hadley.

IN OTHER NEWS . . . NOW 20 (NOVEMBER 1991)

On 24 November **Queen** singer **Freddie Mercury** died at his home in Kensington, West London, aged 44.

The Addams Family opened in cinemas; it would become the seventh-highest grossing film of 1991. In 2005 Wednesday Addams actress Christina Ricci provided vocals for the Beck single 'Hell Yes'.

Alan Bennett's play *The Madness of George III* had its premiere at the National Theatre in London.

8
NOW appearances
'Get Ready for This',
NOW 20, November 1991

'Here I Go',
NOW 30, April 1995

2 UNLIMITED

Formed by producers Jean-Paul De Coster and Phil Wilde, Belgian techno outfit 2 Unlimited had fourteen Top 40 hits between 1991 and 1995. Their debut single, 'Get Ready for This' (*NOW 20*), was a number 2 hit that found its route to the top blocked first by **Bryan Adams**'s '(Everything I Do) I Do It for You', then by **Vic Reeves** and **The Wonder Stuff**'s 'Dizzy' (*NOW 20*). 'Get Ready …' opens with the line, 'Y'all ready for this?', sampled from 'It's Funky Enough' by American rapper The D.O.C.

For their follow-up single 'Twilight Zone' (*NOW 21)* they enlisted Dutch rapper Ray Slijngaard and singer

Anita Doth, who – according to Jean-Paul – had been working as a traffic warden in Amsterdam. Their third appearance was the repetitively negative 'No Limit' (*NOW 24*), which ended **Whitney Houston**'s ten-week stay at the top with 'I Will Always Love You'. Their 1994 number 6 single 'The Real Thing' (*NOW 28*) demonstrated a more highbrow approach, using a riff taken from J.S. Bach's 'Toccata and Fugue In D Minor'.

Their 2 Unlimited guise wasn't the first time that our Belgian studio boffins had been in the UK charts. In 1990 Jean-Paul De Coster had a number 7 hit as **Bizz Nizz** with

'Don't Miss the Party Line' (*NOW 17*). The following year Phil Wilde, under the guise of T99, reached number 14 with 'Anasthasia'.

Unlikely as it may seem, *NOW* has been host to not one but two successful Belgian techno acts. **Technotronic** had nine Top 40 singles and three appearances on *NOW*, though their third, 'Megamix' (*NOW 18*), incorporated elements of their first, 'Pump Up the Jam' (*NOW 16*), and their second, 'This Beat Is Technotronic' (*NOW 17*). We can also thank Belgium for **Lasgo** (two *NOW* appearances), **Milk Inc.** and most recently **Lost Frequencies** (one appearance each).

90s

90s

NOW 22 Did You Know . . .

En Vogue made the first of three appearances with 'My Lovin''. Sampling **James Brown**'s 1973 song 'The Payback', it was their biggest hit, peaking at number 4. Their collaboration with **Salt 'N' Pepa**, 'Whatta Man' (*NOW 28*), was originally recorded in 1968 by Lynda Lyndell. 'Don't Let Go (Love)' (*NOW 37*) was the last of the group's hits to feature Dawn Robinson, who left to join short-lived venture Lucy Pearl. It re-charted in 2011 after the nascent **Little Mix** performed it on *The X Factor*.

NOW 97 Did You Know . . .

Introducing **Stefflon Don**, aka Birmingham rapper Stephanie Allen. Her first *NOW* appearance, 'Instruction', saw her hook up with **Jax Jones** for his third showing and **Demi Lovato** for her fifth. 'Hurtin' Me' (*NOW 98*) was a collaboration with Moroccan-born hip-hop artist **French Montana**, reaching number 7 in October 2017. In March 2018 Stefflon Don became the last artist ever to appear on the front cover of the *NME* music magazine.

14
NOW appearances

'It Only Takes a Minute',
NOW 22, August 1992

'Giants',
NOW 97, July 2017

IN OTHER NEWS . . . NOW 22 (AUGUST 1992)

Birth Announcement: To Mr & Mrs XCX, a daughter, **Charli XCX**. In 2013 she scored her first number 1 with 'I Love It', a collaboration with **Icona Pop**.

Comedian Graham Norton made his debut at the Edinburgh Fringe Festival. His act included wearing a tea towel on his head while impersonating Mother Teresa of Calcutta.

Composer John Cage died, aged 79. Perhaps his best-known work is *4'33"*, which calls on musicians to assemble and not play their instruments for the time specified in the title.

TAKE THAT

Take That opened their *NOW* account with two cover versions, starting with the number 7 hit 'It Only Takes a Minute' (*NOW 22*), originally a US hit for Tavares in 1975 but not released in the UK until 1986, when it peaked at number 46. Take That's version of 'Could It Be Magic' (*NOW 24*) reached number 3, considerably higher than Barry Manilow's number 25 original in 1975 or **Donna Summer**'s number 40 version released the following year.

Six of Take That's twelve number 1s have appeared on *NOW*, starting with 'Pray' (*NOW 26*). Their first of four consecutive 'one-word' number 1s on *NOW*, it was followed by 'Sure' (*NOW 29*), 'Patience' (*NOW 66*) and 'Shine' (*NOW 67*). Keen-eyed readers will notice that the 1993 number 1 'Babe' is missing to complete the set. The *NOW* collection of their number 1s is completed by a mini 'Day' series: 'Greatest Day' (*NOW 72*) and 'These Days' (*NOW 90*).

For their first four appearances plus the 2010 'Robbie's return', 'The Flood' (*NOW 78*), the group were a five-piece. Six appearances saw them as a quartet, and two further entries – 'These Days' (*NOW 90*) and 'Giants' (*NOW 97*) – had them as a trio, following the departure of Jason Orange. In 2016 the trio were augmented by drum and bass duo **Sigma** for the number 21 single 'Cry' (*NOW 94*).

Let's throw **Gary Barlow** and **Robbie Williams**'s 'Shame' (*NOW 77*) into the mix, along with the Diamond Jubilee number 1 single, 'Sing' by Gary Barlow and **The Commonwealth Band** (*NOW 82*), and Gary's only solo appearance, 'Let Me Go' (*NOW 87*). Add his writing credits for **Blue**'s 'Guilty' (*NOW 56*), **Matt Cardle**'s 'Run for Your Life' and **Westlife**'s 'Lighthouse' (both *NOW 80*), and it barely leaves space for the fourth of **Mark Owen**'s six Top 40 releases, 'Four Minute Warning' (*NOW 56*).

From *NOW 3* until George Michael's untimely death in 2016 there were two appearances with **Wham!**, two duets and nine solo appearances, most recently a posthumous and second showing for 'Fastlove' (*NOW 96*). 'Don't Let the Sun Go Down On Me' (*NOW 22*), with **Elton John**, was his fourth post-Wham! number 1 and the first of those two *NOW* duets, both cover versions. This came six years after Elton lent his piano skills to 'The Edge of Heaven' by Wham! (*NOW 7*), and seven years after George provided backing vocals on Elton's own 'Nikita' (*NOW 6*).

'Too Funky' (*NOW 23*) marked George's first unaided solo appearance with a sample from Tony Hancock's classic 1961 comedy 'The Radio Ham' ('Would you stop playing with that radio of yours, I'm trying to get to sleep'). Hancock had adorned the sleeve of **Phil Collins**'s 1990 single 'Something Happened on the Way to Heaven' (*NOW 18*), and another celebrated quote – 'Watch it, mate, or I'll have you with a punch up the bracket' – was swiped by **The Libertines** (a solitary showing – 'Can't Stand Me Now' on *NOW 59*) for the title of their debut album in 2002.

'Freedom' (*NOW 34*) made it to number 2 for **Robbie Williams** in the summer of 1996 and gave the imploring entertainer his first solo appearance with a faithful (bar ditching the '90') rendition of George's number 28 hit 'Freedom '90'. On the same edition, George began a phenomenal run of singles from his number 1 album *Older*. Five singles, five consecutive *NOW*s, two number 1s – 'Jesus to a Child' (*NOW 34*) and 'Fast Love' (*NOW 35*) – and three number 2s – 'Spinning the Wheel' (*NOW 36*), 'Star People '97' (*NOW 37*) and 'You Have Been Loved' (*NOW 38*).

Wham! made the first of their appearances on *NOW 3* with 'Wake Me Up Before You Go-Go', a number 1 single for two weeks in June 1984. The video saw George and Andrew sporting the soon-to-be-ubiquitous Katharine Hamnett 'Choose Life' T-shirts, which would quickly spawn **Frankie Goes to Hollywood**'s own cheeky adaptation, 'Frankie Say'. As for the single's sleeve, it featured photography by Trevor Key – the man responsible for the renowned Virgin signature logo, a brand that adorned every *NOW* release until volume 74.

GEORGE MICHAEL

80s

NOW 22 Did You Know . . .

Electronic made their only appearance with the number 6 'Disappointed', one of their eight Top 40 singles. Two of the song's three writers had already made their *NOW* debut, and the third would be back twelve months later. Johnny Marr was first up with **The Smiths'** 'What Difference Does It Make?' (*NOW 2*), followed by Neil Tennant of **Pet Shop Boys** with 'Opportunities (Let's Make Lots of Money)' (*NOW 7*). Despite an impressive twenty-seven Top 40 singles, Bernard Sumner's **New Order** made only two appearances, beginning with 'Regret' (*NOW 25*).

NOW 96 Did You Know . . .

Julia Michaels made her first appearance as a performer with 'Issues', having already notched up her first five writings credits on the previous five volumes, including **Justin Bieber'**s second number 1, 'Sorry' (*NOW 93*). The same volume included 'Hands to Myself', one of two songs Julia wrote with **Selena Gomez**, the other being 'Good for You' (*NOW 92*), featuring the spell-check confusing **A$AP Rocky**. Julia made her second appearance as an artist alongside **Clean Bandit** with the 2017 number 4 'I Miss You' (*NOW 98*).

IN OTHER NEWS . . . *NOW 96* (APRIL 2017)

There was renewed demand for *NOW That's What I Call Music! 48* after it featured in an episode of the BBC comedy *Peter Kay's Car Share*.

Filmmaker Jonathan Demme died, aged 73. In 1984 he made the acclaimed Talking Heads concert film *Stop Making Sense*, and went on to direct the multi-Oscar winning *Silence of the Lambs* and *Philadelphia*.

In Stockholm, songwriter Bob Dylan received the Nobel Prize for Literature.

11
NOW appearances
'Don't Let the Sun Go Down on Me', George Michael and Elton John, *NOW 22*, July 1992

'Fastlove', *NOW 96*, April 2017

90s

NOW 23 Did You Know . . .

ABBA make their only *NOW* appearance with the 1976 number 1 'Dancing Queen', re-issued to promote their third greatest hits collection, the phenomenal *Gold*. Although it only spends one week at number 1 on release in 1992, it returns to number 1 for five weeks in 1999 when it is reissued to mark the twenty-fifth anniversary of their first hit, 'Waterloo'. It's back at number 1 again in 2008 when the film *Mamma Mia* is released. To date it has spent a total of four-and-a-half years in the Top 40.

NOW 36 Did You Know . . .

The Chemical Brothers make the first of five appearances with the number 1 single 'Block Rockin' Beats'. The song takes its title from the vocal sample 'back with another of those block rockin' beats' in the 1989 Schoolly D song 'Gucci Again'. The band's fourth appearance, 'Galvanize' (*NOW 60*), features rapper **Q-Tip**, formerly of A Tribe Called Quest. You'll also find him on **Janet Jackson**'s 'Got 'til It's Gone' (*NOW 38*) and 'Thank You' by **Busta Rhymes** featuring Q-Tip, **Kanye** and **Lil Wayne** (*NOW 87*).

IN OTHER NEWS . . . NOW 23 (NOVEMBER 1992)

BBC Two broadcast the first episode of *Absolutely Fabulous*. In 2016 it was turned into a film with a theme tune written by **Pet Shop Boys** that appears on *NOW 28*.

In the Album Chart three greatest-hits collections took it in turn to have the number 1 spot: *Glittering Prize 81/91* by **Simple Minds**, *Greatest Hits: 1965–1992* by **Cher** and *Pop! The First 20 Hits* by **Erasure**.

American actress **Miley Cyrus** was born. She initially found fame in the Disney Channel TV series *Hannah Montana*. The theme song, 'Best of Both Worlds', was co-written by **Robbie Nevil**, singer of 'C'est La Vie' on *NOW 9*.

10 NOW appearances
'House of Love', *NOW 23*, November 1992
'Hey Child', *NOW 36*, March 1997

EAST 17

Songwriter Tony Mortimer was so enamoured of his East London roots he named his band **East 17** after the postcode for Walthamstow, which was also the name of their number 1 debut album. It yielded six Top 40 singles and the first four of their ten *NOW* appearances, including the number 10 debut 'House of Love'. In 1996 female duo **Shampoo** included a version of 'House of Love' on their debut album. Shampoo's only *NOW* appearance came on volume 29, with their number 11 single 'Trouble'.

East 17 were managed by Tom Watkins, a role he had previously filled for **Pet Shop Boys** and Bros. In 1996 East 17 scored a number 11 hit with 'West End Girls' (*NOW 25*), a cover of the Pet Shop Boys' 1985 chart topper. Another cover, 'If You Ever' by East 17 featuring **Gabrielle** (*NOW 35*), originally made number 36 in 1992 when released by US R&B quartet Shai. The East 17 version charted at number 2 but was held off the top by **Spice Girls**' second number 1, 'Say You'll Be There' (also *NOW 35*).

The band had their biggest hit with the 1994 Christmas number 1 'Stay Another Day' (*NOW 30*). The following year Tony Mortimer won Songwriter of the Year at the Ivor Novello Awards, though 'Stay Another Day' lost out to 'Parklife' by **Blur** (*NOW 29*) in the Single of the Year category at the 1995 BRIT Awards. In 2002 **Girls Aloud** recorded their version of 'Stay . . .' as the B-side of their debut number 1 'Sounds of the Underground' (*NOW 54*).

In 1998, without Tony Mortimer, the band changed their name to **E17** and landed a number 2 hit with 'Each Time' (*NOW 41*). Singer Brian Harvey managed three solo hits, the most successful of which was the number 20 single 'Loving You (Ole Ole Ole)', a collaboration with The Refugee Crew. In 2005 Brian was badly injured in a freak motoring accident when he ran himself over. He told GMTV News that he fell from the car when he opened the door to be sick, having eaten too many jacket potatoes.

ACE OF BASE

Swedish quartet Ace of Base consisted of siblings Jenny, Jonas and Malin Berggren, along with Ulf Ekberg. Their only number 1, 'All That She Wants' was the first of six *NOW* appearances and twelve Top 40 singles. **The Kooks** recorded a version in 2007 for a collection to mark the fiftieth anniversary of Radio 1. Ace of Base's second appearance, 'The Sign' (*NOW 27*), made it to number 2 but was kept off the top by **Mariah Carey**'s 'Without You', then 'Doop' by **Doop** (also *NOW 27*).

Ace of Base also made the chart with two cover versions, starting with 'Don't Turn Around' (*NOW 28*). The song was originally released as the B-side of **Tina Turner**'s 1986 single 'Typical Male'. In 1988 it had given **Aswad** their only number 1, while Ace of Base had to settle for number 5. In 1998 Ace of Base scored their tenth Top 40 single with a version of **Bananarama**'s 'Cruel Summer'; it reached number 8, matching the original, which appears on *NOW 15*.

Ace of Base are one of twelve Swedish acts to have number 1 singles on *NOW*. The other eleven are **Avicii**, **Zara Larsson**, **Swedish House Mafia**, **Tove Lo**, **Alesso**, **Robyn**, **Basshunter**, **Eric Prydz**, **Icona Pop**, **Rednex** and, of course, **ABBA**. However, Sweden's greatest contribution comes from songwriter Max Martin, who can boast a quite extraordinary SIXTY-SEVEN songs on *NOW*, including fifteen number 1s, starting with 'I Want It That Way' by **Backstreet Boys** on *NOW 43*.

Ace of Base's last appearance was 'Always Have, Always Will' (*NOW 42*), co-written by Jonas Berggren and Mike Chapman. In the early seventies Mike was responsible for hits by The Sweet, Mud and Suzi Quatro, and a few years down the line he was producer on 'Heart of Glass' by Blondie and 'My Sharona' by The Knack. Next time you're at a sports event and they play Tina Turner's 'The Best' (*NOW 16*) over the PA, remember that Mike is getting 50 per cent of the songwriting royalties.

90s

90s

NOW 25 Did You Know . . .

'Everybody Hurts' was the first appearance by **R.E.M.** and the second of eleven Top 10 hits. It was taken from their 1992 number 1 album *Automatic for the People*, as was their second, 'The Sidewinder Sleeps Tonite' (*NOW 26*). Their third and final appearance was the 1994 number 9 'What's the Frequency, Kenneth?' (*NOW 29*). There have been many cover versions of 'Everybody Hurts', including **The Corrs**, **Joe Cocker** and Tina Arena, though the best known is undoubtedly the 2010 number 1 by **Helping Haiti** (*NOW 75*).

NOW 42 Did You Know . . .

'Walk Like a Panther' by **The All Seeing I** featuring **Tony Christie** marked the second of two appearances for 'The I', and the first of three for Tony. The All Seeing I previously appeared on *NOW 39* with their version of Sonny and **Cher**'s 1967 single 'The Beat Goes On'. Tony Christie returned in 2005 with the official Comic Relief single '(Is This the Way to) Amarillo' (*NOW 60*), which had first charted in 1971, and 'Avenues and Alleyways' (*NOW 61*), a reissue of his 1973 number 37 single.

IN OTHER NEWS . . . NOW 25 (AUGUST 1993)

Independent Local Radio scrapped *The Network Chart Show*, presented for the last nine years by David Jensen. David was the voice behind the TV adverts for fourteen volumes of *NOW*, beginning with *NOW 8* in November 1986.

For the first time in history, Buckingham Palace opened its doors to the public.

After 154 episodes, BBC TV pulled the plug on soap opera *Eldorado*.

6
NOW appearances
'All That She Wants', *NOW 25*, August 1993
'Always Have, Always Will', *NOW 42*, March 1999

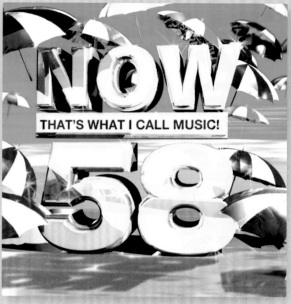

90s

NOW 25 Did You Know . . .

Making their debut are Jamaican reggae duo **Chaka Demus** and **Pliers**, known to their mums as John Taylor and Everton Bonner. 'Tease Me' was the first of six Top 40 hits in fourteen months, a run that saw them appearing on five consecutive volumes of *NOW*. Their biggest hit was a number 1 version of 'Twist and Shout' (*NOW 27*), which also credits **Jack Radics** and **Taxi Gang**. Five years earlier **Salt 'N' Pepa** scored a number 4 with their rendition, which was included on *NOW 13*.

NOW 58 Did You Know . . .

'Hey Ya!', the number 3 single from **OutKast**, was the second and most recent appearance by the R&B outfit from Atlanta, Georgia. Comprising **André 3000** and Big Boi, the duo first popped up on *NOW 49* with the number 2 hit 'Ms. Jackson'. André would be back with two more number 3 hits, 'Millionaire' (*NOW 59*) by **Kelis** featuring André 3000, and 'Dedication to My Ex (Miss That)' (*NOW 81*) by **Lloyd** featuring André 3000 and **Lil Wayne**.

IN OTHER NEWS . . . NOW 58 (JULY 2004)

French crooner Sacha Distel died, aged 71. His only UK Top 10 hit was 'Raindrops Keep Falling on My Head' in 1970, though he is mentioned in the lyrics of Peter Sarstedt's 1969 number 1 'Where Do You Go to My Lovely'.

The first series of the BBC's *Strictly Come Dancing* ended with newsreader Natasha Kaplinsky and her partner Brendan Cole crowned champions.

At the cinema the live-action version of *Thunderbirds* was released. The theme song 'Thunderbirds Are Go' (*NOW 59*) gave **Busted** their fourth number 1 single.

13
NOW appearances

'Dreams',
NOW 25, August 1993

'Stay the Same',
NOW 58, July 2004

GABRIELLE

'Dreams' was the first of thirteen *NOW* appearances and two number 1 singles for the singer born Louise Gabrielle Bobb, in East London. When 'Dreams' was first released in 1991 it included a sample of Tracy Chapman's 1988 number 4 single 'Fast Car', though legal wrangling resulted in that version being withdrawn. 'Fast Car' would eventually find its way onto *NOW 93* when recorded by **Jonas Blue** featuring **Dakota**. 'Dreams' spent three weeks at number 1 before it was replaced by **Take That**'s first chart topper, 'Pray' (*NOW 26*).

Gabrielle's fourth appearance, 'Give Me a little More Time' (*NOW 33*) was co-written by Benjamin Barson, older brother of **Madness** keyboard player Mike. Next up was 'If You Ever' (*NOW 35*), a collaboration with **East 17** and a re-working of the 1992 single 'If I Ever Fall in Love' by Shai. In 1997 Gabrielle had a number 7 hit with 'Walk on By' (*NOW 36*), originally a 1964 number 9 single for Dionne Warwick, though the best chart position for this song belongs to **Sybil**'s number 6 version in 1990.

Gabrielle nabbed her second number 1 in 2000 with 'Rise' (*NOW 45*), which included a sample of Bob Dylan's 1973 number 14 hit 'Knockin' on Heaven's Door', from the soundtrack to the film *Pat Garrett and Billy the Kid*.

In 1991 Guns N' Roses took a version of 'Knockin' on Heaven's Door' up to number 2, though a version featuring Mark Knopfler, released in aid of families affected by the Dunblane school shooting, spent a week at number 1 in 1996.

In 2001 Gabrielle had a fourteenth Top 40 hit with the number 4 'Out of Reach' (*NOW 49*). Taken from the soundtrack to the film *Bridget Jones's Diary*, the same collection gave **Geri Halliwell** her fourth number 1 with 'It's Raining Men' (also *NOW 49*), a cover of **The Weather Girls** song that had first appeared on *NOW 3*. **Martha Wash** of The Weather Girls has two other *NOW* appearances with 'Keep on Jumpin'' (*NOW 34*) and 'Something's Goin' On' (*NOW 37*) credited to **Todd Terry** featuring Martha Wash and **Jocelyn Brown**.

90s

PAUL WELLER

Paul Weller's five appearances on *NOW*, beginning with 'Sunflower' (*NOW 25*), barely begin to scrape the surface of a long and fruitful career. In the forty-plus years since The Jam first charted with 'In the City' there has rarely been a year when Paul hasn't been back in the charts. In total he can boast (at least) seventy-four Top 40 singles, either as a solo artist, with The Jam or **The Style Council**, as part of the original Band Aid line-up, or the 1995 charity project **The Smokin' Mojo Filters**.

NOW's arrival in 1983 was too late to catch any of The Jam's hits, but Paul's haul of five solo appearances is matched by his tally with The Style Council, a run that started with 'You're the Best Thing' (*NOW 3*) in 1984. The Style Council's last showing was a cover of the 1989 Joe Smooth single 'Promised Land' (*NOW 14*). Paul can take comfort that 'You're the Best Thing' has been since covered by boyband **911** and **Lisa Stansfield**.

Paul's latest entry, 2008's 'Have You Made Up Your Mind' (*NOW 70*), was a double A-side single with 'Echoes Round the Sun', a song co-written with Noel Gallagher. Noel was part of The Smokin' Mojo Filters line-up that also included **Paul McCartney**, **Carleen Anderson** and Steve Cradock of **Ocean Colour Scene**; their version of The Beatles' 1969 B-side 'Come Together' appeared on *NOW 32*. Another Beatles cover, 'Sexy Sadie', appeared on the B-side of Paul's 1994 single 'Out of the Sinking' (*NOW 33*).

Paul Weller's admiration for The Beatles extended to asking Sir Peter Blake to create the sleeve for his 1995 album *Stanley Road*. In 2012 Sir Peter reworked his *Sgt. Pepper's Lonely Hearts Club Band* artwork to mark his eightieth birthday, creating a new tableau that included Paul Weller, **Amy Winehouse**, **Paul McCartney**, **Mick Jagger**, **David Bowie**, **Elton John**, Elvis Costello and **Eric Clapton**. Maybe the nice people at *NOW* should give Sir Peter a call?

80s

NOW 25 Did You Know . . .

'Housecall', a number 8 collaboration with **Maxi Priest**, is the last of three *NOW* appearances for **Shabba Ranks**, and the follow-up to his biggest hit, the self-eulogising 1993 number 3 'Mr Loverman' (*NOW 24*). Both songs were originally released a couple of years earlier and failed to break into the Top 20. Shabba first appeared on *NOW 19* when he collaborated with **Scritti Politti** on their cover of The Beatles' 1964 B-side 'She's a Woman'.

NOW 70 Did You Know . . .

'Wearing My Rolex' (*NOW 70*) is the first of eight *NOW* appearances to date for **Wiley**, and his only 'solo' entry thus far. Wiley's third appearance, 'Never Be Your Woman' (*NOW 75*) by **Naughty Boy** presents Wiley featuring **Emeli Sandé**, may include the oldest sample on any *NOW* title. It includes a loop from the 1997 number 1 'Your Woman' (*NOW 36*) by **White Town**, who had sampled the same snippet from the 1932 recording 'My Woman' by Lew Stone and the Monseigneur Band featuring Al Bowlly.

IN OTHER NEWS . . . NOW 70 (JULY 2008)

The Dark Knight, starring Christian Bale as Batman, opened at cinemas. It was sequel to the 2005 film *Batman Begins*, and saw Michael Caine reprise his role as Alfred, the butler. Michael Caine was the subject of a 1984 single by **Madness**, featured on *NOW 2*.

When Judy Finnigan was incapacitated after a knee operation, two *NOW* favourites stepped up to co-host the Channel 4 TV show *Richard & Judy*. Former **Spice Girl Emma Bunton** was first, succeeded by ex-**Hear'Say** warbler Myleene Klass.

As part of the highbrow (and dead posh) BBC Proms season, Radio 3 broadcast a *Doctor Who* concert from the Royal Albert Hall, in London.

5
NOW appearances
'Sunflower',
NOW 25, August 1993
'Have You Made Up Your Mind',
NOW 70, July 2008

90s

NOW 26 Did You Know . . .

'Play Dead' by **Björk** and **David Arnold** was the first *NOW* appearance for the Icelandic singer and songwriter. Taken from the soundtrack of the film *The Young Americans*, it was co-written by former **Public Image Ltd** bass guitarist Jah Wobble, and was the third of Björk's twenty Top 40 hits so far. David Arnold is best known for his film scores, including *Casino Royale* and *Quantum of Solace*. Björk has made two further *NOW* appearances with 'Violently Happy' (*NOW 27*) and 'Possibly Maybe' (*NOW 35*).

NOW 38 Did You Know . . .

'Better Day' was the last appearance to date for Birmingham indie outfit **Ocean Colour Scene**. Chart-wise their two biggest hits were 'The Day We Caught the Train' (*NOW 34*) and '100 Mile High City' (*NOW 37*), both peaking at number 4. The latter was used as the theme tune for the 1998 film *Lock, Stock and Two Smoking Barrels*. However, they are perhaps best known for their second *NOW* appearance, 'The Riverboat Song' (*NOW 35*), as it was frequently used on the Channel 4 TV series *TFI Friday* between 1996 and 2000.

IN OTHER NEWS . . . NOW 26 (NOVEMBER 1993)

Nirvana taped an acoustic performance in New York City for the MTV *Unplugged* television series. Following Kurt Cobain's death the concert was released as a 'live' album, which charted at number 1.

In the cinema Jane Campion's New Zealand-based drama *The Piano* was released. The following year it won three Oscars, including Best Supporting Actress for 11-year-old Anna Paquin.

Anthony Burgess, writer and musician, died, aged 76. He is best known for his 1962 novel *A Clockwork Orange*.

11
NOW appearances
'Stay',
NOW 26, November 1993
'Angel of Mine',
NOW 38, November 1997

ETERNAL

Formed by sisters Easther and Vernie Bennett, with **Kéllé Bryan** and **Louise** Nurding, Eternal had fifteen Top 40 hits between 1993 and 1999, eleven of which can be found on *NOW*, including their only number 1, 'I Wanna Be the Only One' (*NOW 37*). Their first five appearances – 'Stay', 'Save Our Love', 'Just a Step from Heaven', 'So Good' and 'Oh Baby I . . .' – appeared on five consecutive volumes, from *NOW 26* to *NOW 30*. All five were taken from the number 2 album *Always and Forever*.

By the time of their sixth appearance Louise had departed and Eternal were down to a trio. 'Power of a Woman' (*NOW 32*) was written by Carl Sturken and Evan Rogers.

In 2004, on a visit to Barbados, Carl auditioned a trio of singers, including 16-year-old Robyn Fenty. Robyn became **Rihanna**, and Carl and Evan wrote her debut hit 'Pon de Replay' (*NOW 62*), as well as her 2007 number 5 'Shut Up and Drive' (*NOW 68*). You can also credit Carl and Evan for **Boyzone**'s third number 1, 'All That I Need'.

Gospel singer **BeBe Winans** had written and produced a song on each of the group's first two albums, but it was 'I Wanna Be the Only One', a collaboration from their third, that gave BeBe his only Top 40 hit and Eternal their only number 1. Both 'I Wanna Be . . .' and Eternal's last appearance, 'Angel of Mine' (*NOW 38*), were

co-written by Rhett Lawrence, the man who gave us 'Never Be the Same Again' (*NOW 45*), a 2000 number 1 for **Melanie C** and **Lisa 'Left Eye' Lopes**.

Whilst Louise's solo career would yield twelve Top 40 hits, Kéllé Bryan could only manage the one with her 1999 number 14 'Higher than Heaven'. Easther Bennett released one single, 'Shy Guy', with **Aswad** in 2002, but it stalled at number 62. In 2014 Eternal took part in the second series of the ITV show *The Big Reunion*. Also participating were A1, **Damage**, Girl Thing and 'super group' 5th Story, consisting of Kenzie from Blazin' Squad, **Dane Bowers** from **Another Level**, **Adam Rickitt**, **Kavana** and Gareth Gates.

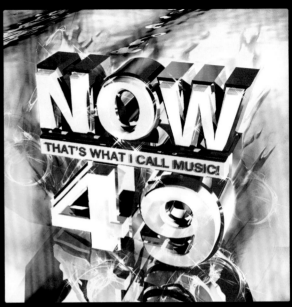

90s

NOW 26 Did You Know . . .

Prior to solo success, **Lisa Stansfield** had co-written and sung on **Coldcut**'s 1989 number 11 'People Hold On'. In October that year she had the first of two number 1 singles with 'All Around the World'. Her second chart topper came in May 1993 when she shared vocals with **George Michael** on a version of the **Queen** song 'These Are the Days of Our Lives'. 'Change' (*NOW 20*) gave her a number 10 hit in 1991, co-written by Lisa with her future husband Ian Devaney, as was her second and final appearance, 'So Natural' (*NOW 26*), a 1993 number 15 single.

NOW 49 Did You Know . . .

Since 1997 **Basement Jaxx** have had eighteen Top 40 singles and three *NOW* appearances, starting with the number 5 hit 'Red Alert' (*NOW 43*). It sampled the 1980 single 'Far Beyond' by US funk-group Locksmith, while the number 13 hit 'Bingo Bango' (*NOW 45*) contains another obscure sample, this time from 'Merengue!' by Bolivar. Their last appearance to date was 'Romeo' (*NOW 49*), a number 6 hit featuring vocals from **Kele Le Roc**. Kele also has two solo *NOW* appearances, 'Little Bit of Lovin'' (*NOW 41*) and 'My Love' (*NOW 42*), both number 8 singles.

IN OTHER NEWS . . . *NOW 49* (JULY 2001)

Former **Spice Girls** singer **Melanie B** hosted a new ITV talent show, *This Is My Moment*. The programme ran for one series only.

Musician and composer Delia Derbyshire died, aged 64. As a member of the BBC Radiophonic Workshop she arranged the original theme music for *Doctor Who*, used from 1963 to 1980.

US rock band The Strokes released their debut album *Is This It*. Guitarist Albert Hammond Jr. is the son of songwriter Albert Hammond, whose credits include 'The Air That I Breathe' by **The Hollies**.

7
NOW appearances
'Creep',
NOW 26, November 1993
'Pyramid Song',
NOW 49, July 2001

RADIOHEAD

Radiohead's debut single 'Creep' (*NOW 26*) failed to chart when it was first released in September 1992 but peaked at number 7 when re-issued twelve months later, and is now their bestselling single. Artists including **Tears for Fears**, **Damien Rice** and the **Glee Cast** have since recorded their own version. Songwriters Albert Hammond and Mike Hazlewood were later added to the credits due to similarities with 'The Air That I Breathe', a 1974 number 2 for **The Hollies**.

Radiohead's second appearance, 'Lucky (Warchild)' (*NOW 32*), was taken from the 1995 charity project *The Help Album*. All the featured songs were recorded on Monday, 4 September, and the album was

available in shops the following Saturday. The same compilation included a new version of 'Fade Away' by **Oasis**. Originally the B-side of their 1994 number 7 'Cigarettes and Alcohol' (*NOW 29*), the new recording featured actor Johnny Depp on guitar and model Kate Moss on backing vocals.

Peter Gabriel also recorded 'Street Spirit (Fade Out)' (*NOW 33*) for his 2010 album of cover versions, *Scratch My Back*. He hoped Radiohead would record one of his songs for a follow-up project, but his request went unheeded. With a title derived from *The Hitchhiker's Guide to the Galaxy*, 'Paranoid Android' (*NOW 37*) reached number 4 in 1997, the band's highest chart

placing to date. In 1981 'Marvin the Paranoid Android' by Marvin (voiced by actor Stephen Moore) peaked at number 52 in the chart.

In 2005 Radiohead's Phil Selway and Jonny Greenwood joined Jarvis Cocker of **Pulp** in *Harry Potter and the Goblet of Fire* as members of the band Weird Sisters; their repertoire included 'Do the Hippogriff'. In 2007 Radiohead made their seventh album, *In Rainbows*, available online, allowing fans to pay whatever they wanted. The *NME* reported that the average sale price was £2.90, while 60 per cent of fans opted to pay zero. When released physically the album became their fifth number 1

'LESSONS IN LOVE'*

Twenty *NOW* observations on being amorous

'Hold Me, Thrill Me, Kiss Me, Kill Me', U2 (*NOW 32*)

'Kiss Me', Sixpence None the Richer (*NOW 44*)

'Kissing with Confidence', Will Powers (*NOW 1*)

'Kiss the Rain', Billie Myers (*NOW 39*)

'French Kissin' in the USA', Deborah Harry (*NOW 8*)

'Kiss the Stars', Pixie Lott (*NOW 81*)

'Kiss the Girl', Peter Andre (*NOW 40*)

'Kiss Me Thru the Phone', Soulja Boy Tell 'Em (*NOW 73*)

* Level 42 (*NOW 7*)

NOW 26 Did You Know . . .

Presenting the first of four appearances from Manchester four-piece **M People**, featuring the distinctive tones of **Heather Small**. Their run starts with the number 6 hit 'One Night in Heaven', taken from their second album *Elegant Slumming*. In 1994 *Elegant Slumming* won the third Mercury Music Prize, beating such no-hopers as **Blur**'s *Parklife* and **Pulp**'s *His 'n' Hers*. M People's other appearances include their biggest hit, the 1993 number 2 'Moving on Up' (*NOW 27*), 'Renaissance' (*NOW 28*) and conclude with 'Sight for Sore Eyes' (*NOW 30*).

NOW 65 Did You Know . . .

Gnarls Barkley, the duo formed by singer **CeeLo Green**, aka Thomas Callaway, and producer Danger Mouse, aka Brian Burton, announced themselves to the *NOW* audience with the number 1 hit 'Crazy' (*NOW 64*), the bestselling single of 2006 and the first to top the chart on download sales alone. Their second appearance came on *NOW 65* with the number 10 single 'Smiley Faces'. CeeLo has since enjoyed four further *NOW* appearances, including the very clean, definitely not rude number 1 'Forget You' (*NOW 77*).

IN OTHER NEWS . . . *NOW 65* (NOVEMBER 2006)

BC Radio broadcast the fifteen-thousandth episode of their rural-drama serial *The Archers*, which first aired in 51. Among the occasional cameo appearances have been *NOW* favourites **Pet Shop Boys** and DJs John Peel, rry Wogan and Chris Moyles.

V announced that the reality TV show *Love Island* was to be axed after just two series. Contestants had included llé Bryan, singer with **Eternal**, and Shane Lynch of **Boyzone**. The original theme tune, 'Wish I', was sung by elsh artist **Jem**, whose one *NOW* appearance came on *NOW 61* with her number 6 hit 'They'.

estlife scored their fourteenth (FOURTEENTH!!) and so far final number 1 with 'The Rose' (*NOW 65*). It would knocked off the number 1 spot in early December by **Take That**'s ninth number 1 'Patience' (*NOW 66*)

MEAT LOAF

Two of the man born Marvin Lee Aday's five *NOW* appearances – 'I'd Do Anything for Love (But I Won't Do That)' (*NOW 26*) and 'Rock and Roll Dreams Come Through' (*NOW 27*) – were lifted from his album *Bat Out of Hell II: Back Into Hell*, while 'It's All Coming Back to Me Now' (*NOW 65*) comes from *Bat Out of Hell III: The Monster Is Loose*. The original 1978 *Bat Out of Hell* album has spent over 520 weeks in the album chart. In 2017 the Official Charts Company reported that it had still averaged 20,000 sales per year in the previous ten years.

Three of Meat Loaf's five *NOW* appearances were written by frequent collaborator Jim Steinman, who wrote all of the first two *Bat Out of Hell* albums and came to *NOW* attention on the very first volume, having penned **Bonnie Tyler**'s number 1 'Total Eclipse of the Heart'. The same song appeared again on *NOW 30* when covered by **Nicki French**, her only *NOW* appearance, though in 2000 she would represent the UK at the Eurovision Song Contest in Stockholm, finishing sixteenth.

Jim Steinman also wrote the lyrics for Andrew Lloyd Webber's 1996 musical *Whistle Down the Wind*, which yielded the song 'No Matter What'. Meat Loaf would record this as the B-side of his 1996 single 'Is Nothing Sacred', though its greatest success came when **Boyzone** made it the fourth of their six number 1s. Their version is included on *NOW 41*. The title song from the musical gave Tina Arena a number 24 hit in 1998.

While Meat Loaf's recording of 'It's All Coming Back to Me Now' peaked at number 6 in 2006, ten years earlier **Céline Dion** had taken the same song to number 3, the eighth of her fourteen Top 10 hits to date. However, the story of the song starts back in 1989 when Jim Steinman recorded it for his project *Pandora's Box*, though this version could only manage to get to number 51.

90s

90s

NOW 26 Did You Know . . .

'Comin' On' was the last appearance by **The Shamen**. The band also popped up with 'LSI (Love Sex Intelligence)' on *NOW 22*, and their only number 1 'Ebenezer Goode' on *NOW 23*. The BBC would eventually ban the song due to blooming obvious drug references, but not before The Shamen had performed it on *Top of the Pops*, where rapper Mr C swapped the line 'Got any salmon?' for 'Got any underlay?' A drug reference – 'salmon and trout' for 'snout' – for a rug reference. See?

NOW 50 Did You Know . . .

While a lot of people now associate the song 'Stuck in the Middle with You' with a rather nasty scene in Quentin Tarantino's 1992 film *Reservoir Dogs*, that didn't deter **Louise** from giving it the disco treatment and landing a number 4 hit and a place on *NOW 50* in 2001. In addition to her ten *NOW* appearances, starting with 'Light of My Life' (*NOW 32*) up to 'Pandora's Kiss' (*NOW 56*), Louise can also lay claim to appearing on the first five of ten appearances by female four-piece **Eternal**.

IN OTHER NEWS . . . *NOW 50* (NOVEMBER 2001)

A man widely regarded as one of the 'all time greats', singer, songwriter, guitarist and former Beatle George Harrison died at the age of 58.

American actor David Boreanaz, vampire Angel in the *Buffy the Vampire Slayer* TV series, married *Playboy* model Jaime Bergman in Palm Springs, California.

ITV launched new soap opera *Night and Day*, revolving around the lives of six south London families. The cast included Lesley Joseph and Gareth Hunt, with a theme song 'Always & Forever' sung by **Kylie Minogue**.

4
NOW appearances
'Too Young to Die',
NOW 26, November 1993

'Little L',
NOW 50, November 2001

JAMIROQUAI

Fronted by every milliner's favourite, Jay Kay, Jamiroquai's debut single was released on the achingly hip Acid Jazz record label, before the band signed to globe-spanning behemoth Sony and scored a number 10 hit at the first attempt with 'Too Young to Die' (*NOW 26*). Jay reportedly started the band after he failed an audition to be singer for **The Brand New Heavies**. Still, he has four *NOW* appearances to their three, so who had the last laugh, eh?

Jamiroquai's second appearance, with 'Virtual Insanity' on *NOW 36*, provided the band with the highest chart placing of their four *NOW* titles, peaking at number 3. Sales of the single were undoubtedly helped by the 'moving floor' video, directed by Jonathan Glazer, and winner of Video of the Year at the 1997 MTV Awards. Glazer's other credits include videos for **Blur**'s 'The Universal', **Radiohead**'s 'Street Spirit (Fade Out)' (both *NOW 33*), and **Richard Ashcroft**'s 'A Song for the

To date Jamiroquai's only number 1 single is 'Deeper Underground', taken from the soundtrack to the 1998 film *Godzilla*. This collection also produced the number 2 single 'Come with Me' by Puff Daddy featuring Jimmy Page, which borrows its monstrous guitar riff from the 1975 Led Zeppelin song 'Kashmir'. Puff Daddy would later change his name to Diddy, not to be confused with **Diddy** who appears on *NOW 37* with 'Give Me Love' (or Ken Dodd's Diddy Men).

Also making his last appearance on *NOW 50* was another famous (hard) hat wearer, **Bob the Builder**. Although his musical career has received fewer plaudits than Jamiroquai's, he can boast two number 1s: 'Can We Fix It?' (*NOW 48*) and 'Mambo No. 5' (*NOW 50*). The former held the coveted Christmas number 1 slot in 2000, holding off **Westlife**'s 'What Makes a Man'. 'Mambo No. 5' was originally written and recorded by Pérez Prado in 1949, though Bob's version is an adaption of **Lou Bega**'s 1999

BLUR

Damon Albarn's *NOW* career started on volume 28, where Blur's breakthrough Top 5 hit 'Girls and Boys' found itself unceremoniously wedged betwixt the third of **M People**'s four entries and denim-bedecked Scots rockers **Stiltskin** (just the one). Blur would go on to score a further eight *NOW* hits, and **Gorillaz** – Albarn's polymorphous side project – a not insignificant five credits in their own right. 'Girls and Boys' heralded the start of a twenty-four month, eight-single run of consecutive Top 20 hits for Blur.

'Parklife' (*NOW 29*) featured the vocal prowess of *Quadrophenia* actor Phil Daniels, one of only two of the film's stars to grace *NOW*, alongside 'Ace Face' and erstwhile **Police** frontman **Sting**. In a curious ragbag of entries, the former Gordon Sumner first appeared on *NOW 18* ('Englishman in New York'), and then with **Pato Banton** on *NOW 30* ('This Cowboy Song') and as part of the **Different Gear** vs Police mash-up on *NOW 46* ('When the World Is Running Down . . .'). Alas, fellow mod Leslie Ash's 1996 number 25 hit with Caroline Quentin ('Tell Him' by Quentin and Ash) was not captured for *NOW* posterity.

Blur's 'Beetlebum' (*NOW 36*) has the dubious distinction of being one of only three number 1 singles to spend just three weeks in the UK Top 40. It shares this record with

Katie Melua and **Eva Cassidy**'s 'What a Wonderful World' (*NOW 69*) and **McFly**'s 'Baby's Coming Back' (*NOW 67*). It was also Blur's last number 1 single to date, with 'Tender' (*NOW 42*) peaking at number 2 two years later. That single was held off the top spot by **Britney Spears**'s pan-global mega hit '. . . Baby One More Time', marking her first appearance two volumes later on *NOW 44*.

It was bassist Alex James, not Damon Albarn, who first landed a side-project appearance, alongside fellow carousers and 'Country House' (*NOW 32*) collaborators Damien Hirst and Keith Allen. The unofficial 1998 World Cup anthem 'Vindaloo' by **Fat Les** – co-written by Alex – reached number 2, beaten only by a timely re-recording of 'Three Lions' by **Baddiel**, **Skinner** and **The Lightning Seeds**. Both tracks can be found rubbing shoulders on *NOW 40*, pre-dating the first Gorillaz appearance, 'Clint Eastwood' (*NOW 48*), by eight volumes.

DOUBLE CD, CASSETTE & MINIDISC

90s

NOW 28 Did You Know . . .

The B-52's (sort of) made their only appearance, as the **BC-52's**, with '(Meet) The Flintstones', the theme from the live-action film version of the cartoon series. It spent three weeks at number 3 in July 1994, a position only bettered by their 1990 number 2 'Love Shack'. Also making a pseudonymous showing were **Pet Shop Boys**, appearing as **Absolutely Fabulous** with 'Absolutely Fabulous', a fund-raiser for Comic Relief incorporating dialogue from Jennifer Saunders's popular show.

NOW 43 Did You Know . . .

James made their seventh and most recent appearance with 'I Know What I'm Here For', their seventeenth Top 40 hit. Their biggest hit was the 1991 number 2 'Sit Down' (*NOW 20*), which also gave them their sixth appearance in a remixed form as 'Sit Down '98' (*NOW 41*). In 2013 a poll for BBC Radio 2 and the Official Charts Company voted 'Sit Down' the nation's fourth-favourite number 2 single. The poll was won by **Ultravox**'s 1981 single 'Vienna' (*NOW 24*), itself denied by 'Shaddap You Face' by Joe Dolce Music Theatre.

IN OTHER NEWS . . . NOW 28 (AUGUST 1994)

The Woodstock '94 music festival took place in New York State. Performers included Bob Dylan, **The Cranberries** and **Joe Cocker**, who had played the original festival twenty-five years earlier.

British actor Peter Cushing died, aged 81. Best known for his roles in the Hammer horror films, in 1977 he played Grand Moff Tarkin in the original *Star Wars* film.

Rapper Christopher 'The Notorious B.I.G.' Wallace married R&B singer **Faith Evans**.

9
NOW appearances
'Girls and Boys', *NOW 28*, August 1994
'Coffee and TV', *NOW 43*, July 1999

NOW 29 Did You Know . . .

Cyndi Lauper is another artist who tops and tails her appearances with the same song, or rather two versions of it. 'Girls Just Want to Have Fun' reached number 2 when **Frankie Goes to Hollywood** were in the middle of their five-week run at the top with 'Relax' (both *NOW 2*). She had a second attempt in 1994 when the slightly more informal 'Hey Now (Girls Just Wanna Have Fun)' (*NOW 29*) made number 4. In between Cyndi had a number 3 with the much-covered 'Time After Time' (*NOW 3*).

NOW 99 Did You Know . . .

It seems **Dua Lipa** can put out singles as quickly as *NOW* can albums. Beginning with 'Hotter than Hell' (*NOW 94*) and most recently 'IDGAF' (*NOW 99*), her first seven Top 40 singles have all made an appearance. In fact, busy Dua managed three songs on *NOW 96*, including collaborations with Dutch DJ **Martin Garrix** – 'Scared to Be Lonely' and Jamaican **Sean Paul** – 'No Lie'. The latter was co-written by American songwriter Emily Warren, who also had a hand in Dua's first number 1, 'New Rules' (*NOW 98*).

IN OTHER NEWS . . . *NOW 29* (NOVEMBER 1994)

Ronald 'Buster' Edwards died, aged 63. In 1963 he was part of the Great Train Robbery gang, and in 1988 his story was made into the film *Buster*, starring **Phil Collins** in the title role.

At the cinema it was Frankenstein vs Dracula, with openings for *Mary Shelley's Frankenstein*, starring Robert De Niro, and *Interview with the Vampire*, starring Tom Cruise.

Songwriter Uzoechi Emenike was born. As **MNEK** he has three *NOW* appearances plus a further nine writing for others.

14
NOW appearances

'Cigarettes and Alcohol',
NOW 29, November 1994

'Live Forever',
NOW 99, March 2018

OASIS

All of Oasis' appearances were Top 10 singles, though we only get four of their eight number 1s. 'Live Forever' made its first belated appearance on *NOW 33,* two years after its original release. Twenty-two years later it returned as an unofficial anthem and tribute to the city of Manchester. The Oasis 'revolving door' policy began after their first number 1 'Some Might Say' (*NOW 31*), when the band said goodbye to drummer Tony McCarroll. By the time they recorded 'The Importance of Being Idle' (*NOW 62*), only Noel and Liam remained from the original line-up, and even Liam doesn't appear on that particular song.

No cover versions among Oasis appearances, though 'Whatever' (*NOW 30*) was subject to a legal battle with erstwhile Rutle and

Bonzo Dog songwriter Neil Innes, who spotted a passing resemblance to his 1973 track 'How Sweet to Be an Idiot'. Innes was successful and now shares a songwriting credit with N. Gallagher. Oasis have been subject to a cover or two themselves, most notably Mike Flowers Pops' 1995 version of 'Wonderwall', which – like the Oasis original on *NOW 34* – made it to number 2. Norwegian singer **Aurora** owes her only appearance to 'Half a World Away' (*NOW 92*), originally the B-side of 'Whatever'.

'Stand by Me' was one of four singles to be held off the number 1 slot by **Elton John**'s 'Candle in the Wind 1997', the biggest-selling single in UK chart history. 'You Have Been Loved' by **George Michael**, 'Sunchyme' by **Dario G** and 'Stay' by **Sash!** featuring **La**

Trec complete the list of frustrated runners-up. All four songs appeared on *NOW 38* and, while a 1988 live version of 'Candle in the Wind' can be found on *NOW 11*, Elton's Diana tribute was never anthologised by *NOW*.

Oasis first appeared with 'Cigarettes and Alcohol' (*NOW 29*), a paean to the pursuit of hedonism, though the *NOW* back pages are littered with musical odes to sin and vice. From the off, **UB40** were extolling the virtues of alcohol on 'Red Red Wine' (*NOW 1*), **Matt Bianco** warned against sloth with 'Get Out of Your Lazy Bed' (*NOW 2*), while **The Gin Blossoms** alerted us to envy with 'Hey Jealousy' (*NOW 27*). Fitting then that the last appearance by a new Oasis song was 'The Importance of Being Idle'.

90s

BOYZONE

90s

The bountiful relationship between Boyzone and *NOW* has spanned forty-one volumes and included all six of their number 1 singles, plus five number 2s, two number 3s, one number 4 and a number 5 – a most impressive average. Even after the group's initial break-up, **Ronan Keating** graced us with another thirteen appearances and a further three number 1 singles, while **Stephen Gately** also managed one more appearance with his 2000 number 3 'New Beginning' (*NOW 46*).

'Love Me for a Reason' (*NOW 30*) was originally a hit for another boyband, The Osmonds; it gave them their only number 1 in 1974. 'Father and Son' (*NOW 33*) seems to be held in particular affection by Boyzone. Their version of the 1970 Cat Stevens song gave them a number 2 hit, and has also featured as a bonus track on three of their other singles. In 2004 Ronan Keating recorded the song once more, this time as a duet with the song's writer, now known as **Yusuf Islam**. Yet another number 2 hit, it appeared on *NOW 60*.

Two more Boyzone cover versions resulted in two more chart toppers. 'Words' (*NOW 35*) was originally a number 8 for the **Bee Gees**, and it provided American singer Rita Coolidge with one of only two Top 40 hits in 1978. In 1999 Boyzone released the official Comic Relief single, a version of 'When the Going Gets Tough, the Tough Get Going' (*NOW 42*). The original by **Billy Ocean** was also a number 1 and appeared on *NOW 7*.

Boyzone's longest spell at the top came with 'No Matter What' (*NOW 41*), staying there for three weeks in August 1998. It was written by Andrew Lloyd Webber, his producer Nigel Wright and frequent **Meat Loaf** collaborator Jim Steinman, for the musical *Whistle Down the Wind*. A concept album of songs from the show also featured 'When Children Rule the World' by original boyband member Donny Osmond.

90s

NOW 30 Did You Know . . .

Tin Tin Out made three *NOW* appearances, each a cover version and each featuring a different singer. 'Always Something There to Remind Me' (*NOW 30*) featured **Espiritu**, with a song that had been a number 1 debut hit for Sandie Shaw in 1964. Their second appearance was the number 7 hit 'Here's Where the Story Ends' (*NOW 39*), featuring **Shelley Nelson**. The original by The Sundays had failed to chart on release in 1990. 'What I Am' (*NOW 44*) featured **Emma Bunton** with a version of the 1989 Edie Brickell and New Bohemians' single.

NOW 71 Did You Know . . .

To date 'Mountains' (*NOW 71*) is the biggest of **Biffy Clyro**'s sixteen Top 40 hits. When first released in January 2010, 'Many of Horror' (*NOW 75*) peaked at number 20; however, the following December it was re-titled 'When We Collide' (*NOW 78*) and was the debut single and Christmas number 1 for *X Factor* winner **Matt Cardle**. Renewed interest and an internet campaign by fans saw the Biffy original re-chart and peak at number 8. The Kilmarnock rockers' most recent appearance came on *NOW 84* with the number 14 hit 'Black Chandelier'.

15
NOW appearances
'Love Me for a Reason', *NOW 30*, April 1995
'Love You Anyway', *NOW 71*, November 2008

IN OTHER NEWS . . . *NOW 30* (APRIL 1995)

DJ Kenny Everett died, aged 50. When BBC Radio 1 launched in 1967 he was one of the original DJs in a line-up that included John Peel, Tony Blackburn and Terry Wogan.

Channel 4 screened the first episode of sitcom *Father Ted*. Its theme music is by **The Divine Comedy**, and later episodes included roles for Brian Eno and Altered Images singer Clare Grogan.

Rapper **2Pac Shakur** married Keisha Morris at the Clinton Correctional Facility in New York, where he was serving nine months in prison. The couple divorced the following year.

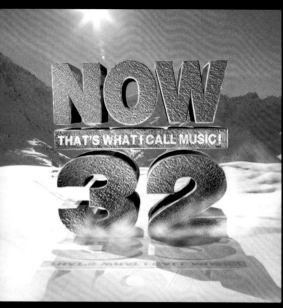

DOUBLE CD, CASSETTE & MINIDISC

90s

NOW 32 Did You Know . . .

Featuring the fabled **Blur** versus **Oasis** battle – only one place separated them in the chart, while **Cast** were the meat in a Britpop sandwich on volume 32. **Everything but the Girl** were making the second of three appearances with the number 3 hit 'Missing'. **Karen Ramirez** had her only *NOW* appearance with a cover of their song 'Looking for Love' (*NOW 40*), while EBTG singer **Tracey Thorn** was the featured vocalist on 'Protection' (*NOW 30*), a number 14 hit for **Massive Attack** in 1995.

NOW 43 Did You Know . . .

In a three-year spell beginning in 1999, former *EastEnders* star **Martine McCutcheon** scored five Top 10 hits, all of them on *NOW*, starting with her solo debut number 1, 'Perfect Moment' (*NOW 43*). Martine had made two previous attempts to crack the charts: in 1994 she was in female trio Milan, who scraped in at number 82 with 'Lead Me On'; the following year she was featured vocalist on 'Are You Man Enough', a number 62 single and the only chart entry for Uno Clio.

IN OTHER NEWS . . . *NOW 32* (NOVEMBER 1995)

At the cinema Pixar Studios released *Toy Story*, the first feature-length computer-animated film. It was awarded an Oscar for Special Achievement.

The actor Paul Eddington died, aged 68. He had been the star of BBC TV sitcoms *The Good Life, Yes, Minister* and its sequel *Yes, Prime Minister*. He received a CBE in the 1987 New Years Honours.

Diana, Princess of Wales, had a candid interview with Martin Bashir on the current-affairs programme *Panorama*. An estimated twenty-two million viewers tuned in.

8
NOW appearances
'Alright',
NOW 32, November 1995

'Beat Mama',
NOW 43, July 1999

CAST

Cast were formed in 1992 by John Power, formerly of **The La's**, and bass player Pete Wilkinson, previously with another critically acclaimed Liverpudlian outfit, Shack. In a four-year spell beginning in 1995, they had ten Top 40 singles, eight of them making it onto *NOW*, including a run of seven consecutive appearances, from volumes 32 to 38. Their first three appearances – 'Alright' (*NOW 32*), 'Sandstorm' (*NOW 33*) and 'Walkaway' (*NOW 34*) – were taken from their number 7 debut album *All Change*.

In the second half of the nineties the number 9 hit 'Walkaway' seemingly became the go-to ballad for film and TV sad scenes. It popped up in a 1996 episode of *EastEnders* and 1998 episode of *Friends* 'The One with Ross's Wedding'. In 1999 a version of 'Walkaway', now with added rap, soundtracked a perhaps best-forgotten TV advert for Swedish furnishers IKEA.

In 1996 Cast scored their highest chart position – number 4 – with the non-album song 'Flying' (*NOW 35*) – not to be confused with 'Flying', the 1967 instrumental by The Beatles. For a genuine Beatles link look no further than Quarry Bank High School, seat of learning for both John Power and John Lennon. Cast's next three appearances – 'Free Me' (*NOW 36*), 'Guiding Star' (*NOW 37*) and 'I'm So Lonely' (*NOW 38*) – were all lifted from their second album, 1997's *Mother Nature Calls*.

John Power's first band, The La's, managed one Top 40 single and one appearance on *NOW* with 'There She Goes' (*NOW 18*). It failed to chart when first released in 1988, but finally made it to number 13 in 1990. In 1999 Texas band **Sixpence None the Richer** scored their second Top 40 hit with a cover of 'There She Goes'. Their only other hit was the 1994 number 4 'Kiss Me', which also gave them their only *NOW* appearance on volume 44.

SPICE GIRLS

Spice Girls should need little introduction, but their *NOW* statistics will really make you want to zig-a-zig-ah: thirty-seven entries in total – ten group appearances, nine of them number 1s, and twenty-seven solo endeavours, including another eight chart toppers. Leading the pack is **Geri Halliwell** with eight solo appearances, followed by **Emma Bunton** with six, five a piece for **Melanie B** and **Melanie C**, and a compact trio for **Victoria Beckham**. In fact, there were Spice treats to be found on every *NOW* between volumes *34* and *51*, barring time off for good behaviour on *NOW 46*.

Whilst Melanie B can claim the first solo entry – 'I Want You Back' (*NOW 41*) with **Missy Elliott** – and Geri has bragging rights for most entries, Victoria has the distinction of being the only Spice Girl never to have a solo number 1 single, even though 'Out of Your Mind' (*NOW 47*), her collaboration with **True Steppers** and **Dane Bowers**, reached number 2 in August 2000, having sold a whopping 180,000 copies. Sadly, still not enough to catch 'Groovejet (If This Ain't Love)' (*NOW 46*) by **Spiller** featuring **Sophie Ellis-Bextor**, who ended the week in pole position.

'Say You'll Be There' (*NOW 35*) was one of two group appearances not to be co-written by either the Biffco or Absolute production teams. The song was penned with Eliot Kennedy, who also co-wrote **S Club 7**'s debut, 'Bring It All Back' (*NOW 43*), and 'When You're Gone' by **Bryan Adams** – a Top 3 duet with Melanie C, ironically unchronicled by *NOW*. Honking his harmonica all over 'Say You'll Be There' was music-industry veteran Judd Lander, extending his *NOW* legacy by thirteen years, having played on **Culture Club**'s 'Karma Chameleon' way back on *NOW 1*.

Gerry and the Pacemakers, **Frankie Goes to Hollywood**, **Jive Bunny and the Mastermixers**, Robson and Jerome . . . schizophrenic bed fellows, but all reached number 1 with their first three singles. In March 1997, Spice Girls became the first act to topple that empire when the double A-side 'Mama' (*NOW 36*) and 'Who Do You Think You Are' (*NOW 37*) followed 'Wannabe', 'Say You'll Be There' and '2 Become 1' to the top of the charts. While Frankie's first three singles are all captured for *NOW* posterity, only Jive Bunny's debut 'Swing the Mood' (*NOW 15*) flies the flag for the Spice Girls' vanquished forebears.

90s

NOW 34 Did You Know . . .

We were treated to two contrasting 'returns', starting with **Mark Morrison**'s number 1 'Return of the Mack'. He returned on *NOW 36* with 'Horny', followed by an enforced absence while he was 'detained at Her Majesty's pleasure'. 'The Mack' (*NOW 95*) saw him return once more in the company of **Nevada** and **Fetty Wap**. West London Britpop outfit **The Bluetones** had their biggest hit in February 1996 with 'Slight Return'. They made just one more appearance with the curiously titled 'Marblehead Johnson' (*NOW 35*).

NOW 47 Did You Know . . .

After six appearances across seven volumes, including three number 1 singles, we said goodbye to **Billie Piper** with 'Walk of Life'. As a child actor she featured in a TV advert for *Smash Hits* magazine, before scoring two number 1s with her first two singles, 'Because We Want To' (*NOW 40*) and 'Girlfriend' (*NOW 41*). Her third number 1, 'Day and Night' (*NOW 46*), was the first to include her surname in the credits, the opposite of the career path chosen by Spice Girls Emma and Geri, who dropped their surnames for their final *NOW* appearances.

IN OTHER NEWS . . . NOW 47 (NOVEMBER 2000)

Charlie's Angels opened at the cinema. The theme tune, 'Independent Women Part 1', gave **Destiny's Child** their first number 1.

Queen guitarist **Brian May** married *EastEnders* actress Anita Dobson at Richmond Registry Office.

Singer Connie Talbot was born. In 2008, aged just seven years old, she had a US number 1 single with a version of **Bob Marley**'s 'Three Little Birds'.

10
NOW appearances
'Wannabe',
NOW 34, August 1996

'Holler',
NOW 47, November 2000

NOW 34 Did You Know . . .

NOW 34 contains the sole appearance by **Gina G**, the (Australian-born) UK representative at the 1996 Eurovision Song Contest, in Oslo. Although the UK finished eighth, 'Ooh Aah . . . Just a Little Bit' topped the UK singles chart, the last UK entry to do so (as of 2018). Also making their debut on *NOW 34* were **Spice Girls**, whose hit 'Wannabe' was one of four number 1 singles on this volume.

NOW 96 Did You Know . . .

Skip Marley's collaboration with **Katy Perry**, 'Chained to the Rhythm', makes him the third member of the Marley massive to grace *NOW*, after grandfather **Bob Marley** (four appearances) and uncle **Damien 'Jr. Gong' Marley** (just the one so far). **George Michael**'s 'Fastlove' made a second appearance on *NOW*, following his death on Christmas Day 2016. Robbie's first solo hit was a cover of George's song 'Freedom'.

IN OTHER NEWS . . . NOW 34 (AUGUST 1996)

The Prince and Princess of Wales completed their divorce proceedings after fifteen years of marriage.

Ossie Clark, the British fashion designer synonymous with the Swinging Sixties, died, aged 54. A velvet and lycra jumpsuit he made for **Mick Jagger** in 1972 is now in the Victoria and Albert Museum collection.

George R. R. Martin's epic fantasy novel *A Game Of Thrones* was published, the first in his series 'A Song of Ice and Fire'.

30
NOW appearances
'Freedom',
NOW 34, August 1996
'Love My Life',
NOW 96, April 2017

ROBBIE WILLIAMS

Presenting Mr Robert Peter Williams, the reigning Heavy Entertainment Champion of *NOW*. Robbie has twenty-five appearances under his own name, one each with **Kylie Minogue**, **Nicole Kidman**, **Pet Shop Boys** and **Gary Barlow**, plus a featured role with **Dizzee Rascal**. Eight of Robbie's appearances were number 1 hits, including a double A-side single that produced a combination so strong we put one song ('She's the One') on *NOW 44* and the other ('It's Only Us') on *NOW 45*.

Robbie sings on five of the fourteen *NOW* appearances by **Take That**, including two number 1 singles, 'Pray' (*NOW 26*) and 'Sure' (*NOW 29*). Robbie also has three number 1s by dint of his contributions to charity projects: **Justice Collective**'s 'He Ain't Heavy, He's My Brother' on *NOW 84*; **Helping Haiti**'s 'Everybody Hurts' on *NOW 75*; and 'Bridge Over Troubled Water' by **Artists for Grenfell** on *NOW 97*. His tally of thirty-nine *NOW* appearances to date is completed by 'My Culture' for **1 Giant Leap**, on *NOW 52*.

One of Robbie's two contributions to *NOW 41*, 'No Regrets', included backing vocals by Neil Hannon of **The Divine Comedy** and Neil Tennant of **Pet Shop Boys**. Pet Shop Boys would work with Robbie once more on *NOW 66*, with their collaboration 'She's Madonna'. Curiously, this marks a very rare 'appearance' on any volume of *NOW* by Madonna. We keep calling her but she must have lost her phone.

Meanwhile, Robbie and one of his two female Australian duet partners, Kylie Minogue, were reunited in 2005, when they voiced characters in the animated film version of *The Magic Roundabout*. There is little else to report from Robbie's acting CV, though look closely at a September 1995 episode of *EastEnders* – that's him playing 'Man Using Queen Vic Telephone'.

00s

PETER ANDRE

Yes, you read it right: Peter Andre's first and last appearances were the same song, 'Mysterious Girl' featuring **Bubbler Ranx**. First released in September 1995, it took nine months to climb to number 2, where it got stuck behind **Fugees**' 'Killing Me Softly'. In 2004, following Peter's stint on *I'm a Celebrity . . . Get Me Out of Here!*, the song was re-released and became Peter's third number 1. The same year, the *Liverpool Echo* reported that Bubbler Ranx was now working in a South London supermarket.

Peter's first number 1 was the 1996 single 'Flava' (*NOW 35*), with a rap from never-to-be-heard-of-again Melbourne singer Cee. 'Flava' also marked the first appearance by one of the 'backroom heroes' of *NOW*, songwriter Wayne Hector. Wayne has written or co-written thirty-seven songs on *NOW*, including hits for **One Direction**, **Olly Murs** and **JLS**. However, our favourite has to be the 2001 number 6 single 'What If' (*NOW 50*); so far the only appearance and only chart hit for actress **Kate Winslet**.

Peter's fourth appearance, 'Lonely' (*NOW 38*), was also courtesy of Wayne Hector, though his fifth came from an entirely different source. The ballad 'Kiss the Girl' (*NOW 40*) had originally featured in the 1989 Walt Disney film *The Little Mermaid*. The single reached number 9, perhaps helped by some formats including a new recording of 'Mysterious Girl', this time round including additional vocals from Orville Burrell, better known to *NOW* fans as **Shaggy**.

When Peter finished third in the 2004 series of *I'm a Celebrity . . .* his fellow contestants included future wife Katie Price, ex-Sex Pistol **John Lydon** and the eventual winner, former **Atomic Kitten** singer Kerry Katona. In 2005 Katie Price was runner-up in the competition to choose a song for the UK to enter in the Eurovision Song Contest. In 2006 Katie and Peter blessed us all with an album of love duets that included their number 12 single 'A Whole New World'.

90s

NOW 34 Did You Know . . .

Making their fourth and final appearance with 'Jazz It Up' were **Reel 2 Real**, essentially a studio project for producer and DJ Erick Morillo. Their first appearance, 'I Like to Move It' (*NOW 27*), was also their biggest hit, reaching number 7 in 1994. A version of it was used in the 2005 film *Madagascar*, sung by actor Sacha Baron Cohen. All of their hits were co-written by Erick and Mark Quashie, aka **The Mad Stuntman**, who was the featured vocalist on their first three appearances.

NOW 57 Did You Know . . .

New York combo **Scissor Sisters** made the first of eight *NOW* appearances with a cover of the 1979 Pink Floyd song 'Comfortably Numb'. This marks one of only two *NOW* credits for Pink Floyd, the other being 'Proper Education' (*NOW 66*) by **Eric Prydz vs Floyd**. It was based on Pink Floyd's only number 1 single, 'Another Brick in the Wall (Part II)', which has the honour of being the last number 1 single of the seventies and the first number 1 of the eighties.

6
NOW appearances

'Mysterious Girl', Peter Andre featuring Bubbler Ranx, *NOW 34*, August 1996

'Mysterious Girl', Peter Andre featuring Bubbler Ranx, *NOW 57*, April 2004

IN OTHER NEWS . . . *NOW 57* (APRIL 2004)

At the cinema, Quentin Tarantino's film *Kill Bill Vol. 2* opened. The soundtrack includes 'Woo Hoo' by Japanese trio The 5.6.7.8's, a number 28 hit in July 2004.

On 1 April Google announced the launch of their Gmail service. Due to the April Fool's Day timing a number of potential users thought it was a hoax.

Caron Keating, *Blue Peter* presenter from 1986 to 1990, died, aged just 41.

90s

NOW 35 Did You Know . . .

Sheryl Crow makes her *NOW* debut with the number 9 hit 'If It Makes You Happy'. It is the first of six appearances, which includes her theme to the eighteenth James Bond film, *Tomorrow Never Dies*. The soundtrack also included a new version of Monty Norman's classic 'James Bond Theme' (*NOW 38*) by **Moby**. In 1999 **Prince** recorded a version of Sheryl's 1996 number 12 'Everyday Is a Winding Road' (*NOW 36*) for his album *Rave Un2 the Joy Fantastic*.

NOW 51 Did You Know . . .

Canadian rockers **Nickelback** make the first of three appearances with the number 4 hit 'How You Remind Me'. Their biggest hit to date is 'Rockstar' (*NOW 69*), with additional vocals by Billy Gibbons of ZZ Top. It spent two weeks at number 2 in February 2008 but was kept off the top spot by 'Now You're Gone' by **Basshunter** featuring **DJ Mental Theo's Bazzheadz**, then by **Duffy**'s 'Mercy' (both *NOW 69*). In 2002 Nickelback singer **Chad Kroeger** teamed up with **Josey Scott** for the number 4 hit 'Hero' (*NOW 53*), the theme to the film *Spider-Man*.

IN OTHER NEWS . . . *NOW 35* (NOVEMBER 1996)

The Sands Hotel in Las Vegas was demolished to make way for The Venetian. The plane crash at the climax of Nicholas Cage film *Con Air* was filmed there shortly before the lobby was knocked down.

Ella Yelich-O'Connor, better known as singer **Lorde**, was born in Auckland, New Zealand.

Music-themed quiz show *Never Mind the Buzzcocks* made its debut on BBC Two, with presenter Mark Lamarr and team captains Sean Hughes and Phill Jupitus.

12
NOW appearances
'I'll Never Break Your Heart',
NOW 35, November 1996

'Drowning',
NOW 51, March 2002

BACKSTREET BOYS

Formed in Florida in 1993, Backstreet Boys have chalked up nineteen Top 40 hits and twelve *NOW* appearances, but despite huge international success, 'I Want It That Way' (*NOW 43*) is their only UK number 1 so far. 'I'll Never Break Your Heart' (*NOW 35*) stalled at number 42 when first released in 1995, but a reissue the following year saw it climb to number 8. The song was co-written by **Eugene Wilde**, who as a solo artist scored one Top 40 hit, the 1984 number 18 'Gotta Get You Home Tonight' (*NOW 4*).

Prior to landing the top spot with 'I Want It That Way' (*NOW 43*), the Boys came 'oh so close' twice, hitting number 2 with 'Quit Playing Games (with My Heart)' (*NOW 37*) and 'All I Have to Give' (*NOW 39*). 'I Want It That Way' was another contribution from relentless hit-writer Max Martin, and spent a week at number 1 in May 1995. It has since been covered by both **JLS** and **One Direction**, which pretty much makes it the ultimate boyband song.

In 'unusual promotion' news, **Britney Spears** included a hidden message on her debut album . . . *Baby One More Time* promoting Backstreet Boys' third album, *Millennium*, and shared snippets of their songs, including 'Show Me the Meaning of Being Lonely' (*NOW 45*) and 'The One' (*NOW 46*). The band's last *NOW* appearance was the 2002 single 'Drowning' (*NOW 51*); taken from a greatest hits compilation, it heralded a two-year break for them.

Both Backstreet Boys and ***NSYNC** were put together and managed by businessman Lou Pearlman. In 2008 Lou was found guilty on various charges, including money laundering, and was sentenced to twenty-five years in prison. In 2011 Backstreet Boys embarked on a world tour with New Kids on the Block, under the catchy title NKOTBSB.

90s

'COUNTING STARS', ONE REPUBLIC (*NOW 86*)

The X Factor and its contribution to *NOW That's What I Call Music*

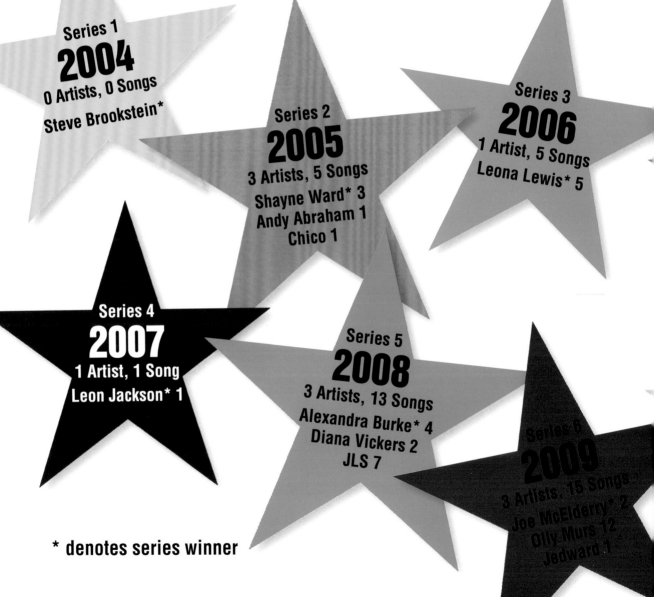

Series 1
2004
0 Artists, 0 Songs
Steve Brookstein*

Series 2
2005
3 Artists, 5 Songs
Shayne Ward* 3
Andy Abraham 1
Chico 1

Series 3
2006
1 Artist, 5 Songs
Leona Lewis* 5

Series 4
2007
1 Artist, 1 Song
Leon Jackson* 1

Series 5
2008
3 Artists, 13 Songs
Alexandra Burke* 4
Diana Vickers 2
JLS 7

Series 6
2009
3 Artists, 15 Songs
Joe McElderry* 2
Olly Murs 12
Jedward 1

* denotes series winner

Series 7
2010
Artists, 14 Songs
Matt Cardle* 2
Cher Lloyd 1
One Direction 11

Series 8
2011
3 Artists, 17 Songs
Little Mix* 15
Amelia Lily 1
Marcus Collins 1

Series 9
2012
3 Artists, 11 songs
James Arthur* 5
Ella Henderson 5
Union J 1

Series 10
2013
1 Artist, 1 Song
Sam Bailey* 1

Series 11
2014
2 Artists, 3 Songs
Ben Haenow* 2
Fleur East 1

Series 12
2015
2 Artists, 4 Songs
Louisa Johnson* 3
Reggie 'n' Bollie 1

Series 13
2016
0 Artists, 0 Songs
Matt Terry*

Series 14
2017
1 Artist, 1 Song
Rak-Su* 1

Special mention for Rowetta (series 1) who sings on Happy Mondays' 'Step On' (*NOW 16*)

TEXAS

Glasgow outfit Texas made their Top 40 debut in 1989, but had to wait eight years for their first *NOW* appearance, when *White on Blonde*, the first of three number 1 albums, gave rise to four Top 10 singles, including 'Say What You Want' (*NOW 36*), 'Halo' (*NOW 37*) and 'Black Eyed Boy' (*NOW 38*). All three were co-written by guitarist Johnny McElhone, who had previously scored six Top 40 hits as a member of Altered Images and another with the band Hipsway.

At the 1998 BRIT Awards, Texas performed 'Say What You Want' in collaboration with rapper Method Man. It was released as a number 4 double A-side single credited to Texas featuring the Wu-Tang Clan, though it was the 'other side', 'Insane', that appeared on *NOW 39*. In 2003 a second rap partnership, 'Carnival Girl' by Texas featuring **Kardinall Offishall**, made it to number 9 and onto *NOW 56*. Kardinall Offishall was also a featured artist, along with **Colby O'Donis**, on **Akon**'s number 8 single 'Beautiful' (*NOW 73*).

'I Don't Want a Lover' (*NOW 49*) was Texas' chart debut in 1989. In 2001 it was re-issued to promote a greatest-hits collection, with a remix by production and songwriting team Stargate. The Norwegian duo of Mikkel S. Eriksen and Tor Erik Hermansen currently have forty-nine *NOW* credits, of which twelve were number 1 singles, including 'Beautiful Liar' (*NOW 67*) by **Beyoncé** and **Shakira**, 'Diamonds' (*NOW 84*) by **Rihanna** and 'Too Good at Goodbyes' (*NOW 98*) by **Sam Smith**.

'Black Eyed Boy' and 'Summer Son' (*NOW 44*) both include a writing credit for Robert Hodgens, previously of Scottish chart-toppers **The Bluebells**. Robert had a hand in writing 'Young at Heart', the 1993 number 1 that appeared on both *NOW 3* and *NOW 24*, as did Siobhan Fahey of **Bananarama**, who first recorded a version of the song for their 1983 album *Deep Sea Skiving*.

90s

NOW 36 Did You Know . . .

Making the first of only two appearances are the duo **Alisha's Attic**, comprising sisters Karen and **Shelly Poole**. As singer with The Tremeloes their father Brian scored a number 1 hit in 1963 with a cover of the Motown classic 'Do You Love Me?' Shelly would appear once more with 'Borderline' (*NOW 65*) by **Michael Gray** featuring Shelly Poole. However, as a songwriter Karen has so far racked up ten appearances, including the number 1 'Lola's Theme' by **The Shapeshifters** (*NOW 58*).

NOW 63 Did You Know . . .

Three more graduates from *The X Factor* school of excellence make their debut, including the winner of series two, **Shayne Ward**. 'That's My Goal' gave Shayne the Christmas 2005 number 1 single, and the first of six Top 40 hits. We were also blessed with another number 1 smash, 'It's Chico Time' by **Chico**, and the slightly less successful 'Hang Up', a disappointing number 63 for singing bin-man **Andy Abraham**. Sadly these would be the only *NOW* appearances for both of them.

IN OTHER NEWS . . . *NOW 36* (MARCH 1997)

Teletubbies made its debut on BBC Two. In December their single 'Teletubbies Say Eh-Oh!' spent two weeks at number 1 but was beaten to the Christmas top spot by **Spice Girls**' 'Too Much' (*NOW 41*).

Camila Cabello was born in Havana, Cuba. In 2012 she joined vocal group **Fifth Harmony**, who finished third on the American version of *The X Factor*.

Wilbert Awdry, better known as the Reverend W. Awbry, creator of *Thomas the Tank Engine*, died, aged 85.

12
NOW appearances
'Say What You Want',
NOW 36, March 1997

'Sleep',
NOW 63, April 2006

90s

NOW 36 Did You Know . . .

No Doubt made their debut with their only number 1 single, 'Don't Speak', and would make just one more appearance with 'Just a Girl' (*NOW 37*). The first of their eleven Top 40 hits, 'Just a Girl' was first released in 1996 but stalled at number 38; it would rise to number 3 the following year on the back of their new-found success. No Doubt last made the Top 40 in 2004 with a cover of the **Talk Talk** single 'It's My Life' (*NOW 18*).

NOW 71 Did You Know . . .

'Somewhere Only We Know' (*NOW 57*) was the first of four appearances on consecutive volumes of *NOW* for **Keane**, a run that included 'Everybody's Changing' (*NOW 58*), 'Bedshaped' (*NOW 59*) and 'This Is the Last Time' (*NOW 60*). All four songs were taken from their number 1 debut album *Hopes and Fears.* Their last appearance to date is 'Spiralling' (*NOW 71*), a 2003 number 23 single. 'Somewhere Only We Know' (*NOW 86*) appeared again in 2013 when a cover version gave **Lily Allen** her third number 1 single.

IN OTHER NEWS . . . *NOW 71* (NOVEMBER 2008)

The American author Michael Crichton died, aged 66. His best-known works include *The Andromeda Strain*, *Westworld* and *Jurassic Park*.

BBC Two broadcast a special edition of their current-affairs programme *Newsnight* to cover the election of Barack Obama as President of the United States. Presenter Jeremy Paxman addressed **Dizzee Rascal** as 'Mr Rascal'.

The Walt Disney animation *Bolt* opened in cinemas. Vocal talent includes **John Travolta** and **Miley Cyrus**, who duet on the original song 'I Thought I'd Lost You'.

8
NOW appearances

'Encore Une Fois',
NOW 36, March 1997

'Raindrops (Encore Une Fois)',
Sash! featuring Stunt,
NOW 71, November 2008

SASH!

Sash! are a German production team fronted by Sascha Lappessen, along with Ralf Kappmeier and Thomas Lüdke. Between 1997 and 2008 they had eleven Top 40 singles, with eight of them appearing on *NOW*. Those eight featured four different vocalists but only **Shannon**, singer on 'Move Mania' (*NOW 41*), saw any other chart action, her biggest hit being 'Let the Music Play', a 1983 number 14. Beginning with 'Encore Une Fois' (*NOW 36*), the trio's first four singles included vocals in French, Spanish, English and Italian.

Sash! never managed to top the charts and had to settle for number 2 on five occasions. 'Encore Une Fois' was held off by 'Don't Speak' by No Doubt, 'Ecuador' (*NOW 37*) got stuck behind 'I'll Be Missing You' by Puff Daddy and **Faith Evans**, 'Adelante' lost out to 'Rise' (both *NOW 45*) by **Gabrielle**, while 'Stay' (*NOW 38*) had the misfortune of coming out at the same time as **Elton John**'s 'Candle in the Wind 1997', the biggest-selling single in UK chart history.

Missing from the list of number 2s, and strangely missing from *NOW*, is 'Mysterious Times', a 1998 collaboration with **Tina Cousins**. Tina has four *NOW* appearances to her name, including two on volume 42. The number 15 hit 'Killin' Time '99' had stalled at number 80 two years earlier when it was plain old 'Killin' Time', while 'Thank ABBA for the Music' was performed at the 1999 BRIT Awards before it gave **Steps**, Tina Cousins, **B*Witched** and **Billie** a number 4 hit.

'Colour the World' (*NOW 42*) included vocals from Dr Alban, another artist who was frustrated in his quest for a number 1 single. He spent three weeks at number 2 in 1992, all the time gazing up at 'Ebeneezer Goode' by **The Shamen** (*NOW 23*). 'Raindrops (Encore Une Fois)' (*NOW 71*) is our last sighting of Sash! As the name suggests, it was a 'mash up' of their first appearance and 'Raindrops', previously a number 51 single for dance duo **Stunt**.

90s

NOW 38 Did You Know . . .

If you're looking for Top 10 hits by Lancastrian anarchists then *NOW* has them (both). Prior to 'Tubthumping' (*NOW 38*), **Chumbawamba**'s best chart showing was 'Enough Is Enough', a number 56 collaboration with **Credit to the Nation** in 1993. 'Tubthumping' spent three weeks at number 2 in August 1997, its path to the summit blocked by **Will Smith**'s 'Men in Black'. Chumbawamba's second hit, 'Amnesia', made it to number 10 and appeared on *NOW 39*.

NOW 65 Did You Know . . .

Simon Webbe's third appearance, 'Coming Around Again', is our most recent sighting of any member of **Blue**, either solo or combined. Blue managed an impressive run of nine appearances, starting with 'All Rise' on *NOW 49* and including 'If You Come Back' (*NOW 50*), one of three number 1 singles, and ending with 'Curtain Falls' (*NOW 59*). Of his ex-bandmates only **Duncan James** has a solo appearance on *NOW*, with the Andrew Lloyd Webber composition 'I Believe My Heart' (*NOW 59*), a duet with **Keedie**.

IN OTHER NEWS . . . *NOW 38* (NOVEMBER 1997)

After sixty-five years BBC One closed down at the end of the day for the last time. Going forward it would broadcast BBC News 24 throughout the night.

Michael Hutchence, singer with Australian Rock group **INXS**, was found dead in a Sydney hotel room.

BBC Two broadcast the first episode of *I'm Alan Partridge*, with Alan now a DJ on the Radio Norwich graveyard shift and living in the Linton Travel Tavern.

8
NOW appearances
'I Know Where It's At',
NOW 38, November 1997

'Rock Steady',
NOW 65, November 2006

Sisters Natalie and Nicole Appleton, Melanie Blatt and Shaznay Lewis scored the first of nine Top 40 hits with the Steely Dan-sampling number 4 'I Know Where It's At'. Follow-up single 'Never Ever' (*NOW 39*) was to be the first of five number 1s, and also bagged them two BRIT Awards in 1998 for Single and Video of the Year. *NOW 40* features a number 1 double-A-side coupling of cover versions: 'Lady Marmalade' – originally a number 17 hit for La Belle in 1974 – and 'Under the Bridge' – a Red Hot Chili Peppers number 13 in 1992.

Their third number 1 in a row came with 'Bootie Call' (*NOW 41*), followed by a slight drop in standards with the number 7 hit 'War of Nerves' (*NOW 42*). Normal service was resumed with 'Pure Shores' (*NOW 47*), which spent two weeks at the top in early 2000, and was the second-bestselling single of the year behind 'Can We Fix It?' (*NOW 48*) by **Bob the Builder**. 'Pure Shores' was taken from the soundtrack to the film *The Beach*, a number 1 album that also featured 'Porcelain' by **Moby** (*NOW 46*).

90s

All Saints would register their last number 1 in October 2000 with 'Black Coffee', and call it a day shortly after. However, in 2006 they were – as *Smash Hits* would have it – 'back! Back! BACK!' with a number 3 hit, 'Rock Steady', written by Shaznay Lewis with Greg Kurstin. Greg has another nineteen writing credits on *NOW*, including **Liam Gallagher**'s first solo hit, 'Wall of Glass' (*NOW 98*). Liam married Nicole Appleton in 2008, and her sister Natalie married Liam Howlett of **The Prodigy** in 2002.

Away from All Saints, Natalie and Nicole have three Top 40 hits as **Appleton**, starting with the number 2 single 'Fantasy' (*NOW 53*), followed by 'Don't Worry' (*NOW 54*), a 2003 number 5, and 'Everything Eventually' (*NOW 55*). Neither 'Twenty Four Seven', Melanie's 2001 number 6 collaboration with **Artful Dodger**, nor 'Never Felt Like This Before', Shaznay's 2004 number 8, made it onto a *NOW* album, though Shaznay can claim a co-writing credit for the number 3 single 'Black Heart' by **Stooshe** (*NOW 82*).

ALL SAINTS

AQUA

Where to start with the legend that is 'Barbie Girl', the first of Aqua's three consecutive chart toppers and seven Top 40 hits? It spent four weeks at number 1 in late 1997 and was the second-bestselling single that year, even though it was voted 'Worst Single of the Year' at the *NME* Awards. Affronted by the saucy lyrics, the manufacturers of the namesake doll filed a lawsuit against Aqua's record label in 2000 for allegedly damaging the reputation of their brand.

Up next we have the Indiana Jones-referencing 'Doctor Jones' (*NOW 40*), and continuing our cinematic theme, third appearance 'Turn Back Time' (*NOW 41*) was

included on the soundtrack to the 1998 Gwyneth Paltrow film *Sliding Doors*. The video for the song includes footage from the film, with additional scenes shot at Holborn tube station. There is currently no plaque to commemorate this event. Aqua's last *NOW* appearance was the 2000 number 7 'Cartoon Heroes' (*NOW 45*).

Aqua began their pop career as Joyspeed, and released a dance version of the nursery rhyme 'Itzy Bitzy Spider'. Singer Lene Nystrøm had her first taste of fame as a glamorous assistant on Norwegian TV, spinning the *Wheel of Fortune*. Although Lene and shaven-headed co-singer René Dif were 'an item',

she later married keyboard player Søren Rasted. René can console himself in the knowledge that there is a street in Bornholm, Denmark, named after him.

In 2001 Aqua, along with **Safri Duo**, provided the half-time entertainment at the Eurovision Song Contest in Copenhagen. Aqua's four listings make them the current '*NOW* Champions of Denmark', just ahead of **MØ**, **Alphabeat** and **Whigfield**, with three appearances each. Also flying the flag for the Nordic kingdom are **Cartoons** (two appearances), Safri Duo, **Junior Senior**, **DJ Aligator** and **Lukas Graham,** who have one appearance each.

90s

NOW 39 Did You Know . . .

Notable 'one *NOW* wonders' on this volume include Leicester combo **Cornershop**. Originally released in August 1997, 'Brimful of Asha' had peaked at number 60 but topped the year-end John Peel Festive Fifty. However, a **Norman Cook** remix (a rare occurrence of him not using a pseudonym) saw it go straight in at number 1 the following February. Elsewhere on volume 39, ska music legend **Prince Buster** scored his second Top 40 hit with 'Whine and Grine', a mere thirty-two years after his first.

NOW 45 Did You Know . . .

German trance outfit **Fragma** made the first of four appearances, a sequence that began and ended with the number 1 hit 'Toca's Miracle'. It was a re-working of their 1999 debut 'Toca Me' with elements from 'I Need a Miracle', a 1997 number 37 for Coco. The latter was co-written by a *NOW* unsung hero, former Mud guitarist Rob Davis. His glittering résumé includes 'Groovejet (If This Ain't Love)' (*NOW 46*) by **Spiller** featuring **Sophie Ellis-Bextor**, and **Kylie Minogue**'s 'Can't Get You Out of My Head' (*NOW 50*).

IN OTHER NEWS . . . *NOW 45* (APRIL 2000)

Cinemagoers had their first chance to assess the acting abilities of Kristen Stewart. The ten-year-old had a brief role in *The Flintstones in Viva Rock Vegas*.

A Second World War Enigma cipher machine was stolen from the Bletchley Park Museum. The thief demanded a £25,000 ransom but eventually returned the machine (ransom unpaid), minus a few missing parts.

The 'Big Number Change' updated local telephone numbers in Cardiff, Coventry, London, Northern Ireland, Portsmouth and Southampton, where

4
NOW appearance

'Barbie Girl',
NOW 39, April 1998

'Cartoon Heroes',
NOW 45, April 2000

00s

NOW 39 Did You Know . . .

From *Neighbours* to *NOW*, on a list that includes **Kylie Minogue**, **Jason Donovan** and Natalie Bassingthwaighte of **Rogue Traders** (number 3 in 2006 with 'Voodoo Child', as if you need reminding), we can add **Natalie Imbruglia**. Her debut single 'Torn' made number 2 in 1997, though it was first recorded in 1993 by Danish singer Lis Sørensen as 'Brændt' (or 'Burned'). Natalie has since clocked up another nine Top 40 hits, including 'Big Mistake' (*NOW 40*) and 'Shiver' (*NOW 61*).

NOW 51 Did You Know . . .

allSTARS* made the second of two appearances with a cover of the **Bucks Fizz** 1981 number 1 'The Land of Make Believe'. They first appeared with 'Things that Go Bump in the Night' (*NOW 50*), taken from the 2002 film *Scooby-Doo*. Like **ABBA**, the 'STARS' element of the band's name derived from the first letter of each member's name – Sam, Thaila, Ashley, Rebecca and Sandy. In 2001 the band (allSTARS*, not ABBA) had their own television show on Children's ITV.

IN OTHER NEWS . . . *NOW 51* (MARCH 2002)

Comedian and musician Dudley Moore died, aged 66. With Peter Cook he had a Top 20 single in 1965 with 'Goodbye-ee', the closing music to their TV show *Not Only . . . But Also*.

The digital radio station BBC 6 Music launched, the BBC's first new national music station in thirty-two years.

An official ceremony was held to rename Speke Airport as Liverpool **John Lennon** Airport.

14
NOW appearances
'5,6,7,8',
NOW 39, April 1998
'Words Are Not Enough',
NOW 51, March 2002

STEPS

Purveyors of pure pop, Steps' first appearance, '5,6,7,8', 'only' made it to number 14, but after that it was Top 10 smashes all the way. Next up was 'Last Thing on My Mind' (*NOW 40*), which peaked at number 6, though it was a cover of a 1992 **Bananarama** single that had stalled at number 71. Their third and sixth appearances – 'Heartbeat' (*NOW 41*) and 'Tragedy' (*NOW 44*) – were a double A-side combination, and the first of their two number 1s. Producer Pete Waterman appears in the 'Tragedy' video as a wedding-reception DJ.

'Tragedy' was also the first of two Steps singles written by **Bee Gees** Barry, Maurice and Robin Gibb, along with the 2001 number 2

'Chain Reaction' (*NOW 50*), originally a 1986 number 1 for **Diana Ross**. Like Steps, Diana has two number 1 singles, though hers were fifteen years apart. The sleeve of Steps' second number 1, 'Stomp' (*NOW 47*), includes the message 'A Tribute to Bernard Edwards and **Nile Rodgers**'. The **Chic**-style melody seemingly doffs its cap to the US act's 1978 number 9 'Everybody Dance'.

In 1999 Steps partnered with **Tina Cousins**, **Cleopatra**, **B*Witched** and **Billie** for the tribute single 'Thank ABBA for the Music' (*NOW 42*). Their love of all things Björn and Benny has also seen them record 'Dancing Queen', 'Lay All Your Love on Me', 'Story of a Heart' and 'I

Know Him So Well'. The latter was another double A-side release, with 'Words Are Not Enough' (*NOW 51*), their most recent appearance on *NOW*.

Out of the Steps shadow, **Lisa Scott-Lee** has two solo appearances – 'Lately' (*NOW 55*) and 'Too Far Gone' (*NOW 56*) – and is featured vocalist on the 2004 number 23 'Get It On' (*NOW 59*) by **Intenso Project**. 'Get It On' samples David Joseph's 1983 number 13 'You Can't Hide (Your Love from Me)', while Intenso Project's only other appearance, 'Luv da Sunshine' (*NOW 52*), is built around the riff from 10cc's third number 1, 'Dreadlock Holiday'.

00s

FATBOY SLIM

In 1998 Fatboy Slim cooked up a tasty mix of two guitar samples for the number 6 hit 'The Rockafeller Skank'. A dash of funk from the 1972 northern-soul favourite 'Sliced Tomatoes' by The Just Brothers is combined with some twangy guitar from John Barry's theme to the 1960 film *Beat Girl*. Lord Finesse, aka New York rapper Robert A. Hall Jr, delivered the 'right about now' vocal that introduces 'The Rockafeller Skank'.

'Gangster Trippin' (*NOW 41*) samples the 'what we're doing . . .' vocal from 'Rinse', a 1997 song by Manchester band Dust Junkys, whose singer Nicky Lockett previously went by the name MC Tunes. In 1990 MC Tunes vs **808 State** had a number 10 with 'The Only Rhyme that Bites', which sampled the theme from 1958 Western *The Big Country*. Elsewhere, Fatboy Slim's only number 1, 'Praise You' (*NOW 42*), includes a vocal from 'Take Yo Praise', a 1975 song by Camille Yarbrough.

'Right Here, Right Now' (*NOW 43*) includes orchestration from 'Ashes the Rain and I', a 1970 recording by James Gang, a US band that included Joe Walsh, future guitarist with The Eagles. The 'Right Here, Right Now' title is spoken by actress Angela Bassett, with dialogue taken from the 1995 film *Strange Days*. In 1994 Angela was nominated for the Best Actress Oscar for her role as **Tina Turner** in the film *What's Love Got to Do with It*.

Before **Norman Cook** adopted his rotund nom de plume, he already had four appearances with **The Housemartins**, beginning with 'Happy Hour' on *NOW 7*. He also had one under his own name in partnership with **MC Wildski** (*NOW 15*), and one each as a member of **Beats International** (*NOW 17*) and **Freak Power** (*NOW 30*). In addition he has a remix credit for **Cornershop**'s only appearance, 'Brimful of Asha' (*NOW 39*), plus a co-writing credit for **Rizzle Kicks'** number 2 single 'Mama Do the Hump' (*NOW 81*).

90s

5
NOW appearances

'The Rockafeller Skank', NOW 40, August 1998

'Eat Sleep Rave Repeat (Calvin Harris Remix)', NOW 86, November 2013

90s

NOW 40 Did You Know . . .

Phil Collins established the 'successful rock drummer turned solo star' trend with the very first song on *NOW 1*. Thirteen years later **Don Henley**, drummer with The Eagles, had a number 12 hit with a reissue of 'The Boys of Summer', the same position he reached when it was originally released in 1985. In 2003 a dance version by **DJ Sammy** reached number 2 and appeared on *NOW 54*, the second of the Spanish DJ's three appearances.

NOW 86 Did You Know . . .

'Lost Generation' is the most recent of five appearances by Brighton duo **Rizzle Kicks**. They first appeared as featured vocalists on **Olly Murs**'s number 1 'Heart Skips a Beat' (*NOW 80*). When the single was released in the US, Philadelphia rappers Chiddy Bang replaced Rizzle Kicks' Sussex tones. Also on *NOW 80* was 'Down with the Trumpets', with said instrument played by one Jack Birchwood, who also plays on **Emeli Sandé**'s 'Hurts' (*NOW 95*). For their *NOW 81* appearance, 'When I Was a Youngster', the trumpets were sampled from 'Revolution Rock', a 1979 song by **The Clash**.

IN OTHER NEWS . . . *NOW 40* (AUGUST 1998)

ITV launched a new Saturday morning schedule, featuring *SMTV Live* and music programme *CD:UK*, with both shows hosted by Cat Deeley, Ant McPartlin and Declan Donnelly.

Jane McDonald, star of BBC documentary series *The Cruise*, released her first album, which spent three weeks at number 1.

The Independent Television Commission upheld a viewer's complaint after a member of **B*Witched** used a phrase on Nickelodeon TV more usually associated with *Father Ted*.

STEREOPHONICS

Stereophonics' nine appearances mark them out as the most frequent visitors from Wales, two ahead of their one-time collaborator **Tom Jones**. 'Just Looking' was the sixth of their twenty-six Top 40 hits, and one of two songs – along with 'Pick a Part That's New' (*NOW 43*) – to be taken from their second album *Performance and Cocktails*, which was the first of five consecutive number 1 studio albums for the band; they enjoyed a sixth number 1 with their 2015 release *Keep the Village Alive*.

90s

Tom Jones has seven appearances on *NOW*, all collaborations, four of which originally appeared on his 1999 album *Reload*, including 'Mama Told Me Not to Come' (*NOW 45*) with Stereophonics. Their version peaked at number 4, one better than their next two appearances, 'Mr Writer' (*NOW 48*) and 'Have a Nice Day' (*NOW 49*). The latter was included on the soundtrack to the 2004 zombie film *Dawn of the Dead*.

On 'Handbags and Gladrags' (*NOW 51*) the band line-up is augmented by Jools Holland and His Rhythm and Blues Orchestra. The song was written by Manfred Mann singer Mike d'Abo and first recorded by Chris Farlowe in 1967, when it made number 33. An arrangement by 'Big George' Webley is used for the BBC series *The Office*, with vocals by Scottish rocker Fin Muir of the band Waysted. Big George also wrote the theme for the satirical quiz show *Have I Got News for You*.

In March 2005 'Dakota' became Stereophonics' first and so far only number 1 when it dislodged 'Over and Over' by **Nelly** featuring **Tim McGraw** (both *NOW 60*). Their most recent appearance, 'It Means Nothing' (*NOW 68*), is one of three Stereophonics singles to include a Beatles cover ('Helter Skelter') as a B-side. The other two are 'Mr Writer' ('Don't Let Me Down') and the 2001 single 'Step On My Old Size Nines' ('I'm Only Sleeping').

9
NOW appearances

'Just Looking',
NOW 42, March 1999

'It Means Nothing',
NOW 68, November 2007

NOW 42 Did You Know . . .

The Corrs make their second and most recent appearance with the number 3 single 'What Can I Do'. They had first appeared four months earlier with their number 6 version of the 1977 **Fleetwood Mac** song 'Dreams' (*NOW 41*), written by singer **Stevie Nicks**. Stevie made one solo appearance on *NOW 15* with 'Rooms on Fire', which she wrote with Rupert Hine. Rupert was previously in one-hit wonders Quantum Jump, who had a number 5 with 'The Lone Ranger' in 1979.

NOW 68 Did You Know . . .

Dutch DJ **Fedde Le Grand** has three Top 10 hits, all of them *NOW* appearances, starting with his 2006 number 1 'Put Your Hands Up for Detroit' (*NOW 65*), a re-working of the 1999 single 'Hands Up for Detroit' by Matthew Dear. In 2007 he hit number 7 with a remix of **Camille Jones**'s 2004 single 'The Creeps' (*NOW 66*). His most recent appearance was on *NOW 68* with another remix, 'Let Me Think About It' by Danish singer **Ida Corr** (no relation).

IN OTHER NEWS . . . *NOW 68* (NOVEMBER 2007)

The MTV Europe Music Awards were held in Munich, where **Avril Lavigne**'s 'Girlfriend' won Best Single and **Nelly Furtado**'s *Loose* won Best Album.

Amazon launched their Kindle e-book reading device.

Actor Christopher Biggins won series 7 of *I'm a Celebrity … Get Me Out Of Here!* Contestants include singer **Cerys Matthews** and former England footballer Rodney Marsh.

00s

NOW 43 Did You Know . . .

New Radicals make their sole appearance with their only Top 40 hit, the number 5 single 'You Get What You Give'. Their singer-songwriter Gregg Alexander had previously released two unsuccessful solo albums before a brief one-album, two-single stint as New Radicals. He would have later success writing songs for others, as evidenced by nine more credits on *NOW*, including **Ronan Keating**'s second solo number 1 'Life Is a Rollercoaster' (*NOW 47*).

NOW 52 Did You Know . . .

Between 2000 and 2009 Manchester band **Doves** had two number 1 albums and nine Top 40 singles, including 'Pounding', the first of their two *NOW* appearances. Comprising brothers Andy and Jez Williams with Jimi Goodwin, the trio had previously been together as **Sub Sub** and scored the 1993 number 3 dance hit 'Ain't No Love (Ain't No Use)' (*NOW 24*), with featured vocalist **Melanie Williams**. Doves' only other appearance is the number 6 single 'Black and White Town' (*NOW 60*).

IN OTHER NEWS . . . *NOW 43* (JULY 1999)

American crime drama *The Sopranos* made its British television debut on Channel 4.

The horror film *The Blair Witch Project* opened in cinemas. It cost a reported $60,000 to make and has since taken $250 million at the box office.

After standing empty for 158 years the fourth plinth in London's Trafalgar Square was used to display the sculpture *Ecce Homo* by Turner Prize-winning artist Mark Wallinger.

9
NOW appearances

'Bring It All Back',
NOW 43, July 1999

'You',
NOW 52, July 2002

S CLUB 7

Springing fully formed from the CBBC drama *Miami 7*, S Club 7 scored the first of four number 1 singles with their debut smash 'Bring It All Back'. Their second number 1 was the 2000 Children in Need single 'Never Had a Dream Come True' (*NOW 48*), one of their five singles co-written by **Cathy Dennis**, a list that also includes their fourth number 1 'Have You Ever' (*NOW 51*). In total S Club 7 had nine Top 10 singles, with 'Natural' (*NOW 47*) peaking the lowest and 'only' getting to number 3.

The quartet of chart toppers is completed by 'Don't Stop Movin'' (*NOW 49*), which they performed in 2002 at the Party at the Palace event staged to celebrate the Queen's Golden Jubilee. They took to the same stage as **Cliff Richard** and **Brian May** on a version of Cliff's 1958 single 'Move It'. In 2004 **The Beautiful South** recorded a version of 'Don't Stop Movin'' for an album of cover versions that also included 'Don't Fear the Reaper' by Blue Öyster Cult.

00s

Our tally of nine *NOW* appearances is open to debate as, following the departure of Paul Cattermole in 2002, the remaining members rebranded themselves as **S Club** and popped up twice more, with the number 5 hit 'Alive' (*NOW 54*) and the farewell ballad 'Say Goodbye' (*NOW 55*). In 2001 **S Club Juniors** joined the party, counting among their ranks Frankie Bridge, later singer with **The Saturdays**. After S Club split in 2003, S Club Juniors morphed into **S Club 8**.

Post-S Club, **Rachel Stevens** has seven Top 40 hits and five appearances on *NOW*. Jo O'Meara had one Top 40 hit with 'What Hurts the Most', and occasionally performs as S Club 3 with Bradley McIntosh and Paul Cattermole. In 2018 Paul put his two S Club 7 BRIT Awards up for sale on eBay. Hannah Spearritt appeared in the BBC time-travel/dinosaur drama *Primeval*. In 2012 Tina Barrett was featured vocalist on a single by astrologer Russell Grant. Jon Lee has been a contestant on *Celebrity Dinner Date*.

BRITNEY SPEARS

The girl from McComb, Mississippi, can boast an impressive nineteen *NOW* appearances, eighteen of them as a solo artist. Ten of her appearances were on consecutive volumes (*NOW 44* to *53*) and all six of Britney's number 1 singles appear on *NOW* albums. While all eighteen of the relevant *NOW* albums can boast number 1 album chart positions, Britney has yet to top that particular tree, with five of her albums stalling at number 2.

'. . . Baby One More Time' was written by Swedish pop Svengali Max Martin and was originally intended for R&B trio TLC. The video was shot at Venice High School in California, which also doubled as Rydell High School for the 1978 film *Grease*. Perpetually wet Scottish indie outfit **Travis** recorded a version of '. . . Baby One More Time' as a B-side for their 1999 single 'Turn'.

One of Britney's first breaks in 'showbiz' came in 1992 when she joined the cast of *The All New Mickey Mouse Club*. Fellow 'Mouseketeers' included **Christina Aguilera** (five *NOW* appearances), **Justin Timberlake** (fourteen solo *NOW* appearances) and JC Chasez (three appearances alongside Justin as a member of ***NSYNC**). Another noteworthy Mouseketeer was actor Ryan Gosling, who – while he has yet to grace a *NOW* album – can boast a number 1 record courtesy of the *La La Land* soundtrack.

Britney's most recent appearance on *NOW*, 'Scream & Shout', a collaboration with **will.i.am**, is also her last number 1 single to date. With thirty-three *NOW* appearances between them, both artists obviously know how to score a hit, but we think this could have been so much better if it were a medley of 'Scream' by **Usher** (*NOW 82*) and 'Shout' by **Ant & Dec** (*NOW 36*).

90s

NOW 44 Did You Know . . .

After Britney announced her arrival with '. . . Baby One More Time', it was followed on *NOW 44* by **Shania Twain** with 'That Don't Impress Me Much'. However, Britney was impressed enough to record Shania's song 'Don't Let Me Be the Last to Know' (*NOW 49*). All four of Shania's *NOW* appearances were co-written by ex-husband Robert Lange; his first credit came on *NOW 7* as co-writer of **Billy Ocean**'s number 1 'When the Going Gets Tough, the Tough Get Going'.

NOW 84 Did You Know . . .

Both of **Gabrielle Aplin**'s *NOW* appearances were on volume 84, including her number 1 single 'The Power of Love', a cover of **Frankie Goes to Hollywood**'s third and, so far, last number 1. Frankie's version didn't make the *NOW* cut when first released in 1984, but popped up on volume 46 when it re-charted following the release of a greatest-hits collection. Other eulogies to the strength of affection that have appeared on *NOW* include 'Faith (In the Power of Love)' by **Rozalla** (*NOW 20*) and 'The Power of Love' by **Céline Dion** (*NOW 29*).

IN OTHER NEWS . . . *NOW 84* (MARCH 2013)

After fifty-three years the iconic BBC Television Centre in West London closed, and all BBC radio and television news services moved to the older Broadcasting House building, near Oxford Circus.

David Bowie released *The Next Day*, his first studio album in over ten years. It entered the album chart at number 1, and remained in the Top 40 for eight weeks. It re-entered the Top 40 in November when an expanded deluxe edition was issued.

Jason Donovan left commercial radio station Heart, to tour the UK in the stage musical *Priscilla, Queen of the Desert*.

19
NOW appearances

'. . . Baby One More Time', *NOW 44*, November 1999

'Scream & Shout', will.i.am featuring Britney Spears, *NOW 84*, March 2013

00s

NOW 45 Did You Know . . .

'Killer 2000' was the third and most recent appearance by **ATB**, aka German techno DJ André Tanneberger. An update of the 1990 number 1 by **Adamski** featuring **Seal**, the ATB version included vocals by Drue Williams, a veteran of the West End stage who appeared in the original 1984 production of *Starlight Express*. ATB made their *NOW* debut on volume 43 with the number 1 hit '9PM (Till I Come)'. As with 'Don't Stop' (*NOW 44*), it featured uncredited vocals from Yolanda Rivera.

NOW 99 Did You Know . . .

Making his third appearance with the gospel/grime crossover song 'Blinded By Your Grace, Part 2' is **Stormzy**. Featuring fellow South Londoner **MNEK**, it is probably unique in the history of *NOW* as the lyrics namecheck both his mum, Abigail, and his co-writer Fraser T. Smith. Fraser has more than a dozen other writing credits on *NOW*, including the number 1s 'Break Your Heart' (*NOW 74*) by **Taio Cruz** and 'Set Fire to the Rain' (*NOW 80*) by **Adele**.

IN OTHER NEWS . . . *NOW 45* (APRIL 2000)

Nintendo announced they had sold their hundred-millionth *Game Boy* hand-held console.

After twelve years of playing Ricky Butcher, actor Sid Owen made his last appearance in *EastEnders*. Three months later he had a number 14 single with a cover of Sugar Minott's 1981 hit 'Good Thing Going'.

DJ Janice Long began presenting the midnight show on BBC Radio 2. Her stint on the programme would last seven years.

11
NOW appearances

'Fill Me In',
NOW 45, April 2000

'I Know You', Craig David
featuring Bastille,
NOW 99, March 2018

CRAIG DAVID

You wait ages for a Craig David track and two come along at once . . . That's how it started on *NOW 45* when we were treated to both 'Fill Me In' by Craig David and 'Re-Rewind (The Crowd Say Bo Selecta)' by **Artful Dodger** featuring Craig David. The latter made the schoolboy error of coming out in December and had to settle for the number 2 slot behind **Cliff Richard**, while 'Fill Me In' gave Craig the first of two number 1s in April 2000.

Craig's second number 1 also came in 2000, when he shared far too many personal details on '7 Days' (*NOW 47*). We waited seven years for his next appearance, with 'Hot Stuff (Let's Dance)', which sampled **David Bowie**'s 1983 number 1 'Let's Dance', and then had to wait another nine years for 'When the Bassline Drops' (*NOW 93*) by Craig David and **Big Narstie**. Normal service was resumed on *NOW 94*, where we got both 'One More Time' and 'Nothing Like This' by **Blonde** and Craig David.

Adam Englefield and Jacob Manson are the Bristol duo behind Blonde. They also co-wrote 'Lay It All on Me' by **Rudimental** featuring **Ed Sheeran** (*NOW 92*). On *NOW 95* Craig gave us both 'All We Needed', the official Children in Need single for 2016, and 'Ain't Giving Up', his collaboration with **Sigala**. The Norfolk-born DJ has six other *NOW* appearances, including his 2015 number 1 'Easy Love' (*NOW 92*), which samples The Jackson 5's 1970 number 8 'ABC'.

Seemingly a sociable individual, Craig wrote 'Heartline' (*NOW 98*) in 2017 with **Jonas Blue** and RØMANS. His latest chums had previously co-written 'Mama' (*NOW 97*) for Jonas Blue featuring **William Singe**. Staying on volume 97, Craig was one of the many contributors to 'Bridge over Troubled Water' by **Artists for Grenfell**, a cast that included **Bastille**, Craig's most recent 'partners in rhyme' on 'I Know You' (*NOW 99*).

00s

ATOMIC KITTEN

According to **OMD**'s Andy McCluskey, he put Atomic Kitten together at the suggestion of Karl Bartos from Kraftwerk, an idea that led to fourteen Top 40 hits, including three number 1s, and eleven appearances on *NOW*. The band's first two appearances were written by Andy with OMD colleague Stuart Kershaw and the Kitten's **Liz McClarnon**, though 'I Want Your Love' (*NOW 46*) also credits Bill Drummond and Jimmy Cauty of **The KLF**, as it samples their 1991 number 2 'Justified and Ancient' (*NOW 21*).

Shortly after the release of their first number 1, 'Whole Again' (*NOW 48*), Kerry Katona left the group and was replaced by Jenny Frost, previously a singer with all-female five-piece **Precious.** The new line-up immediately scored a second number 1 with 'Eternal Flame' (*NOW 49*), a cover of The Bangles' 1989 ballad. It proved too strong for 'Bootylicious' (*NOW 50*) by **Destiny's Child** – complete with a sample of **Stevie Nicks**'s 1981 single 'Edge of Seventeen' – which stuck behind them at number 2.

Another cover version gave Atomic Kitten their third number 1, with 'The Tide Is High (Get the Feeling)' (*NOW 53*); first recorded in 1967 by The Paragons, it had given Blondie their fifth number 1 in 1980. While their next appearance, 'Love Doesn't Have to Hurt' (*NOW 54*), was an original, it was another

song by Susannah Hoffs of The Bangles. Their one *NOW* collaboration was with **Kool and the Gang**, a re-working of their 1979 hit 'Ladies' Night' (*NOW 57*). It peaked at number 8, one place higher than the original.

The group had planned to bow out with the 2004 single 'Someone Like Me' (*NOW 58*), but were back the following year with 'Cradle' (*NOW 60*), a charity single and a remix of a song recorded for their 2000 debut album. Since then only Liz McLarnon has graced *NOW*, with her cover of Barbra Streisand's 1980 number 1 'Woman in Love' (*NOW 63*). For three years Jenny Frost presented the BBC TV show *Snog Marry Avoid?* In 2013 the original Atomic Kitten line-up reformed for the ITV show *The Big Reunion.*

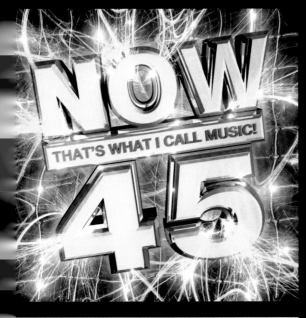

NOW 45 Did You Know . . .

Moloko made their second and most recent appearance with their biggest hit, the number 2 'The Time Is Now'. 'Never Be the Same Again' by **Melanie C** featuring **Lisa 'Left Eye' Lopes** kept it off the top spot. Moloko's only other appearance was 'Sing It Back' (*NOW 44*), but singer **Róisín Murphy** also featured on 'Never Enough' (*NOW 49*) by German DJ **Boris Dlugosch**, while 'the other Moloko' Mark Brydon produced 'House Arrest' (*NOW 11*), a 1987 number 3 for **Krush**.

NOW 60 Did You Know . . .

Making a rare but welcome appearance was **LL Cool J** (short for Ladies Love Cool James, of course), who had the first of his seventeen Top 40 hits back in 1987. His 2005 number 3 single 'Hush' featured an even rarer artist credit for **7 Aurelius**, a frequent production partner for **Ja Rule** and **Ashanti**. LL Cool J's first appearance was 'Phenomenon' (*NOW 38*), which provides a sole *NOW* credit for Bill Withers, as it samples his 1972 song 'Who Is He (And What Is He to You)?'

N OTHER NEWS . . . *NOW 60* (MARCH 2005)

John Travolta and Uma Thurman starred in *Be Cool*, the sequel to the 1995 film *Get Shorty*. The cast also included singer **Christina Milian** and André Benjamin of **OutKast**.

Rock DJ Tommy Vance died, aged 64. Born Richard Anthony Crispian Francis Preu Hope-Weston, in July 1985 he had announced the acts as they took to the stage at Live Aid.

After a gap of nine years *Doctor Who* returned to BBC TV, with Christopher Eccleston playing the ninth Doctor and **Billie Piper** as

11
NOW appearances

'See Ya',
NOW 45, April 2000

'Cradle',
NOW 60, March 2005

00s

NOW 46 Did You Know . . .

Making the Top 10 with his debut solo single was **Richard Ashcroft**. 'A Song for the Lovers' reached number 3 in April 2000 and was the first of his four *NOW* appearances. The number 3 spot was as good as it got for Richard; he hit it again in 2006 with his final *NOW* appearance, 'Break the Night with Colour' (*NOW 63*). However, he did get to number 1 with 'The Drugs Don't Work' (*NOW 38*), one of four Top 10 singles and five *NOW* appearances for **The Verve**.

NOW 97 Did You Know . . .

Twenty-one of the forty-five songs on volume 97 are credited as 'featuring' at least one more artist; that's the most on any volume so far. In fact the first nine songs on this volume all feature a 'featuring'. There are twenty-seven different artists 'featured', with **Justin Bieber** 'featuring' on two songs, while **Katy Perry** 'features' **Migos** on 'Bon Appetit' and is 'featured' on the **Calvin Harris** song 'I'm the One'.

IN OTHER NEWS . . . *NOW 46* (JULY 2000)

In cinemas *Nutty Professor II: The Klumps* opened. Starring alongside Eddie Murphy are **Janet Jackson** and soul music legend Freda Payne, who had a number 1 hit in 1970 with 'Band of Gold'.

Jennifer Aniston married Brad Pitt in Malibu, California. They would separate and divorce in 2005.

Paul Young, singer with Sad Café and Mike and the Mechanics, died, aged 53.

20
NOW appearances

'Yellow',
NOW 46, July 2000

'Something Just Like This',
The Chainsmokers
featuring Coldplay,
NOW 97, July 2017

COLDPLAY

Only six acts have clocked up more *NOW* appearances than Coldplay, and one of those is **Rihanna**, who shares a credit with them for the number 4 hit 'Princess of China' (*NOW 82*). From their first appearance with the number 4 single 'Yellow' (*NOW 46*), the band had to wait six years for their first number 1, 'Viva la Vida' (*NOW 71*). Patience was also required for their second chart topper, 'Paradise' (*NOW 81*), which took ten weeks from entering the chart at number 14 to reach the summit.

Coldplay might have hoped to top the charts a little earlier, but in 2002 'In My Place' was runner-up to **Darius**'s 'Colourblind' (both *NOW 53*), and they would have got away with it in 2005 if that pesky **Crazy Frog** and his 'Axel F' hadn't kept 'Speed of Sound' (both *NOW 61*) at number 2. It may be some consolation to Coldplay that all seven of their studio albums have made it to number 1. They have also won the BRIT Award for Best British Group four times.

'Princess of China' lists Brian Eno as co-writer, while Coldplay's ninth appearance, 'Talk' (*NOW 63*), includes a credit for German synthesiser-pioneers Kraftwerk, as it samples elements of their 1981 number 1 'Computer Love' (a double A-side single with 'The Model'). Brian Eno is also co-writer of **David Bowie**'s iconic single 'Heroes' (*NOW 93*). When 'Heroes' was first released in 1977 the B-side was the instrumental 'V-2 Schneider', a tribute to Kraftwerk founder Florian Schneider.

Chris Martin sang on both the Band Aid 20 and Band Aid 30 number 1 singles. He is co-writer of **Jamelia**'s number 5 song 'See It in a Boy's Eyes' (*NOW 58*), and 'Homecoming' (*NOW 69*) by **Kanye West** featuring Chris Martin, while Coldplay collectively wrote 'Gravity' (*NOW 59*) for **Embrace**. Away from the day job Chris and guitarist Jonny Buckland both played zombies in the 2004 comedy film *Shaun of the Dead*, while drummer Will Champion popped up in a 2013 episode of *Game of Thrones*.

'YOU'RE MY NUMBER ONE'

Twenty artists who had one number 1 hit (and one *NOW* appearance) but never made the Top 75 again.*

M/A/R/R/S, 'Pump Up the Volume' (*NOW 10*, October 1987)

Doop, 'Doop' (*NOW 27*, March 1994)

Hale & Pace & The Stonkers, 'The Stonk' (*NOW 19*, March 1991)

Mister Oizo, 'Flat Beat' (*NOW 42*, April 1999)

Baz Luhrmann, 'Everybody's Free (To Wear Sunscreen)' (*NOW 43*, June 1999)

DJ Pied Piper & Master of Ceremonies, 'Do You Really Like It?' (*NOW 49*, June 2001)

Las Ketchup, 'Aserejé (The Ketchup Song)' (*NOW 53*, October 2002)

Michael Andrews feat. Gary Jules, 'Mad World' (*NOW 56*, December 2003)

Frankee, 'F.U.R.B.' (*NOW 58*, May 2004)

3 of a Kind, 'Baby Cakes' (*NOW 59*, August 2004)

Yolanda Be Cool & D Cup, 'We No Speak Americano' (*NOW 76*, July 2010)

Gotye feat. Kimbra, 'Somebody that I Used to Know' (*NOW 81*, February 2012)

Storm Queen, 'Look Right Through (MK Vocal Edit)' (*NOW 86*, November 2013)

Magic!, 'Rude' (*NOW 89*, August 2014)

Nizlopi, 'JCB Song' (*NOW 63*, December 2005)

Sak Noel, 'Loca People' (*NOW 80*, October 2011)

Sam & The Womp, 'Bom Bom' (*NOW 83*, September 2012)

Sam Bailey, 'Skyscraper' (*NOW 87*, December 2013)

David Zowie, 'House Every Weekend' (*NOW 91*, July 2015)

* Date shown is the month it reached Number 1, not the date it appeared on *NOW*.

Westlife had already seen their first seven singles go to number 1 before they made their *NOW* debut with 'Uptown Girl'. The 2001 Comic Relief single gave them the eighth of fourteen number 1s, while Billy Joel's 1983 original is his only chart topper. Billy included his future wife Christie Brinkley in his video, while the Westlife boys shared their screen with Claudia Schiffer. Although Billy has fifteen Top 40 singles he has never appeared on *NOW* and his only other credit is 'She's Always A Woman' (*NOW 76*), **Fyfe Dangerfield**'s cover of a 1977 song.

We had a gap of almost five years and four number 1s before Westlife returned with 'You Raise Me Up' (*NOW 62*). Their thirteenth number 1 was originally recorded by Irish-Norwegian duo Secret Garden for their 1992 album *Once in a Red Moon*, and provided another Irishman, Daniel O'Donnell, with one of his sixteen Top 40 hits in 2003. It was Westlife's first single without **Brian McFadden**, who as a solo artist landed four Top 40 singles, including 'Almost Here' (*NOW 60*), a duet with yet another escapee from *Neighbours*, **Delta Goodrem**.

Westlife's fourteen number 1 singles is the most by any artist who has appeared on *NOW*, a record they share with **Cliff Richard**. Their most recent was 'The Rose' (*NOW 65*), a 1980 single for Bette Midler that was a number 1 in the US but failed to chart in the UK. Bette's biggest UK hit is the 1989 number 5 'Wind Beneath My Wings', also a Top 40 entry for actor Bill Tarmey, who played Jack Duckworth in *Coronation Street* for thirty-one years.

In 2007 Westlife had a number 3 hit with 'Home', a song co-written by **Michael Bublé** that had given him his first Top 40 hit two years earlier. In 2011 Michael sang 'Home' as a duet with **Gary Barlow** for an ITV Christmas show, and it was Gary who would write Westlife's most recent appearance, 'Lighthouse' (*NOW 80*). Of the twenty-six Westlife singles to make the Top 40 this has the dubious honour of being the least successful, peaking at number 32.

00s

NOW 50 Did You Know . . .

American rock band **Wheatus** made their second appearance with a cover of **Erasure**'s 1988 single 'A Little Respect', reaching number 3 – one place higher than the original, which appeared on *NOW 13*. In 1992 it was also a number 25 hit for **Björn Again**, giving them their only appearance on *NOW 23*. Wheatus' only other appearance came with 'Teenage Dirtbag' (*NOW 49*), which spent two weeks at number 2, gazing up at **Atomic Kitten**'s 'Whole Again' (*NOW 48*).

NOW 80 Did You Know . . .

Thirteen years on from its 1998 chart debut, 'Iris' by **Goo Goo Dolls** peaked at number 3, following performances by contestants on *The X Factor*. It was originally written for the soundtrack to the Nicolas Cage and Meg Ryan film *City of Angels*. In 2006 **Ronan Keating** took the same song to number 15, and in 2011 it reached number 8 as one of three covers on an EP by **Leona Lewis**, alongside 'Hurt', originally by Nine Inch Nails, and a **Counting Crows** song, 'Colorblind'.

IN OTHER NEWS . . . *NOW 50* (NOVEMBER 2001)

Microsoft launched their Xbox games console, and the game *Halo: Combat Evolved*, the first of that particular franchise.

American author Ken Kesey died, aged 66. He is best known for his 1962 novel *One Flew Over the Cuckoo's Nest*. The 1975 film adaptation won five Oscars, including Best Actor and Best Actress for Jack Nicholson and Louise Fletcher.

The Kumars at No. 42 made its debut on BBC Two. The cast featured on the number 1 2003 Comic Relief single 'Spirit in the Sky', alongside Gareth Gates.

6
NOW appearances

'Uptown Girl',
NOW 50, November 2001

'Lighthouse',
NOW 80, November 2011

00s

NOW 52 Did You Know . . .

Two dance acts made their debut on *NOW 52*, with both taking inspiration from late-seventies British rock acts. **Intenso Project**'s 'Luv Da Sunshine' was based on the 1978 10cc chart-topper 'Dreadlock Holiday', while 'The Logical Song' by **Scooter** was a reworking of the 1979 number 7 hit from Supertramp. Intenso Project returned on *NOW 59*, partnering with 20 per cent of **Steps**, **Lisa Scott-Lee**, while Scooter graced us with their presence on another four volumes.

NOW 75 Did You Know . . .

By 2010 it was all about 1981. Some bright spark thought pairing **Jedward** with **Vanilla Ice** for a cover of the **Queen** and **David Bowie** hit 'Under Pressure' was a good idea. And guess what? It reached number 2, so it MUST have been a good idea. Meanwhile, the cast of US television series *Glee* also scored a number 2 with the **Glee Cast** rendition of 'Don't Stop Believin' by **Journey**. Just for good measure, Journey's original version also appeared on *NOW 75*.

IN OTHER NEWS . . . NOW 52 (JULY 2002)

On 25 July Queen Elizabeth II opened the Commonwealth Games at the City of Manchester Stadium. **S Club 7** and opera singer Russell Watson were among the acts performing at the opening ceremony.

On the big screen it was a good month for sequels, with both *Men in Black II* and *Stuart Little 2* opening in cinemas.

American actor Rod Steiger died at the age of 77. His extensive career included roles in *On the Waterfront*, *Oklahoma!* and *Doctor Zhivago*, and he won the 1967 Best Actor Oscar for *In the Heat of the Night*.

19
NOW appearances

'Freak Like Me',
NOW 52, July 2002

'About a Girl',
NOW 75, March 2010

SUGABABES

How many girls in a pop trio? Who said three? When the trio in question is Sugababes, the answer is six. The original threesome consisted of Siobhán Donaghy, **Mutya Buena** and Keisha Buchanan. When the girls made their *NOW* debut on volume 53 with the number 1 hit 'Freak Like Me', Siobhán had left to be replaced by Heidi Range, briefly a member of another pop trio, **Atomic Kitten**. The 'Babes' last appearance was eight years later, with 'About a Girl', on *NOW 75*. By that time the line-up was Heidi with Amelle Berrabah and former UK Eurovision hopeful Jade Ewen.

Sugababes managed a total of nineteen appearances on *NOW*, including five number 1 singles, one of which was their 2007 cover of 'Walk this Way', a collaboration with **Girls Aloud**. Their *NOW* debut 'Freak Like Me' was originally a number 33 hit in 1995 for Adina Howard. This original included a sample of legendary funkateer Bootsy Collins's 'I'd Rather Be with You'. Producer **Richard X** added a

sample of the Tubeway Army number 1 'Are "Friends" Electric?' to the Sugababes version, which consequently credits twelve different writers!

Sugababe number 5 Amelle Berrabah was the featured artist on **Tinchy Stryder**'s number 1 hit 'Never Leave You'. The song appeared on *NOW 74* in 2009, and marks the only time that a member of the Sugababes has achieved a UK number 1 single outside of the group.

While Sugababes were saying 'hello' to *NOW* on volume 52, it was time to say goodbye to Richard Hall, better known as **Moby**. He made his chart debut in 1991 with 'Go' (*NOW 20*), which sampled Angelo Badalamenti's 'Laura Palmer's Theme' from the TV series *Twin Peaks*, and a vocal from a 1987 **Jocelyn Brown** song. The promo video for Moby's fifth and most recent appearance, 'We Are All Made of Stars', features a host of cameos including JC Chasez of ***NSYNC** and actor Sean Bean.

00s

NOW 54 Did You Know . . .

Five artists who first featured on volume 54 have gone on to make a combined total of fifty-two appearances. Chipping in with the first of three appearances were female duo **t.A.T.u.** Already a hit in their native Russia, the girls hit number 1 with their first English-language single 'All the Things She Said', with assistance from über-producer Trevor Horn. Spending four weeks at the top, the single kept three other *NOW 54* debutants in the number 2 slot, including **Justin Timberlake** and **Kelly Rowland.**

NOW 99 Did You Know . . .

Late to the party is Seattle rapper **Macklemore**. With frequent collaborator Ryan Lewis, a DJ and record producer, he already has a first number 1 single, the 2013 hit 'Thrift Shop', plus a further five Top 40 chart entries. However, 'These Days' by **Rudimental** featuring **Jess Glynne**, Macklemore and **Dan Caplen** marks his first appearance on *NOW*. Conversely making their first appearance with their first Top 40 hit is **Portugal. The Man**, as far as we know the only Alaskan band to grace *NOW*.

IN OTHER NEWS . . . *NOW 54* (APRIL 2003)

Motown soul legend Edwin Starr died aged 61. His biggest hit, the 970 number 3 'War', has been covered by **Frankie Goes to Hollywood**, Bruce Springsteen and **Boyz II Men**.

Club 7 announced that they were to split after four years, four number 1 singles and nine *NOW* appearances. (Spoiler Alert: they reform in 2014.)

Apple Inc. launched the iTunes Music Store, offering 200,000 songs to download and play on your portable electronic device.

15
NOW appearances

'Like I Love You',
NOW 54, April 2003

'Say Something',
Justin Timberlake featuring Chris Stapleton,
NOW 99, March 2018

JUSTIN TIMBERLAKE

Justin Timberlake opened his *NOW* account in 2003 with the number 2 hit 'Like I Love You'. The single features an uncredited rap by Clipse, aka the brothers Gene 'No Malice' Thornton and Terrence 'Pusha T' Thornton. On the subject of 'uncredited', Justin's current tally of fifteen appearances would be sixteen if his writing and vocal contribution to **Black Eyed Peas'** 'Where Is the Love?' (*NOW 56*) was given bigger billing.

Justin grabbed the headlines in 2004 while performing 'Rock Your Body' (*NOW 56*) with **Janet Jackson** at the half-time show during Super Bowl XXXVIII. The 'wardrobe malfunction' was witnessed by an estimated ninety-million people, though Justin was invited back again in 2018. He had also courted controversy the previous year at The BRIT Awards when he appeared to get a little fruity with **Kylie Minogue** during their rendition of Blondie's 1981 number 5 'Rapture'.

NOW has played host to three of Justin's four number 1 singles – 'SexyBack' (*NOW 65*), 'Give It to Me' (*NOW 67*) by **Timbaland** featuring Justin Timberlake and **Nelly Furtado**, and 'Mirrors' (*NOW 85*). His fifth appearance, 'I'm Lovin' It' (*NOW 57*), only managed to get to number 79, yet it may be his most familiar song as it started life as a jingle for a hamburger advert. For reasons that no one can explain it was a number 1 single in Belgium.

Justin's film credits include providing voices for Boo-Boo Bear in *Yogi Bear* (2010), Arthur Pendragon in *Shrek the Third* (2007) and Branch in *Trolls* (2016). The latter also included roles for **Gwen Stefani** and **Icona Pop**, and provided Justin with his fourteenth *NOW* appearance, 'Can't Stop the Feeling!' (*NOW 94*). Although it is currently Justin's bestselling UK single it had to settle for four weeks at number 2 in 2016, stuck behind 'One Dance' (*NOW 95*) by **Drake** featuring **WizKid** and **Kyla**.

00s

NOW 54 Did You Know . . .

On which we say 'Hello' to two promising newcomers, **Beyoncé** and **Justin Timberlake**. Fittingly, '03 Bonnie & Clyde' by **Jay-Z** featuring Beyoncé Knowles includes a sample from the 1987 **Prince** song 'If I Was Your Girlfriend'. By spooky coincidence Justin Timberlake's last single with ***NSYNC** was the number 2 hit 'Girlfriend', a chart placing he would match with his solo debut, 'Like I Love You', here on NOW 54. Sadly, after enough appearances to guarantee a place in this book, we wave goodbye to both **Erasure** and **Queen**.

NOW 84 Did You Know . . .

Despite being one of the biggest bands on the planet, **Fleetwood Mac** have only had three UK Top 40 hits during the life of NOW. One of these – 'Everywhere' – re-charted in 2013 following its use on a mobile-phone advert and resulted in the band's only NOW showing to date. Another Fleetwood Mac song, 'Dreams', provided **The Corrs** with one of their two NOW appearances on volume 41, and **Wild Colour** with their only entry on NOW 32.

IN OTHER NEWS . . . NOW 84 (MARCH 2013)

Actor Richard Griffiths died, aged 65. Best known for two 'uncle' roles, he appeared in five of the Harry Potter films as Vernon Dursley, and in Withnail and I as Monty.

BBC Red Nose Day raised over £75 million for charity. During the telethon event Manchester band **James** performed their 1991 number 2 'Sit Down' (NOW 20) with comedian **Peter Kay**.

To mark the fortieth anniversary of Pink Floyd's Dark Side of the Moon album, radio station Smooth 70s ('All 70s, all the time') played the album in full.

21
NOW appearances

'Sound of the Underground',
NOW 54, April 2003

'Something New',
NOW 84, March 2013

GIRLS ALOUD

Girls Aloud currently wear the collective crown of female group with the most appearances on *NOW*, providing twenty hit singles plus a further entry with 'Walk This Way' by **Sugababes** vs. Girls Aloud, the 2007 charity single for Comic Relief. Emerging from the ITV talent show *Popstars: The Rivals*, 'The Girls' made their debut on *NOW 54*, as did their male counterparts, **One True Voice**, though the boys would take a bow after one more contribution on *NOW 55*.

Neither Nicola Roberts nor **Kimberley Walsh** originally made the *Popstars* Final 10, but were given a second chance when the original contestants were either eliminated on age grounds or chose to quit. Outside of the group, Kimberley's only chart showing to date is 'Like U Like' (*NOW 78*), a collaboration with Brazilian rapper **Aggro Santos**. Nicola has two Top 40 singles of her own but, sadly for us, neither made it onto *NOW*.

Post-Girls Aloud, the artist occasionally known as **Cheryl** has proved the most durable, notching up more solo UK hits and *NOW* appearances than her four former bandmates combined. All five of her UK number 1 singles have appeared on *NOW* albums, along with her two collaborations with **will.i.am**, and one with **Tinie Tempah**.

The majority of Girls Aloud's hits were written by the hugely successful Xenomania team. Xenomania have also contributed songs to such illustrious *NOW* alumni as **Bananarama**, **Cher**, **Kaiser Chiefs**, **Kylie Minogue**, **Little Mix**, **Pet Shop Boys**, **Texas** and **The Wanted**. Three further Girls Aloud hits were cover versions of songs that had featured on earlier volumes of *NOW*: 'Walk This Way' by **Run-D.M.C.** was on *NOW 8*, 'I Think We're Alone Now' by **Tiffany** was on *NOW 12* and 'I'll Stand by You' by **The Pretenders** was on *NOW 28*.

00s

BEYONCÉ

Beyoncé's *NOW* story begins with her duet on **Jay-Z**'s number 2 ''03 Bonnie & Clyde', which samples the 1996 song 'Me and My Girlfriend' by **2Pac**. 2Pac's *NOW* appearances include the 2005 number 1 'Ghetto Gospel' featuring **Elton John**, which samples the latter's 1971 song 'Indian Sunset'. The distinctive brass riff that introduces Beyoncé's first solo number 1 'Crazy in Love' (*NOW 56*) is sampled from The Chi-Lites' 1970 song 'Are You My Woman (Tell Me So)'.

In 2006 Beyoncé had the second of five number 1s with 'Déjà Vu' (*NOW 65*), written and produced with Rodney Jerkins, a service he had previously provided for the **Spice Girls**' ninth number 1 'Holler' (*NOW 47*). Beyoncé's next appearance, 'Irreplaceable' (*NOW 66*), a co-write with **Ne-Yo**, peaked at number 4 but was her fourth chart topper in the US. However, she only had to wait six months for her next UK number 1, 'Beautiful Liar' (*NOW 67*), a duet with **Shakira** that spent three weeks at the top.

The ballad 'Halo' (*NOW 73*) was another release to halt at number 4, though it is currently Beyoncé's bestselling single, and has been covered by the likes of **Westlife** and Jasmine Thompson. In 'highbrow news', 'Sweet Dreams' (*NOW 74*) begins with a melody from Johannes Brahms's 1868 lullaby 'Guten Abend, Gute Nacht'. Meanwhile Beyoncé's most recent appearance, 'Runnin' (Lose It All)' (*NOW 92*) by **Naughty Boy** featuring Beyoncé and **Arrow Benjamin**, soundtracked a TV advert for the Chanel perfume Gabrielle.

Beyoncé had fourteen Top 40 hits with **Destiny's Child**, including two number 1s, one of which – 'Survivor' (*NOW 49*) – is among their three *NOW* appearances. Another ex-Child, **Kelly Rowland**, also has two number 1s in her list of thirteen Top 40 hits. They are 'Dilemma' (*NOW 54*) with **Nelly**, and 'When Love Takes Over' (*NOW 73*) with **David Guetta**. Third member Michelle Williams has a bit of catching up to do, having waited until 2018 to get her first Top 40 hit with 'A Million Dreams'.

00s

NOW 54 Did You Know . . .

Richard X has two Top 40 singles, including the number 3 hit 'Being Nobody' by Richard X vs **Liberty X**, which used lyrics from the 1983 number 8 single 'Ain't Nobody' by Rufus and Chaka Khan, over a backing track taken from **The Human League**'s 1982 number 6 'Being Boiled'. He also sampled The Human League for his second appearance, 'The Finest' (*NOW 56*) featuring **Kelis**, pairing their 1981 tune 'The Things That Dreams Are Made Of' with lyrics from the 1986 number 17 'The Finest' by The S.O.S. Band.

NOW 92 Did You Know . . .

Continuing our homage to Rufus and Chaka Khan, *NOW 93* includes the only appearance by **Felix Jaehn** featuring **Jasmine Thompson** with their number 2 version 'Ain't Nobody (Loves Me Better)'. Songwriter David 'Hawk' Wolinski also benefits from a 1997 number 8 version by **The Course** on *NOW 37*. Away from Rufus (a band, not a person, incidentally) Chaka's biggest hit was the 1984 number 1 'I Feel for You', written by **Prince**, with harmonica by Stevie Wonder and rap by **Melle Mel**.

IN OTHER NEWS . . . *NOW 92* (NOVEMBER 2015)

New Orleans musician Allen Toussaint died, aged 77. His compositions include 'Here Come the Girls', originally recorded by Ernie K-Doe and sampled by **Sugababes** for their 2008 number 3 'Girls' (*NOW 71*).

Graham Norton hosted the television special *Adele at the BBC*. It was **Adele**'s her first TV performance for over two years.

The British crime-comedy *Kill Your Friends*, a dark satire about the seedy side of the music industry, opened at cinemas, starring Nicholas Hoult and James Corden.

8
NOW appearances

''03 Bonnie & Clyde',
Jay-Z featuring Beyoncé Knowles,
NOW 54, April 2003

'Runnin' (Lose It All)',
Naughty Boy featuring Beyoncé
& Arrow Benjamin,
NOW 92, November 2015

90s

NOW 55 Did You Know . . .

NOW 55 served up the sophomore efforts of **Girls Aloud** and **One True Voice** following their battle for the Christmas number 1. As documented elsewhere in these pages, the former would go on to have twenty-one *NOW* appearances, though this would be our last glimpse of 'OTV'. Although The Bard doesn't get a writing credit for their number 10 hit 'Shakespeare's (Way with) Words', **Rick Astley** does. This marks one of only two entries in the *NOW* ledger for Rick, alongside his 1991 number 7 'Cry for Help' (*NOW 19*).

NOW 70 Did You Know . . .

Making the first of nine appearances is **Dizzee Rascal**, previously a member of the **Roll Deep** crew (three *NOW* appearances), alongside fellow MC **Wiley** (eight *NOW* appearances). Four of Dizzee's five number 1 singles appear on *NOW*, including 'Dance wiv Me' (*NOW 70*), a collaboration with **Calvin Harris** and **Chrome**, 'Bonkers' (*NOW 73*), his project with **Armand Van Helden**, 'Holiday' (*NOW 74*) and 'Dirtee Disco' (*NOW 75*). In 2010 Dizzee was a judge on Sky TV talent show *Must Be the Music*, alongside pianist **Jamie Cullum** and **Texas** singer Sharleen Spiteri.

IN OTHER NEWS . . . *NOW 55* (JULY 2003)

Soul legend Barry White died aged 58. He scored seventeen Top 40 singles, including the number 1 'You're the First, the Last, My Everything'. **Robbie Williams**'s 2000 number 1 'Rock DJ' (*NOW 47*) samples Barry's 'It's Ecstasy When You Lay Down Next to Me'.

The British spy comedy *Johnny English* opened at cinemas. Starring Rowan Atkinson and **Natalie Imbruglia**, it also includes the vocal talents of DJ Chris Tarrant and newsreader Trevor McDonald.

The BBC screen a new series of *Mastermind*, the first since 1997, with John Humphrys replacing Magnus Magnusson as presenter. Specialist subjects on the first episode include 'the music of **The Smiths**'.

MARIAH CAREY

There was a long gap between Mariah's chart debut 'Vision of Love' in 1990 and her first appearance on *NOW 55*. By that time she already had twenty-eight Top 40 hits including two number 1s: a cover of the Badfinger song 'Without You' – previously a 1972 number 1 for Nilsson – and her duet with **Westlife**, 'Against All Odds', the original of which had appeared on *NOW 3* as a number 2 hit for **Phil Collins**.

Mariah's first *NOW* listing, 'Boy (I Need You)' was based on the **Cam'ron** song 'Oh Boy'. Both recordings included a sample from the 1976 single 'I'm Going Down' by Rose Royce, taken from the soundtrack to the film *Car Wash* and written by Norman Whitfield, whose illustrious CV includes such Motown classics as 'I Heard It through the Grapevine' and 'Papa was a Rollin' Stone'. Cam'ron's only other *NOW* listing to date is 'Hey Ma' by Cam'ron featuring **Julez Santana**, **Freekey Zekey** and **Toya** on volume 54.

Mariah's second appearance also owes something to a sample. 'It's Like That' (*NOW 61*) borrows the hook 'It's like that, y'all' from 'Hollis Crew (Krush Groove 2)' on **Run-D.M.C.**'s 1984 debut album. Run-D.M.C. also enjoyed a *NOW* entry with a song entitled 'It's Like That' when a **Jason Nevins** remix gave them their only UK number 1 in 1998, and a place on *NOW 39*. Mariah's four appearances are completed by 'We Belong Together' (*NOW 62*) and 'Touch My Body' (*NOW 70*).

Like a few other yuletide classics, Mariah's most enduring hit, 'All I Want for Christmas Is You', stalled at number 2. In 1994 it lost out to **East 17**'s 'Stay Another Day' (*NOW 30*). In 1984 Wham's 'Last Christmas' was denied by Band Aid's 'Do They Know It's Christmas', while 'Fairytale of New York' (*NOW 10*) by **The Pogues** and **Kirsty MacColl** was frustrated in 1987 by **Pet Shop Boys**' 'Always on My Mind' (*NOW 11*). This trend seemingly began in 1980 when a re-release of John and Yoko's 'Happy Xmas (War Is Over)' got stuck behind 'There's No One Quite Like Grandma' by St Winifred's School Choir.

90s

4
NOW appearances

'Boy (I Need You)', Mariah Carey featuring Cam'ron, *NOW 55*, July 2003

'Touch My Body', *NOW 70*, July 2008

WILL YOUNG

Just eighteen months after his *Pop Idol* win, Will Young had his fourth and most recent number 1 with 'Leave Right Now'. His previous chart toppers were all cover versions (**Westlife**, The Doors and The Beatles, if you wondered), but this fresh hit was penned by Francis 'Eg' White. Francis first had chart success as a member of **Brother Beyond**, while his other writing credits include another number 1 single, 'Once' (*NOW 76*) for **Diana Vickers**, and **Natalie Imbruglia**'s 'Shiver' (*NOW 61*).

A wealth of talent contributed to 'Switch It On' (*NOW 62*), including Mark Feltham, harmonica player with Nine Below Zero, who can also be heard on **Oasis**' fourth number 1, 'All Around the World'. 'All Time Love' (*NOW 63*) was written by Jamie Hartman, who is yet to have major success with his own band Ben's Brother but can also claim responsibility for co-writing **Marlon Roudette**'s 'When the Beat Drops Out' (*NOW 90*) and **Rag'n'Bone Man**'s debut hit 'Human' (*NOW 96*).

'Who Am I' (*NOW 64*) and 'Changes' (*NOW 71*) are also Francis 'Eg' White songs, though on 'Who Am I' he shares writing duties with **Lucie Silvas**, who can boast two appearances of her own, 'What You're Made Of' (*NOW 59*) and 'Breathe In' (*NOW 60*). The latter was written by Lucie with Judie Tzuke, a one-hit wonder by dint of her 1979 number 16 'Stay with Me till Dawn'. 'Changes' is one of three appearances that Will has co-written.

The 2011 number 5 'Jealousy' (*NOW 80*) is both Will's most recent *NOW* and Top 40 appearance. It was co-written by Will with Jim Eliot and Mima Stilwell, who also wrote '2 Hearts' (*NOW 68*) and 'All the Lovers' (*NOW 76*) for **Kylie Minogue**, and 'Glitterball' (*NOW 92*) for **Sigma** featuring **Ella Henderson**. And speaking of 'Henderson', in 2005 Will had his first big-screen starring role alongside Bob Hoskins and Judi Dench in the Oscar-nominated *Mrs Henderson Presents*.

00s

00s

NOW 57 Did You Know . . .

Georgian-born singer **Katie Melua** made the first of three appearances with 'The Closest Thing to Crazy'. Like 'Nine Million Bicycles' (*NOW 62*), it was written and produced by Mike Batt, the talent behind a plethora of hits including those by The Wombles and Art Garfunkel's 1979 number 1 'Bright Eyes'. Katie's only number 1 came in 2007 with 'What a Wonderful World' (*NOW 69*), on which Mike created a duet by adding a new vocal from Katie to a recording by the late **Eva Cassidy**.

NOW 80 Did You Know . . .

Maroon 5 singer **Adam Levine** made the first of two solo appearances as featured vocalist on 'Stereo Hearts' by **Gym Class Heroes**. His second was 'Locked Away' (*NOW 92*), a collaboration with **R. City** and their only showing to date. 'Locked Away' samples the melody of 'Do That to Me One More Time', a 1980 number 7 for American duo Captain and Tennille. Maroon 5 currently have ten appearances, including their only number 1, 'Payphone' (*NOW 82*) featuring **Wiz Khalifa**.

6

NOW appearances

'Leave Right Now',
NOW 57, April 2004

'Jealousy',
NOW 80, November 2011

IN OTHER NEWS . . . *NOW 80* (NOVEMBER 2011)

Maverick film director Ken Russell died, aged 84. His music-related projects include the 1975 Academy Award nominee *Tommy*, starring The Who alongside **Elton John** and **Tina Turner.**

The Twilight Saga: Breaking Dawn Part 1 opened in cinemas. 'It Will Rain' by **Bruno Mars**, the lead single from the soundtrack, reached number 14.

Singer Ashlee Simpson divorced **Fall Out Boy** bassist Pete Wentz after two-and-a-half years of marriage.

00s

NOW 58 Did You Know . . .

In May 2004 the number 1 single 'F**k It (I Don't Want You Back)' by **Eamon** was replaced at the top by the 'answer record', 'F.U.R.B. (F U Right Back)' by **Frankee**. It was such a beautiful relationship that the two songs sat next to each other on *NOW 58*. In 2010 **Katy Perry** told *Rolling Stone* magazine that 'California Gurls' (*NOW 76*) was an answer record to 'Empire State of Mind', a 2009 number 2 by **Jay-Z** featuring **Alicia Keys**, written as a tribute to New York City.

NOW 84 Did You Know . . .

Christina Perri has only made two appearances but neither could be considered a flash in the pan. 'A Thousand Years' had already spent fifty-six weeks in the chart before it peaked at number 11 in September 2013. By comparison her debut single 'Jar of Hearts' (*NOW 80*) was a bit of a sprinter, taking a mere eight weeks to reach number 4 but then hanging around in the Top 40 for thirty-one weeks.

IN OTHER NEWS . . . *NOW 58* (JULY 2004)

American composer Jerry Goldsmith died, aged 89. His film scores include *Basic Instinct* and *L.A. Confidential*. He was nominated for eighteen Academy Awards but won only one, for *The Omen* in 1976.

Actor Nicholas Cage, 40, married his third wife, 20-year-old waitress Alice Kim. His previous marriage to Lisa Marie Presley lasted less than four months.

David Bowie was forced to pull out of the T in the Park festival in Scotland following emergency heart surgery in Germany.

15
NOW appearances
'Five Colours in Her Hair',
NOW 58, July 2004
'Love Is Easy',
NOW 84, March 2013

McFLY

Since 2004 McFly have notched up twenty-one Top 40 singles, including seven number 1s, and *NOW* has got all *eight* of them – 'All About You' (*NOW 60*) and 'You've Got a Friend' (*NOW 61*) were actually a double A-side coupling, one of their three chart toppers with two designated lead tracks. They are also responsible for one of English rapper **Taio Cruz**'s eleven appearances due to their collaboration on 'Shine a Light' (*NOW 78*), which made number 4 in November 2010.

Three of McFly's number 1s have been cover versions. Their recording of Carole King's 'You've Got a Friend' (*NOW 61*) was the official Comic Relief single in 2005. It stayed at the top for just one week before it was dislodged by the 'unofficial' single '(Is This the Way to) Amarillo' (*NOW 60*) by **Tony Christie**. In 2006 they were back at number 1 with 'Don't Stop Me Now' (*NOW 64*), originally a number 9 for **Queen** in 1979, while their last chart topper to date is 'Baby's Coming Back' (*NOW 67*), which reached number 51 for Jellyfish in May 1991.

In 2001 Tom Fletcher auditioned to join **Busted**, and although he lost out he did get to co-write some of their singles, including the number 1s 'Who's David?' (*NOW 57*) and 'Thunderbirds Are Go' (*NOW 59*). In 2014 **Matt Willis** and James Bourne of Busted (who had co-written McFly's first two number 1s – try to keep up) joined forces with McFly to form supergroup **McBusted**. They had one Top 40 single with 'Air Guitar' (*NOW 90*).

In 2005 McFly made cameo appearances on both *Casualty* and a *Doctor Who* episode, 'The Sound of Drums'. In 2011 bassist Dougie Poynter won the eleventh series of *I'm a Celebrity . . . Get Me Out of Here!*, while back on BBC One, band-mate Harry Judd won series nine of *Strictly Come Dancing*. In 2014 Tom Fletcher and Dougie Poynter became bestselling authors with their children's book *The Dinosaur that Pooped a Planet*.

00s

KANYE WEST

00s

Kanye's thirty-five Top 40 hits feature contributions from twenty-five other artists, including three from **Jay-Z**, two from **Rihanna** and one from Otis Redding. Otis's whistle, as originally heard at the end of '(Sittin' On) The Dock of the Bay', can be heard on **De La Soul**'s 'Eye Know' (*NOW 16*). Kanye's debut hit 'Through the Wire' sampled Chaka Khan's 1985 single 'Through the Fire', co-written by Cynthia Weil who, along with husband Barry Mann, wrote **The Righteous Brothers**' 1965 number 1 'You've Lost That Lovin' Feelin'' (*NOW 19*).

'Diamonds from Sierra Leone' (*NOW 62*) samples Don Black and John Barry's 1971 James Bond theme 'Diamonds Are Forever', and consequently gives Shirley Bassey her only (uncredited) *NOW* appearance. Elsewhere, 'Stronger' (*NOW 68*), one of Kanye's three number 1s (all on *NOW*), samples **Daft Punk**'s 2001 single 'Harder, Better, Faster, Stronger', which in turn sampled 'Cola Bottle Baby', a 1979 song by Edwin Birdsong. 'Heartless' (*NOW 72*) was covered by Colorado Rock band **The Fray**, who released their version as a single in 2009.

Another number 1, 'American Boy' (*NOW 70*) by **Estelle** featuring Kanye West, is one of three collaborations with English artists, the others being 'Homecoming' (*NOW 69*) with **Chris Martin**, and 'Supernova' (*NOW 74*) with **Mr Hudson**. And in 'seventies Greek psychedelia news', that third number 1, 'Run This Town' (*NOW 74*) by Jay-Z featuring Rihanna and Kanye West, includes a guitar sample from a (very) obscure release by The 4 Levels of Existence. No, us neither . . .

Staying with obscure influences, the video for 'E.T.' (*NOW 78*) by **Katy Perry** featuring Kanye West begins with a snippet of the 1938 recording 'Where in the World' by Midge Williams and her Jazz Jesters. 'Thank You' (*NOW 87*) by **Busta Rhymes** featuring **Q-Tip**, Kanye and **Lil Wayne** took a more mundane approach, sampling a 1981 disco song, 'I Want to Thank You' by Alicia Myers. However, it gives us a chance to mention Q-Tip from A Tribe Called Quest, whose only other appearance was as featured artist on 'Galvanize' (*NOW 60*), the 2005 number 18 from **The Chemical Brothers**.

00s

NOW 58 Did You Know . . .

Country singer **LeAnn Rimes** made her fourth appearance with 'Last Thing on My Mind', a number 5 duet with **Ronan Keating**. Her 1998 debut was 'How Do I Live' (*NOW 39*), a number 7 hit that spent thirty weeks in the Top 40. In common with her only number 1, 'Can't Fight the Moonlight' (*NOW 47*), it was written by Diane Warren, who has a total of twelve writing credits on *NOW*, including hits for **Meat Loaf** and **Daniel Bedingfield**.

NOW 87 Did You Know . . .

Our most recent sighting of 2002 Mercury Music Prize winner **Ms Dynamite**, as featured vocalist on the number 3 single 'Dibby Dibby Sound' by **DJ Fresh** vs **Jay Fay**, her second *NOW* collaboration following 'Lights On' (*NOW 78*) with **Katy B**. The prize-winning album *A Little Deeper* gave us 'It Takes More' (*NOW 52*) and her signature tune 'Dy-Na-Mi-Tee' (*NOW 53*), which was covered in a 'unique' style-ee by The Ukulele Orchestra of Great Britain in 2003.

11

NOW appearances

'Through the Wire',
NOW 58, July 2004

'Thank You',
Busta Rhymes featuring Q-Tip, Kanye and Lil Wayne,
NOW 87, April 2014

IN OTHER NEWS . . . *NOW 87* (APRIL 2014)

Novelist Sue Townsend died, aged 68. When her bestselling book *The Secret Diary of Adrian Mole, Aged 13¾* was adapted for TV, the theme tune, 'Profoundly in Love with Pandora' gave Ian Dury a number 45 single.

Good Morning Britain launched on ITV. Presenters included journalist Susanna Reid, who finished as runner-up on *Strictly Come Dancing* the previous year.

DJs Jo Whiley and Steve Lamacq were reunited on Radio 2 for a weeklong series of programmes celebrating the twentieth anniversary of Britpop.

00s

NOW 60 Did You Know . . .

Dance outfit **Uniting Nations** made their one appearance with 'Out of Touch', a re-working of Daryl Hall and John Oates's 1984 single. Five of Hall and Oates' six Top 40 hits pre-date *NOW*, and they have yet to appear as artists, though **De La Soul**'s 'Say No Go' (*NOW 15*) samples their 1981 number 8 'I Can't Go for That (No Can Do)', and 'Take Control' (*NOW 67*) by **Amerie** includes elements of their 1980 song 'You Make My Dreams'.

NOW 98 Did You Know . . .

'Rain' was the seventh appearance for Irish trio **The Script**, and their tenth Top 40 single. Their first three appearances were written with producer Andrew Frampton, who also contributed to hits by **Steps** and more recently co-wrote 'The Club Is Alive' (*NOW 76*), a 2010 number 1 for **JLS**. The Script's only number 1, 'Hall of Fame' (*NOW 83*), was a collaboration with **will.i.am**, while their 2008 number 2 single 'The Man Who Can't Be Moved' found its route to the top blocked by **Katy Perry**'s 'I Kissed a Girl' (both *NOW 71*).

IN OTHER NEWS . . . *NOW 60* (MARCH 2005)

The US version of Ricky Gervais and Stephen Merchant's TV comedy *The Office* debuted on NBC. It ran for 201 episodes, while the original UK series ran for 14.

American engineer John DeLorean died, aged 80. He is best known for his DMC-12 sports car, made famous by the *Back to the Future* film trilogy.

Radio 1 DJ Edith Bowman won the charity talent contest *Comic Relief Does Fame Academy*, performing the **Oasis** song 'Champagne Supernova'.

7
NOW appearances

'Somebody Told Me (King Unique Vocal Mix)', *NOW 60*, March 2005

'The Man', *NOW 98*, November 2017

THE KILLERS

The Killers 'found' their name on a drum kit belonging to a fictitious band in the video for 'Crystal', **New Order**'s 2001 number 8 single. Their debut appearance 'Somebody Told Me' had floundered at number 28 when first released in March 2004, but went straight in at number 3 when re-issued the following year, remixed by King Unique, aka DJ Matt Thomas. Second appearance 'Smile Like You Mean It' (*NOW 61*) was originally the B-side of their debut single, 'Mr Brightside'.

Although The Killers are yet to have a chart topper, they came close in 2006 with 'When You Were Young' but were thwarted by **Scissor Sisters**' only number 1, 'I Don't Feel Like Dancin'' (*NOW 65*). Former **Blue** singer **Simon Webbe** covered 'When You Were Young' for Radio 1's *Live Lounge* and released it as the B-side to his 2007 single 'My Soul Pleads for You'. The same year 'Read My Mind' (*NOW 66*) was remixed by **Pet Shop Boys** as a B-side of The Killers' number 15 single.

'Tranquilize' (*NOW 68*) featured **Lou Reed**, and gave him only his fourth 'solo' visit to the Top 40 in thirty-four years, a run that started with 'Walk on the Wild Side' in 1973. The Killers' 'catchy sing-along' 2008 number 3 'Human' (*NOW 72*) spent twenty weeks in the Top 40, and frequently returns to the lower reaches, though it will have a hard job catching up with 'Mr Brightside', which spent a mere six weeks in the Top 40 but clocked up its two-hundredth week in the Top 100 in March 2018.

The Killers' 2017 single 'The Man' (*NOW 98*) samples 'Spirit of the Boogie', a 1975 single by **Kool and the Gang**, who have two appearances of their own with 'Cherish' (*NOW 5*) and 'Ladies' Night' (*NOW 57*), their 2003 collaboration with **Atomic Kitten**. Their original 1979 version of 'Ladies' Night' was sampled by **Samantha Mumba** for her number 5 'Baby Come on Over' (*NOW 50*), while **Luniz**'s 'I Got 5 on It' (*NOW 33*) samples Kool and the Gang's 1973 single 'Jungle Boogie'.

00s

PHARRELL WILLIAMS

Pharrell already had five Top 40 hits with **N.E.R.D.**, including 'She Wants to Move' (*NOW 57*) and 'Maybe' (*NOW 58*), when he hit number 3 with his first solo single, 'Can I Have It Like That' featuring **Gwen Stefani**. He has since notched up a further eighteen solo Top 40 hits, while his six *NOW* appearances include all four of his number 1s. 'One (Your Name)' (*NOW 76*) first appeared as an instrumental on **Swedish House Mafia**'s debut album before Pharrell added a vocal and gave the DJ collective their first chart hit.

'Get Lucky' was both Pharrell and **Daft Punk**'s first number 1, spending four weeks at the top in May 2013. He was only absent from the summit for one week before 'Blurred Lines' (both *NOW 85*), his collaboration with **Robin Thicke** and **T.I.**, became his second chart topper. This also spent four weeks at the top before dropping down to number 2 for two weeks, only to rise up for one more week in July. 'Blurred Lines' and 'Get Lucky' would finish 2013 as the first- and second-bestselling singles of the year.

And so to 'Happy' (*NOW 87*), with no featured artists, samples or co-writers, a genuine solo hit. 'Happy' also managed four weeks at number 1, though split into three stints between January and March 2014, and once again it became that year's bestselling single. Pharrell's most recent number 1 was 'Feels' (*NOW 97*) by **Calvin Harris** featuring Pharrell Williams, **Katy Perry** and **Big Sean**. This was Big Sean's second appearance, following on from 'Wild' (*NOW 85*), his 2013 collaboration with **Jessie J** and **Dizzee Rascal**.

In addition to six artist appearances, Pharrell has eighteen credits as a writer, starting with 'Caught Out There' (*NOW 45*) by **Kelis** in 2000. *NOW 57* included three of his songs: 'I'm Lovin' It' by **Justin Timberlake**, **Jamie Cullum**'s only appearance with 'Frontin' (Live)', alongside 'She Wants To Move', one of Pharrell's two appearances as N.E.R.D. He will also share the spoils of number 1 hits by **Ed Sheeran** – 'Sing' (*NOW 88*) – and **Camila Cabello** featuring **Young Thug** – 'Havana' (*NOW 98*). However, way back in 1993 a young Pharrell rapped on 'Right Here' (*NOW 26*), the only appearance by **SWV**.

10s

NOW 62 Did You Know . . .

Electro duo **Goldfrapp** debuted with their biggest hit, the number 4 single 'Ooh La La'. Alongside singer Alison Goldfrapp is Will Gregory who, as a saxophonist, played on hit albums by **Tears for Fears** and **The Cure**. Alison and Will co-wrote their second appearance, 'Ride a White Horse' (*NOW 63*), with Nick Batt. Nick was previously half of the duo **DNA**, who had a 1990 number 2 hit with their remix of 'Tom's Diner' (*NOW 18*) by **Suzanne Vega**.

NOW 97 Did You Know . . .

Both 'Did You See' and 'Bouff Daddy' (*NOW 99*) were taken from **J Hus**'s number 6 album *Common Sense*. The London-born rapper first broke into the Top 40 on the 2017 number 22 'Bad Boys' by **Stormzy** featuring Ghetts and J Hus. Both *Common Sense* and Stormzy's debut album *Gang Signs and Prayer* were shortlisted for the 2017 Mercury Music Prize but lost out to a third Londoner, Sampha and his debut album *Process*.

10s

**6
NOW appearances**

'Can I Have It Like That', Pharrell featuring Gwen Stefani, *NOW 62*, November 2005

'Feels', Calvin Harris featuring Pharrell Williams, Katy Perry and Big Sean, *NOW 97*, July 2017

IN OTHER NEWS . . . NOW 62 (NOVEMBER 2005)

Tony Meehan, original drummer with The Shadows, died aged 62. In 1963 Tony and another ex-Shadow, Jet Harris, had a number 1 single with the instrumental 'Diamonds'.

The annual BBC 1 *Children in Need* event included a cast of BBC newsreaders performing **Queen**'s 1975 and 1991 number 1 'Bohemian Rhapsody'.

The first *Guitar Hero* video game launched for PlayStation 2. Players could try their hand at thirty songs including **Sum 41**'s 'Fat Lip' (*NOW 50*) and **Franz Ferdinand**'s 'Take Me Out' (*NOW 57*).

TEN X TEN = NOW 100

Ten 'Big Questions'

1 **Duran Duran**, 'Is There Something I Should Know?' (*NOW 1*)
2 **The Clash**, 'Should I Stay or Should I Go?' (*NOW 19*)
3 **Charles & Eddie**, 'Would I Lie to You?' (*NOW 23*)
4 **The Human League**, 'Don't You Want Me?' (*NOW 32*)
5 **Spice Girls**, 'Who Do You Think You Are?' (*NOW 37*)
6 **DJ Pied Piper**, 'Do You Really Like It?' (*NOW 49*)
7 **Black Eyed Peas**, 'Where Is the Love?' (*NOW 56*)
8 **Busted**, 'Who's David?' (*NOW 57*)
9 **Tony Christie**, '(Is This the Way to) Amarilo?' (*NOW 60*)
10 **Justin Bieber**, 'What Do You Mean?' (*NOW 92*)

Ten Career Opportunities

1 **The Commentators**, 'N-N-Nineteen Not Out' (*NOW 5*)
2 **Doctor and the Medics**, 'Spirit in the Sky' (*NOW 7*)
3 **Maxi Priest**, 'Wild World' (*NOW 12*)
4 **The Spin Doctors**, 'Two Princes' (*NOW 26*)
5 **Crash Test Dummies**, 'Mmm Mmm Mmm Mmm' (*NOW 29*)
6 **Athlete**, 'Wires' (*NOW 60*)
7 **Bob the Builder**, 'Can We Fix It' (*NOW 48*)
8 **Usher**, 'Scream' (*NOW 82*)
9 **Professor Green feat. Tori Kelly**, 'Lullaby' (*NOW 89*)
10 **Rag 'n' Bone Man**, 'Human' (*NOW 96*)

Ten Queen Vic vs Rovers Return

1 **Nick Berry**, 'Every Loser Wins' (*NOW 8*): Simon Wicks in *EastEnders*
2 **Adam Rickitt**, 'I Breathe Again' (*NOW 43*): Nick Tilsley in *Coronation Street*
3 **Michelle Gayle**, 'Sweetness' (*NOW 29*): Hattie Tavernier in *EastEnders*
4 **Keith Duffy of Boyzone**, 'Words' (*NOW 35*): Ciaran McCarthy in *Coronation Street*
5 **Sean Maguire**, 'Suddenly' (*NOW 30*): Aidan Brosnan in *EastEnders*
6 **Kym Marsh**, 'Cry' (*NOW 54*): Michelle Connor in *Coronation Street*
7 **Martine McCutcheon**, 'Perfect Moment' (*NOW 43*): Tiffany Mitchell in *EastEnders*
8 **Sarah Harding of Girls Aloud**, 'The Promise' (*NOW 71*): Joni Preston in *Coronation Street*
9 **Matt Willis**, 'Up All Night' (*NOW 64*): Luke Riley in *EastEnders*
10 **Status Quo**, 'In the Army Now' (*NOW 8*): Les Battersby's wedding band in *Coronation Street*

Ten 'As Seen on TV'

1 **The Bluebells**, 'Young at Heart' (*NOW 24*): Volkswagen Golf, 1993
2 **Stiltskin**, 'Inside' (*NOW 28*): Levi's, 1994
3 **Etta James**, 'I Just Want to Make Love to You' (*NOW 33*): Diet Coke, 1996
4 **Ladysmith Black Mambazo**, 'Inkanyezi Nezazi (The Star and the Wiseman)' (*NOW 42*): Heinz Baked Beans, 1999
5 **Wiseguys**, 'Ooh La La' (*NOW 43*): Budweiser, 1999
6 **Phil Collins**, 'In the Air Tonight' (*NOW 68*): Cadbury Dairy Milk, 2007
7 **Sugababes**, 'Girls' (*NOW 71*): Boots, 2007
8 **Fleetwood Mac**, 'Everywhere' (*NOW 84*): Three Mobile, 2013
9 **Tom Odell**, 'Real Love' (*NOW 89*): John Lewis, 2014
10 **Grace featuring G-Eazy**, 'You Don't Own Me' (*NOW 92*): House of Fraser, 2015

Ten Comic Relief Number 1s

1 **Hale & Pace and The Stonkers**, 'The Stonk' (1991, *NOW 19*)
2 **Cher, Chrissie Hynde, Neneh Cherry & Eric Clapton**, 'Love Can Build a Bridge' (1995, *NOW 30*)
3 **Spice Girls**, 'Mama' (1997, *NOW 36*)
4 **Boyzone**, 'When the Going Gets Tough' (1999, *NOW 42*)
5 **Westlife**, 'Uptown Girl' (2001, *NOW 50*)
6 **McFly**, 'You've Got a Friend' (2005, *NOW 61*)
7 **The Proclaimers feat. Brian Potter & Andy Pipkin**, 'I'm Gonna Be (500 Miles)' (2007, *NOW 66*)
8 **Vanessa Jenkins, Bryn West & Sir Tom Jones feat. Robin Gibb**, 'Barry Islands in the Stream' (2009, *NOW 72*)
9 **One Direction**, 'One Way or Another (Teenage Kicks)' (2013, *NOW 84*)
10 **Sam Smith**, 'Lay Me Down' (2015, *NOW 90*)

Ten Songs that Borrowed from the Classics

1 **Queen**, 'It's a Hard Life' (R. Leoncavallo, 'Pagliacci', 1892) (*NOW 4*)
2 **Take That**, 'Could It Be Magic' (F. Chopin, 'Prelude in C Minor', 1839) (*NOW 24*)
3 **UB40**, '(I Can't Help) Falling in Love with You' (J.P. Égide-Martini, 'Plaisir d'Amour', 1784) (*NOW 26*)
4 **2 Unlimited**, 'The Real Thing' (J. S. Bach, 'Toccata and Fugue in D Minor', 1707) (*NOW 28*)
5 **Coolio**, 'I'll See You when U Get There' (J Pachelbel, 'Canon in D', c.1706) (*NOW 37*)
6 **Warren G**, 'Prince Igor' (A. Borodin, 'Prince Igor', 1890) (*NOW 39*)
7 **Jem**, 'They' (J.S. Bach 'Prelude in F Minor', 1742) (*NOW 61*)
8 **N-Dubz feat. BodyRox**, 'We Dance On' (J. Pachelbel, 'Canon in D', c.1706) (*NOW 79*)
9 **Lady Gaga**, 'Alejandro' (V. Monti, 'Csárdás', 1904) (*NOW 79*)
10 **Plan B**, '**iLL Manors**' (Shostakovich, 'Symphony No. 7 in C Major', 1940) (*NOW 82*)

Ten Songs about Someone Else

1 **Madness**, 'Michael Caine' (*NOW 2*)
2 **The Special AKA**, 'Nelson Mandela' (*NOW 3*)
3 **Bananarama**, 'Robert De Niro's Waiting' (*NOW 3*)
4 **Weezer**, 'Buddy Holly' (*NOW 31*)
5 **Gorillaz**, 'Clint Eastwood' (*NOW 48*)
6 **Mika**, 'Grace Kelly' (*NOW 66*)
7 **Robbie Williams with Pet Shop Boys**, 'She's Madonna' (*NOW 66*)
8 **Duck Sauce**, 'Barbra Streisand' (*NOW 77*)
9 **Chiddy Bang**, 'Ray Charles' (*NOW 81*)
10 **Charlie Puth**, 'Marvin Gaye' (*NOW 92*)

Ten Artists to Make You Peckish

1 **Blancmange**, 'Don't Tell Me' (*NOW 3*)
2 **Hot Chocolate**, 'You Sexy Thing' (*NOW 9*)
3 **Jellybean feat. Steven Dante**, 'The Real Thing' (*NOW 10*)
4 **Vanilla Ice**, 'Play That Funky Music' (*NOW 19*)
5 **Lolly**, 'Viva La Radio' (*NOW 43*)
6 **Nelly featuring City Spud**, 'Ride with Me' (*NOW 49*)
7 **Jean-Jaques Smoothie**, '2 People' (*NOW 50*)
8 **Fast Food Rockers**, 'Fast Food Song' (*NOW 55*)
9 **David Guetta vs The Egg**, 'Love Don't Let Me Go' (*NOW 65*)
10 **Hot Chip**, 'Ready for the Floor' (*NOW 69*)

TEN X TEN = *NOW 100*

Ten Motown Cover Versions

1 **Phil Collins**, 'You Can't Hurry Love' (*NOW 1*): The Supremes
2 **Paul Young**, 'Wherever I Lay My Hat' (*NOW 1*): Marvin Gaye
3 **Kim Wilde**, 'You Keep Me Hanging On' (*NOW 8*): The Supremes
4 **Robert Palmer**, 'Mercy Mercy Me/I Want You' (*NOW 19*): Marvin Gaye
5 **Incognito**, 'Don't You Worry 'Bout a Thing' (*NOW 22*): Stevie Wonder
6 **Music Relief**, 'What's Goin' On?' (*NOW 29*): Marvin Gaye
7 **Go West**, 'The Tracks of My Tears' (*NOW 26*): The Miracles
8 **DJ Luck & MC Neat feat. JJ, 'Masterblaster 2000'** (*NOW 46*): Stevie Wonder
9 **Tom Jones & Heather Small**, 'You Need Love Like I Do' (*NOW 47*): Gladys Knight & the Pips
10 **BeatFreakz**, 'Somebody's Watching Me' (*NOW 64*): Rockwell

Ten Artists from the Aviary

1 **The Housemartins**, 'Happy Hour' (*NOW 7*)
2 **Robin S**, 'Show Me Love' (*NOW 24*)
3 **Babybird**, 'You're Gorgeous' (*NOW 35*)
4 **Sheryl Crow**, 'If It Makes You Happy' (*NOW 35*)
5 **Eagle Eye Cherry**, 'Save Tonight' (*NOW 40*)
6 **Doves**, 'Pounding' (*NOW 52*)
7 **Raven Maize**, 'Fascinated' (*NOW 53*)
8 **Taylor Swift**, 'Love Story' (*NOW 72*)
9 **Owl City**, 'Fireflies' (*NOW 75*)
10 **Duck Sauce**, 'Barbra Streisand' (*NOW 77*)

NOW 62 Did You Know . . .

David Gray made his most recent appearance with 'The One I Love', the eighth of his nine Top 40 hits. When his first two albums sold poorly he was dropped by his record company, and he released his 1998 album *White Ladder* himself. It took eighteen months before it entered the chart at number 69 and a further thirteen months before it finally made number 1 in August 2001. It spawned five Top 40 singles, including 'Babylon' (*NOW 47*), and has now sold over three-million copies.

NOW 73 Did You Know . . .

'Evacuate the Dancefloor' was German dance group **Cascada**'s only number 1, and their only *NOW* appearance that isn't a cover version. 'Everytime We Touch' (*NOW 65*) had been a single for Scottish singer Maggie Reilly, who sang on **Mike Oldfield**'s 1983 number 4 'Moonlight Shadow' (*NOW 1*). Cascada's next appearance, 'Truly Madly Deeply' (*NOW 66*), hit number 4, as had the 1998 original by **Savage Garden**. Their only other appearance was a version of 'What Hurts the Most' (*NOW 69*), the 2005 debut solo single for Jo O'Meara, late of **S Club 7**.

10s

6
NOW appearances

'Don't Cha',
Pussycat Dolls featuring Busta Rhymes,
NOW 62, November 2005

'Jai Ho! (You Are My Destiny)',
A.R. Rahman and Pussycat Dolls featuring Nicole Scherzinger,
NOW 73, July 2009

IN OTHER NEWS . . . *NOW 73* (JULY 2009)

American guitarist Les Paul died, aged 94. The solid-body Gibson electric guitar that he pioneered was named after him.

A public memorial service for **Michael Jackson**, who died on 25 June, was held at the Staples Center in Los Angeles. **Mariah Carey**, Stevie Wonder and **Lionel Richie** all sang at the event.

Ice Age: Dawn of the Dinosaurs opened at cinemas. The voice of Ellie, a woolly mammoth, was provided by rapper Queen Latifah, who had a 1990 number 14 hit with 'Mama Gave Birth to the Soul Child', a collaboration with **De La Soul**.

PUSSYCAT DOLLS

Written by **CeeLo Green**, 'Don't Cha' was a 2004 single for Tori Alamaze, previously a backing singer for **OutKast**. When it failed to chart, the song was given to PCD, now with an added rap by **Busta Rhymes**, and became the first of their two number 1s. 'Beep' (*NOW 63*), their collaboration with **will.i.am**, samples 'Evil Woman', a 1976 number 10 for Electric Light Orchestra. ELO have yet to appear on *NOW*, but the band's Jeff Lynne co-wrote and played on **Roy Orbison**'s 1989 number 3 'You Got It' (*NOW 14*), his first Top 40 single for twenty years.

'Buttons' (*NOW 76*) was the fourth single from their debut album *PCD*. Remixed with additional rap from **Snoop Dogg**, it gave him his first *NOW* appearance and twentieth Top 40 single. 'I Don't Need a Man' (*NOW 65*) was co-written by Rich Harrison, with a little help from Kara DioGuardi and **Nicole Scherzinger**. Rich was co-writer of 'Crazy in Love' (*NOW 56*) by **Beyoncé** featuring **Jay-Z**, while Kara co-wrote another number 1, **Kylie Minogue**'s 'Spinnin' Around' (*NOW 46*).

The 2008 number 3 'When I Grow Up' (*NOW 71*) samples 'He's Always There', a 1966 album track by The Yardbirds, and has additional vocals by brothers Theron and Timothy Thomas, also known as **R.City**. They have one appearance of their own with

'Locked Away' (*NOW 92*) featuring **Maroon 5** singer **Adam Levine**. In its original form 'Jai Ho! (You Are My Destiny)' (*NOW 73*) featured in the 2008 film *Slumdog Millionaire*, and won an Oscar for Best Original Song.

By the time 'Jai Ho! . . .' was included on *NOW 73* Nicole Scherzinger already had two of

eight 'solo' appearances under her belt, a tally that includes the 2011 number 1 'Don't Hold Your Breath' (*NOW 79*). Of the other Dolls, only **Kimberly Wyatt** has so far graced *NOW*, as featured vocalist on 'Candy' (*NOW 76*) by **Aggro Santos**. She can also boast winning *Celebrity MasterChef* 2015, beating **Mica Paris** and Sarah Harding from **Girls Aloud** in the process.

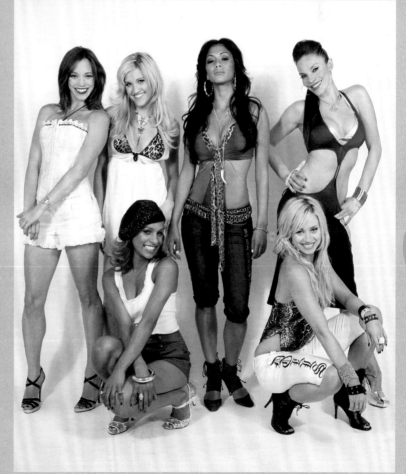

10s

177

RIHANNA

With twenty-seven songs on twenty-one different volumes Rihanna is currently the most prodigious female artist to appear on *NOW*, and second overall. Seven of her nine number 1s are on *NOW*, including her bestselling hit 'We Found Love' (*NOW 80*) featuring **Calvin Harris**, which spent six weeks at the top. In total those seven songs have spent twenty-three weeks at the summit, with the first of them, 'Umbrella' (*NOW 67*) featuring **Jay-Z**, chipping in with a whopping ten weeks.

'Umbrella' was co-written by Terius Nash, also known by his stage name **The-Dream**, his title of choice when he featured on 'Cookie Jar' (*NOW 71*), the 2008 number 6 by **Gym Class Heroes**. **McFly** covered 'Umbrella' as the B-side of 'The Heart Never Lies' (*NOW 68*), **JLS** gave it a go for 'Beat Again' (*NOW 74*) and in 2007 **Taylor Swift** recorded it in New York for an iTunes 'live' session. In 2008 **Manic Street Preachers** gave their version away as an *NME* covermount after they won that magazine's 'Godlike Genius' award.

00s

Rihanna is obviously a big fan of eighties pop, as 'SOS' (*NOW 64*) includes elements of Soft Cell's only number 1, 'Tainted Love', while 'Shut Up and Drive' (*NOW 68*) credits **New Order** and their 1983 number 9 'Blue Monday', and 'Don't Stop the Music' (*NOW 69*) samples **Michael Jackson**'s 'Wanna Be Startin' Something' from the same year. We have no explanation for the use of Geoff Mack's 1959 country-and-western song 'I've Been Everywhere' in Rihanna's 2011 number 6 'Where Have You Been' (*NOW 82*).

Rihanna's twenty-seven appearances make her by far the most successful Barbadian in *NOW* history. **Mark Morrison** has three to his name, including his 1996 number 1 'Return of the Mack' (*NOW 34*), as does **Shontelle**, whose 2010 number 9 'Impossible' (*NOW 77*) was covered by **James Arthur** for his debut number 1 and first appearance on *NOW 84*. **Cover Drive**'s 2012 number 1 'Twilight' is one of their two appearances, while **Grandmaster Flash** has popped up twice with 'White Lines (Don't Do It)' (*NOW 3 & 31*). And a big 'Hello' to **Rayvon**, who featured on two of **Shaggy**'s sixteen Top 40 hits, including 'In the Summertime' (*NOW 31*).

00s

NOW 62 Did You Know . . .

Kelly Clarkson, winner of the first series of *American Idol* in 2002, made her debut with 'Since U Been Gone'. Her eight appearances include her only number 1, 'My Life Would Suck without You' (*NOW 72*), and her bestselling UK single 'Stronger (What Doesn't Kill You)' (*NOW 81*). 'Stronger . . .' was co-written by David Gamson, previously a member of **Scritti Politti** and co-writer of their hits 'The Word Girl' (*NOW 5*) and 'Dear Patti (Don't Feel Sorry for Loverboy)' (*NOW 12*).

NOW 94 Did You Know . . .

DNCE made their only appearance to date with the 2016 number 4 'Cake by the Ocean'. The band were formed by Joe Jonas who made his first appearance as one of the **Jonas Brothers**, alongside siblings Kevin and **Nick Jonas**, and their 2008 number 13 'S.O.S.' (*NOW 70*). 'Cake by the Ocean' was co-written by Justin Tranter, whose other *NOW* credits include Nick Jonas's second solo appearance, 'Close' (*NOW 94*), featuring **Tove Lo**, and **Justin Bieber**'s second number 1, 'Sorry' (*NOW 93*).

27
NOW appearances

'Pon de Replay', *NOW 62*, November 2005

'This Is What You Came For', Calvin Harris featuring Rihanna *NOW 94*, July 2016

IN OTHER NEWS . . . *NOW 94* (JULY 2016)

Actor Ken Barrie died, aged 83. For thirty-seven years he provided the voice of *Postman Pat* in the BBC TV series. In 1982 his recording of the show's theme tune made number 44 in the chart.

Actress Gwyneth Paltrow and **Coldplay** singer **Chris Martin** were divorced after twelve years of marriage.

Japanese consumer electronics company Funai announced they were stopping production of video cassette recorders (VCRs).

00s

NOW 63 Did You Know . . .

Once more *NOW* captured a never-to-be-heard-of-again number 1 artist in its net when volume 63 included 'JCB Song' by **Nizlopi**. The English folk duo were denied the Christmas chart topper by a late appearance from the 2011 *X Factor* winner **Shayne Ward** with 'That's My Goal'. More recent one-hit wonders preserved by *NOW* for posterity are **Sam Bailey** (*NOW 87*), **Magic!** (*NOW 89*), **Storm Queen** (*NOW 86*) and **Sam and the Womp** (*NOW 83*).

NOW 94 Did You Know . . .

After nine writing credits, beginning with **Will Powers**'s 'Kissing with Confidence' (*NOW 1*), **Nile Rodgers** finally got his name on the sleeve with 'Give Me Your Love' by **Sigala** featuring **John Newman** and Nile Rodgers. He'd come close with his 'day job' when **The Shapeshifters** and **Chic**'s 'Sensitivity' made it onto *NOW 64*, and his two writing credits each with **Sister Sledge** – 'Thinking of You' (*NOW 3*) and 'Lost in Music (Sure Is Pure Remix Edit)' (*NOW 24*) – and **Modjo** – 'Lady Hear Me Tonight' (*NOW 47*) and 'Chillin'' (*NOW 48*).

IN OTHER NEWS . . . NOW 63 (APRIL 2006)

Singer **Gene Pitney** died, aged 66. His only number 1 came in 1989 with 'Something's Gotten Hold of My Heart' (*NOW 14*), a duet with **Marc Almond**. It had originally been a number 5 hit for Gene in 1967.

BBC TV launched the talent show *How Do You Solve a Problem Like Maria?* The search to find an unknown singer to appear in a new production of *The Sound of Music* was won by 23-year-old Connie Fisher.

Comedian Russell Brand presented the first of his own Sunday-morning radio shows on BBC 6 Music.

14
NOW appearances

'Beep', Pussycat Dolls featuring will.i.am, *NOW 63*, April 2006

'Boys & Girls', will.i.am featuring Pia Mia, *NOW 94*, July 2016

will.i.am

00s

Perhaps a future contender for King of *NOW* is the boy from Boyle Heights, Los Angeles: will.i.am. He has fourteen appearances as a 'solo' artist, a further fifteen with **The Black Eyed Peas**, and two more writing credits. His only real solo entry is 'Bang Bang' (*NOW 86*), his 2013 number 3 that samples **Cher**'s 1966 song of the same name, which also peaked at number 3. He has twelve different *NOW* collaborators, with only **Cheryl Cole** having the honour of sharing two songs with him.

NOW is home to all five of will.i.am's number 1 singles, each with a different collaborator (of course). The collection includes 'OMG' (*NOW 76*) featuring **Usher**, 'This Is Love' (*NOW 82*) with Dutch singer **Eva Simons**, 'Scream & Shout' (*NOW 84*) featuring **Britney Spears** and 'It's My Birthday' (*NOW 84*) with **Cody Wise**. It's only on 'Hall of Fame' (*NOW 83*) that will.i.am is the 'featured' artist, alongside **The Script**. will.i.am also hosted **Mick Jagger**'s only solo appearance on 'T.H.E. (The Hardest Ever)' (*NOW 81*).

Although **Nicole Scherzinger** can only look back upon 'Baby Love' (*NOW 68*) as her sole will.i.am collaboration, she was also a member of **Pussycat Dolls** when a featured role on their 2006 number 2 'Beep' (*NOW 63*) gave him his first solo chart entry. 'Beep' also provides a rare *NOW* credit for **Jeff Lynne** of ELO, whose 1976 number 10 'Evil Woman' is sampled here. On *NOW 60* 'Shine' by **The Lovefreekz** samples ELO's 1979 number 6 'Shine a Little Love'.

The Black Eyed Peas' five number 1s can all be found on *NOW*. Of the thirty-one songs on *NOW* that will.i.am appears on, only 'Mas Que Nada' (*NOW 64*) by **Sérgio Mendes** featuring The Black Eyed Peas doesn't credit him as a co-writer, but dig a little deeper and you'll see he did sing on it, play bass and drums, arrange it and produce it. The Black Eyed Peas' most recent number 1, 'The Time (Dirty Bit)' (*NOW 78*), includes a sample of '(I've Had) the Time of My Life' (*NOW 19*) by **Bill Medley** and **Jennifer Warnes**.

00s

NOW 64 Did You Know . . .

Mousse T, aka German producer Mustafa Gündogdu, made the last of his four appearances, reaching number 17 with 'Horny as a Dandy', a mash-up of his 1998 number 2 'Horny' (*NOW 40*) with 'Bohemian Like You' (*NOW 50*), originally a 2005 number 5 for **Dandy Warhols**. In 2000 Mousse T helped **Tom Jones** score his thirty-second Top 40 hit with the number 3 'Sex Bomb' (*NOW 46*). Mousse T is now a judge on the German equivalent of *Pop Idol*.

NOW 99 Did You Know . . .

Wyclef Jean made his first appearance for almost twelve years as featured artist, along with **Naughty Boy**, on 'Dimelo', the debut single for **Rak-Su**, 2017 winners of *The X Factor*. He last appeared in 2006 with **Shakira** on her number 1 single 'Hips Don't Lie' (*NOW 65*), though in the 'missing' years he attempted to run for President in his native Haiti. His only other appearance is 'Perfect Gentleman' (*NOW 50*), a number 4 hit in 2001.

IN OTHER NEWS . . . *NOW 64* (JULY 2006)

Former *Baywatch* actress Pamela Anderson married singer **Kid Rock** in St Tropez.

Pirates of the Caribbean: Dead Man's Chest opened at cinemas, taking more than $55 million on its first day.

Milan Williams, keyboard player with soul group the Commodores, died, aged 58. He wrote the band's first hit single, the 1974 number 20 'Machine Gun'.

13
NOW appearances
'Who Knew',
NOW 64, July 2006
'Beautiful Trauma',
NOW 99, March 2018

The artist born Alecia Moore got the party started without *NOW* and already had thirteen Top 40 hits before she made her first appearance. 'Who Knew' is one of six *NOW* songs that P!nk wrote with Swedish maestro Max Martin, a list that includes her third number 1 single 'So What' (*NOW 71*). The video for 'So What' includes a role for her husband, freestyle motocross rider Carey Hart. In 2003 the pair both appeared in the film *Charlie's Angels: Full Throttle*.

P!nk's biggest seller is 'Just Give Me a Reason' (*NOW 84*) featuring **Nate Reuss**, singer with **fun.** The 2003 number 2 was frustrated in its quest for the top by 'Let's Get Ready to Rhumble' (*NOW 85*) by **PJ & Duncan**, which crashed back into the chart when it was re-released to benefit the ChildLine charity and performed on the ITV show *Ant & Dec's Saturday Night Takeaway*. fun. (always lower case, full stop) have two *NOW* appearances, including the 2012 number 1 'We Are Young' (*NOW 82*) featuring **Janelle Monáe**.

P!NK

Both 'Just Give Me a Reason' and 'We Are Young' were co-written by Jeff Bhasker. The American songwriter also had a hand in 'Uptown Funk' (*NOW 90*) by **Mark Ronson** featuring **Bruno Mars** – the bestselling single of 2015 – and **Harry Styles**'s debut solo number 1 'Sign of the Times' (*NOW 97*). P!nk's appearances include a second duet, 'True Love' (*NOW 85*) featuring **Lily Allen** – though at this time the latter was going by the name Lily Rose Cooper.

P!nk rekindled her film career in 2011 when she voiced Gloria, a penguin, in *Happy Feet Two*. For good measure she also sang the theme tune, as she did for the 2006 film *Alice Through the Looking Glass*, the source of her 2016 number 19 'Just Like Fire' (*NOW 94*). In the video of her most recent appearance, 'Beautiful Trauma' (*NOW 99*), P!nk got to dance with Channing Tatum, star of the films *Step Up* and *21 Jump Street*.

NE-YO

Ne-Yo's *NOW* debut 'So Sick' was the first of five number 1s, all of which appear on *NOW*. Four of the five – including 'Closer' (*NOW 70*) and 'Let Me Love You (Until You Learn to Love Yourself)' (*NOW 83*) – were written with the Norwegian production team Stargate. *NOW 82* features the 2012 number 2 'Let's Go', a collaboration with **Calvin Harris** that was prevented from adding to both artists' tally of chart toppers by **Carly Rae Jepsen**'s 'Call Me Maybe' (both *NOW 83*).

Born Shaffer Smith, Ne-Yo was given his nom de plume by record producer Big D Evans, who said he had the super power to see music where others couldn't. The 2010 number 1 'Beautiful Monster' (*NOW 77*) is from Ne-Yo's fourth album, *Libra Scale*. A concept album, it tells the story of three garbage men who are granted super powers but are forced to decide between love and fame, money and power. All pretty standard, then.

00s

Originally employed as a staff writer by Columbia Records, Ne-Yo had his first taste of success co-writing 'That Girl', the 2003 debut single for R&B singer Marques Houston. His first *NOW* credit was as co-writer of 'Let Me Love You' (*NOW 61*), a 2005 number 2 for **Mario**. He has since given his writing skills to **Beyoncé** for 'Irreplaceable' (*NOW 66*), and **Rihanna** for her second number 1 single 'Take a Bow' (*NOW 70*).

Long before his music career, an 8-year-old Shaffer Smith appeared in the TV series *21 Jump Street*, starring Johnny Depp. Ne-Yo continues to make forays into film and TV, and in 2015 appeared with Common and **Mary J. Blige** in a TV production of *The Wiz*, playing Tin Man. *The Wiz* is a musical version of L. Frank Baum's classic children's book *The Wonderful Wizard of Oz* and was first filmed in 1978, starring **Diana Ross** as Dorothy and **Michael Jackson** as Scarecrow.

NOW 64 Did You Know . . .

Despite sixteen Top 40 hits since 1977 Elvis Costello has yet to appear on *NOW*, but he has two writing credits. Australian group **Rogue Traders** had a number 3 hit in 2006 with 'Voodoo Child', which samples Elvis's 1978 single 'Pump It Up'. In 1989 Elvis helped **Paul McCartney** to his eighteenth solo Top 40 hit (excluding The Beatles and Wings) when he co-wrote 'My Brave Face' (*NOW 15*).

NOW 90 Did You Know . . .

American trio **Haim** made their debut, providing vocals for **Calvin Harris**'s number 35 single 'Pray to God'. Their first appearance in their own right came on *NOW 97* with 'Want You Back'. Danielle, the second (or middle) of the three Haim sisters, played in the touring band of Julian Casablancas, singer with The Strokes, and in 2010 had a spell playing guitar with another all-female outfit, Scarlet Fever, backing band for **CeeLo Green**.

14
NOW appearances

'So Sick',
NOW 64, July 2006

'Coming with You',
NOW 90, March 2015

IN OTHER NEWS . . . *NOW 90* (MARCH 2015)

Andy Fraser, bass guitarist and songwriter with **Free**, died, aged 62. Free's 1970 single 'All Right Now' (*NOW 19*) re-charted in 1991 after it featured in a TV advert for chewing gum.

The BBC suspended *Top Gear* host Jeremy Clarkson after what it called a 'fracas' with a TV producer.

Electro Velvet were selected to represent the United Kingdom in the Eurovision Song Contest 2015 with their song 'Still in Love with You'. In the Eurovision final they received 5 points and were placed twenty-

00s

NOW 65 Did You Know . . .

Two (or three) very different 'one *NOW* wonders' made their only appearance here. 'Ridin'' gave **Chamillionaire** and **Krayzie Bone** (of Bone Thugs-n-Harmony) a number 3 hit and won them a Grammy Award for Best Rap Performance by a Duo or Group. Former *Baywatch* and *Knight Rider* star **David Hasselhoff** released his first single in 1983, had his only other chart hit in 1993 and made his only *NOW* appearance in 2006 with the number 3 single 'Jump in My Car'.

NOW 69 Did You Know . . .

Utah Saints' original version of 'Something Good' made number 4 in 1992, when it appeared on *NOW 22*. It takes its title and includes a sample from **Kate Bush**'s 1985 number 20 'Cloudbusting', from her number 1 album *Hounds of Love*. The same album gave Kate the first of three appearances with 'Running Up That Hill (A Deal with God)' (*NOW 6*). Utah Saints' only other appearance, 'I Want You' (*NOW 25*), samples 'War Ensemble' by American thrash-metal band Slayer.

IN OTHER NEWS . . . *NOW 69* (MARCH 2008)

Andy Abrahams, *The X Factor* runner-up in 2005, was chosen to represent the United Kingdom at the Eurovision Song Contest in Belgrade. In the final he finished twenty-fifth out of twenty-five.

Former **Hear'Say** singer Suzanne Shaw won the third series of the ITV talent show *Dancing on Ice*.

Producer and musician Norman 'Hurricane' Smith died, aged 85. He began his career as engineer for The Beatles before graduating to producer of the first Pink Floyd album. In 1973 he had a number 4 hit with his single 'Oh, Babe, What Would You Say?'

6
NOW appearances

'Rehab',
NOW 65, November 2006

'Love Is a Losing Game',
NOW 69, March 2008

Amy Winehouse's collection of six appearances began with her Top 40 debut 'Rehab', produced by **Mark Ronson** and taken from her second album *Back to Black*. That the album has sold over three-and-three-quarter million copies may explain why Amy never had a number 1 single. A 2007 compilation of recordings for the Radio 1 *Live Lounge* sessions included **Paolo Nutini**'s cover of 'Rehab', along with **Arctic Monkeys** performing 'You Know I'm No Good' and Amy's acoustic version of 'Valerie'.

When Amy released 'You Know I'm No Good' (*NOW 66*) as a single, remixes by **Hot Chip** and Ghostface Killah of Wu-Tang Clan were also made available. 'Back to Black' (*NOW 67*) originally reached number 25 when first released in 2007, but eventually peaked at number 8 after Amy's untimely death in 2011. In 2013 **Beyoncé** and **André 3000** of **OutKast** recorded a version of 'Back to Black' for the soundtrack to **Baz Luhrmann**'s film *The Great Gatsby*.

Mark Ronson and Amy recorded 'Valerie' for his 2007 album *Version*, as the name might suggest a collection of (mainly) covers, which also included **Lily Allen** performing **The Kaiser Chiefs**' debut single 'Oh My God'. 'Valerie' gave Amy her best chart position, stalling at number 2 behind **Sugababes**' 'About You Now' (both *NOW 68*). Originally recorded by **The Zutons**, 'Valerie' (*NOW 64*) was also their best chart placing, reaching number 9 in 2006.

'Tears Dry on Their Own' (*NOW 68*) sampled 'Ain't No Mountain High Enough', written by Nicholas Ashford and Valerie Simpson, and a number 6 hit for **Diana Ross** in 1970. Amy's last appearance was 'Love Is a Losing Game' (*NOW 69*), which failed to make the Top 40 when first released in December 2007 but reached number 33 after her death. In 2015 **Sam Smith** released his version of 'Love Is a Losing Game' on the deluxe edition of his debut album, *In the Lonely Hour*.

00s

AMY WINEHOUSE

DAVID GUETTA

Since his debut on *NOW 65* French DJ David Guetta has notched up twenty-four appearances over just thirty-two volumes. He has collaborated with twenty-one different artists yet still managed to work three times with **Nicki Minaj** – 'Where Them Girls At' (*NOW 79*), 'Turn Me On' (*NOW 82*) and 'Hey Mama' (*NOW 91*) – and three times with **Sia** – 'Titanium' (*NOW 81*), 'She Wolf (Falling To Pieces)' (*NOW 83*) and 'Bang My Head' (*NOW 93*).

When he's not 'spinning the wheels of steel' (or whatever it is that DJs do these days) David Guetta earns a bit of extra pocket money by sitting in the producer's chair. Among the *NOW* songs that he's manned the mixing desk for are 'I Gotta Feeling' (*NOW 74*) and 'Rock That Body' (*NOW 76*) for **Black Eyed Peas**, plus one for **Kelis**, with 'Acapella' (*NOW 76*).

David Guetta obviously knows how to pick his collaborators. That group of twenty has so far notched up more than 170 *NOW* appearances between them. The list includes fellow serial collaborator **Snoop Dogg**. The rapper born Calvin Broadus has five *NOW* entries, all of them joint ventures; in addition to Guetta the hook-ups are with **Pussycat Dolls** (*NOW 64*), **Akon** (*NOW 67*), **Katy Perry** (*NOW 76*) and **Jason Derulo** (*NOW 88*).

The numbered *NOW*s have largely managed to steer clear of football-related songs, though David Guetta managed to sneak one onto *NOW 94*. 'This One's for You', the official song of UEFA Euro 2016 coincided with the tournament in France and featured Swedish singer **Zara Larsson**. Other football-related entries include 'Three Lions '98' by **Baddiel, Skinner and The Lightning Seeds** and 'Vindaloo' by **Fat Les**. Both appeared on *NOW 40* in 1998 when the FIFA World Cup was also held in France.

10s

24
NOW appearances

'Love Don't Let Me Go', David Guetta vs. The Egg, *NOW 65*, November 2006

'2U (Radio Edit)', David Guetta featuring Justin Bieber, *NOW 97*, July 2017

NOW 65 Did You Know . . .

'Promiscuous' by **Nelly Furtado** featuring **Timbaland** was the latter's first *NOW* credit as an artist. His first credit came on volume 51 as co-writer of **Aaliyah**'s number 1 'More than a Woman'. Aaliyah's life was cut tragically short when she died in a plane crash in 2001; she was just 22 years old. In January 2002 'More than a Woman' became the first posthumous number 1 by a female artist, staying there for just one week before George Harrison's 'My Sweet Lord' replaced it. The first time in chart history that one posthumous number 1 has replaced another.

NOW 97 Did You Know . . .

No fewer than fifteen artists made their debut on volume 97, including two ex-members of **One Direction**, **Liam Payne** and **Harry Styles**. Liam, along with former bandmate **Louis Tomlinson**, was among a host of music stars that contributed to the **Artists for Grenfell** charity project, in support of The London Community Foundation. Co-ordinated by Simon Cowell, the single – a version of the Simon and Garfunkel hit 'Bridge Over Troubled Water' – was recorded in response to the tragic Grenfell Tower fire, in West London.

IN OTHER NEWS . . . *NOW 65* (NOVEMBER 2006)

The painting *No. 5, 1948* by American artist Jackson Pollock sold for $140 million, a record that stood for five years. The Stone Roses mention the painting in the lyrics of their 1989 song 'Going Down'.

Casino Royale – the twenty-first James Bond film and the first starring Daniel Craig – opened in cinemas. The theme song, 'You Know My Name', gave Soundgarden and Audioslave singer Chris Cornell his only solo Top 40 hit.

Former Radio 1 DJ Alan 'Fluff' Freeman died at the age of 79. His occasional acting roles included 'DJ Call Me Cobber' in the 1986 musical *Absolute Beginners*. The title song from the film would provide **David Bowie** with one of his four *NOW* appearances on volume 7.

CALVIN HARRIS

So far Calvin's thirty-plus Top 40 hits have spent over seven-and-a-half years in the singles chart, and in all likelihood he will soon surpass **Robbie Williams** and **McFly**'s tally of eight number 1s on *NOW*, and equal the record of nine, held by the **Spice Girls** since 'Holler' (*NOW 47*) appeared back in the year 2000. Of Calvin's twenty-six *NOW* appearances, eight have been 'solo' efforts, including two of his number 1s: the rather ironically titled 'I'm Not Alone' (*NOW 73*) and seasonal banger 'Summer' (*NOW 88*).

Nine of Calvin's *NOW* appearances were taken from his third album, *18 Months*. All of these – 'Bounce' (*NOW 79*), 'We Found Love' and 'Feel So Close' (both *NOW 80*), 'Let's Go' (*NOW 82*), 'Sweet Nothing' and 'We'll Be Coming Back' (both *NOW 83*), 'Drinking From the Bottle' (*NOW 84*), 'I Need Your Love' (*NOW 85*) and 'Thinking About You' (*NOW 86*) – reached the Top 10 of the UK Singles Chart, breaking a record previously held by **Michael Jackson**, whose album *Dangerous* produced seven Top 10 singles.

Calvin's twenty-three *NOW* collaborators can boast a total of 169 appearances between them, and include such luminaries as **Rihanna**, **Katy Perry**, **Tinie Tempah**, **Ne-Yo** and **Ellie Goulding**, though only Rihanna and Ellie get more than one look-in. Rihanna and Calvin's second collaboration, 'This Is What We Came For' (*NOW 94*) was co-written by Calvin with **Taylor Swift**, who used the pseudonym Nils Sjöberg.

Rumours of Calvin having the odd day off may be exaggerated. His writing credits for other artists include **Kylie Minogue**'s 'In Your Arms' (*NOW 70*), **Dizzee Rascal**'s 'Holiday' (*NOW 74*), Rihanna's 'Where Have You Been' and **Cheryl Cole**'s 'Call My Name' (both *NOW 82*). He has his own record label, Fly Eye Records, and was one of the original sixteen co-owners of the music-streaming service Tidal. Not bad for a young man who started his career stacking shelves in his local supermarket.

10s

26 NOW appearances

'Acceptable in the 80s',
NOW 66, April 2007

'The Weekend (Funk Wav Remix)',
SZA x Calvin Harris
NOW 99, March 2018

NOW 66 Did You Know . . .

'I'm Gonna Be (500 Miles)' by **The Proclaimers** featuring **Brain Potter** and **Andy Pipkin** was the twelfth of nineteen Comic Relief charity singles to appear on *NOW*. The first sighting was 'Help!' (*NOW 14*) by **Bananarama** and **Lananeeneenoonoo** (actually French and Saunders with Kathy Burke), while the most recent was 'Lay Me Down' (*NOW 90*) by **Sam Smith**. Comedian Peter Kay has sung on two of the singles, once in the guise of Brian Potter and once as **Geraldine McQueen** on 'I Know Him So Well' (*NOW 78*), a duet with **Susan Boyle** (her only *NOW* appearance).

NOW 99 Did You Know . . .

'These Days' by **Rudimental** featuring **Jess Glynne**, **Macklemore** and **Dan Caplen** is Jess Glynne's ninth appearance on *NOW* and her ninth Top 10 hit. She first came to our attention with 'My Love' (*NOW 87*), a collaboration with **Route 94** and her first number 1 single. Since then she has topped the charts another four times: two solo outings, 'Hold My Hand' (*NOW 90*) and 'Don't Be So Hard on Yourself' (*NOW 92*), and two further collaborations, 'Rather Be' (*NOW 88*) with **Clean Bandit** and 'Not Letting Go' (*NOW 91*) with **Tinie Tempah**. After **Cheryl Cole**, she is only the second British female solo artist to have five number 1s.

10s

IN OTHER NEWS . . . *NOW 66* (APRIL 2007)

Avril Lavigne released her third album, *The Best Damn Thing*. A prophetic title, it would go on to be the bestselling album of 2007 worldwide.

ITV launched a new reality talent show, *Grease Is the Word* – a search for two actors to play Danny and Sandy in a new stage production of *Grease* eventually won by Danny Bayne and Susan McFadden.

American singer Bobby 'Boris' Pickett died, aged 69. With his band The Crypt-Kickers he had a number 3 hit in 1973 with 'Monster Mash', a song originally released in 1962.

ADELE

Adele made both her chart and *NOW* debut with 'Chasing Pavements', which spent three weeks at number 2 in January 2008, held off the top all that time by 'Now You're Gone' (*NOW 69*) by **Basshunter** featuring **DJ Mental Theo's Bazzheadz**. Her second appearance, 'Make You Feel My Love' (*NOW 77*) was written by Bob Dylan for his 1997 album *Time Out of Mind* and has also been covered by Billy Joel, country-music superstar Garth Brooks and singing DIY-enthusiast Nick Knowles, but Adele's number 4 version is the only one to chart.

'Rolling in the Deep' charted at number 2, behind **Bruno Mars**'s 'Grenade' (both *NOW 78*), but didn't have time to leave the Top 5 before 'Someone Like You' (*NOW 79*) went to number 1 a month later. It spent four weeks at the top before it was briefly dislodged by **Nicole Scherzinger**'s 'Don't Hold Your Breath' (also *NOW 79*), only to return to the summit one week later. 'Someone Like You' spent forty weeks in the Top 40, the best showing by any Adele single to date.

Adele wrote 'Rolling in the Deep' with Paul Epworth, who also co-wrote **Florence and the Machine**'s only number 1, 'Spectrum (Say My Name)' (*NOW 83*), while 'Someone Like You' was written with Dan Wilson of **Semisonic**, who made their only appearance with 'Secret Smile' (*NOW 43*). 'Set Fire to the Rain' (*NOW 80*) could only manage number 11 in the UK but became her third consecutive US number 1, and won Adele a Grammy Award for Best Solo Pop Performance.

'Someone Like You' was the bestselling single of 2011, taken from Adele's second album *21*, the bestselling album that year. With sales of more than three-and-a-half million, *21* sold more than the next three albums combined, though one of those was her 2008 debut album, *19*. One of the few records that Adele can't claim is 'First Adele to Appear on *NOW*' – that honour goes to **Adele Bertei**, featured vocalist on 'Just a Mirage' (*NOW 12*), one of four Top 40 singles for **Jellybean**.

NOW 69 Did You Know . . .

The first *NOW* of 2008 saw **OneRepublic** (always OneWord) make their debut and second appearance with 'Stop and Stare' and 'Apologize', their 2007 number 3 with **Timbaland**. Their only number 1 to date, 'Counting Stars' (*NOW 86*), spent two separate weeks at the top in October 2013, split briefly by **Miley Cyrus**'s 'Wrecking Ball' (*NOW 87*). OneRepublic frontman Ryan Tedder also had a hand in number 1 singles for **Leona Lewis**, 'Bleeding Love' (*NOW 68*), **Ellie Goulding**, 'Burn' (*NOW 86*), and **Ella Henderson**, 'Ghost' (*NOW 88*).

NOW 80 Did You Know . . .

Both 'Video Games' and **Lana Del Rey**'s second single 'Born to Die' (*NOW 81*) peaked at number 9, though the former stayed in the Top 40 for an impressive twenty-two weeks. Lana's biggest hit to date is 'Summertime Sadness' (*NOW 86*); remixed by French DJ **Cedric Gervais**, it reached number 4 in August 2013 and won a Grammy Award for Best Remix. It is also mentioned in the lyrics of **The Chainsmokers**' 2014 chart debut '#SELFIE' (*NOW 87*).

5

NOW appearances

'Chasing Pavements',
NOW 69, March 2008

'Set Fire to the Rain',
NOW 80, November 2011

N OTHER NEWS . . . *NOW 80* (NOVEMBER 2011)

Absolute Radio launched dedicated sixties and seventies digital radio stations.

Coronation Street became the first prime-time TV show to use 'paid for' product placement after agreeing to install a Nationwide Building Society cash machine.

Actor John Neville died, aged 86. Considered 'one of the most potent classical actors' of his day, in his later years he starred in the films *The Adventures of Baron Munchausen* and *The Fifth Element*.

10s

NOW 71 Did You Know . . .

Fantasia Barrino won series three of *American Idol*, while the contestant finishing in a lowly seventh place was one **Jennifer Hudson**. She can boast six Top 40 singles and three *NOW* appearances, beginning here with 'Spotlight', co-written by **Ne-Yo** and the hugely successful Stargate production team. Her second appearance, 'Go All Night' (*NOW 90*), was a collaboration with **Gorgon City** and co-written by Canadian singer **Kiesza**, whilst the third, 'Trouble' (*NOW 91*), saw her linking up with **Iggy Azalea**.

NOW 98 Did You Know . . .

Charlie Puth seems to be establishing himself as a *NOW* regular. 'How Long' on *NOW 98* is his sixth appearance following a run of five consecutive showings from volumes 91 to 95. His debut appearance, 'See You Again' by **Wiz Khalifa** featuring Charlie Puth, was also his first number 1. Written for the soundtrack of the 2015 film *Furious 7* as a tribute to the late actor Paul Walker, the video has had over 3.4 billion views on YouTube, breaking the record previously held by **Psy**'s 'Gangnam Style' (*NOW 83*).

IN OTHER NEWS . . . *NOW 71* (NOVEMBER 2008)

After finishing fifth in the final race of the season, the Brazilian Grand Prix, 23-year-old Lewis Hamilton became the youngest ever Formula 1 World Champion. He has since won another three World Championships.

Barack Obama was elected the forty-fourth President of the United States. The first African-American to hold the highest seat in the land, he was born in 1961 in Honolulu, Hawaii, and was previously United States Senator for Illinois.

Slumdog Millionaire, directed by Danny Boyle, opened in cinemas. The closing theme 'Jai Ho!' won an Oscar for Best Original Song, and an English-language version credited to **A.R. Rahman** and **Pussycat Dolls** featuring **Nicole Scherzinger** reached number 3, and appeared on *NOW 73*.

20 NOW appearances

'I Kissed a Girl', *NOW 71*, November 2008

'Swish Swish', Katy Perry featuring Nicki Minaj, *NOW 98*, November 20

KATY PERRY

Katy Perry's impressive run of twenty *NOW* appearances in just twenty-seven volumes began with two songs on *NOW 71*, 'I Kissed a Girl' and 'Hot n Cold'. The former was the first of five number 1 singles, a list that includes 'Roar' (*NOW 86*), her bestselling single to date. The three remaining pop toppers are 'California Gurls' (*NOW 76*), an alliance with **Snoop Dogg**, 'Part of Me' (*NOW 82*) and 'Feels' (*NOW 97*) by **Calvin Harris** featuring **Pharrell Williams**, Katy Perry and **Big Sean**.

Katy co-wrote eighteen of her twenty *NOW* appearances, with only 'Starstrukk' (*NOW 75*) by **3OH!3** featuring Katy Perry and 'If We Ever Meet Again' (*NOW 75*) by **Timbaland** featuring Katy Perry, on which she lent her vocal talents only, being the exceptions. Thirteen of Katy's own compositions have benefitted from input by Swedish super-scribbler Max Martin; Max first graced the *NOW* credits as long ago as 1997 when he co-wrote 'Quit Playing Games (with My Heart)' by **Backstreet Boys** (*NOW 37*).

Katy Perry made her film debut providing the voice of Smurfette for *The Smurfs* in 2011. The script calls on Smurfette to utter the strangely familiar phrase, 'I kissed a Smurf, and I liked it.' In 1978, sadly five years too early to be included on the first *NOW* album, 'The Smurf Song' by Father Abraham and the Smurfs spent six weeks at number 2 in the charts. It was kept off the top spot by 'You're the One that I Want' by **John Travolta** and **Olivia Newton-John**, which DID make it onto *NOW 40* by dint of its inclusion in 'The Grease Megamix'.

Katy is not the only Perry to have a girl/gurl-related entry in *NOW* history. Step forward 'Big Girl' by **Precocious Brats featuring Kevin & Perry** (*NOW 45*), written for the film *Kevin & Perry Go Large* by DJ Judge Jules with help from Harry Enfield and Matt Smith. Peaking at number 16, this was Harry's second Top 40 appearance, following on from 'Loadsamoney (Doin' Up the House)', a number 4 hit in 1988.

10s

LADY GAGA

We are kicking off with the first of four number 1s, three of which appear on *NOW*. 'Just Dance' features additional vocals from fellow New Yorker **Colby O'Donis**, and was co-written by Lady Gaga with **Akon** and RedOne. Colby also lent his vocal talents to 'Beautiful' (*NOW 73*), Akon's number 8 single that featured both Colby and **Kardinall Offishall**. RedOne, aka Moroccan-born Nadir Khayat, also assisted Lady Gaga with the writing of two more of her number 1s, 'Poker Face' (*NOW 73*) and 'Bad Romance' (*NOW 75*).

Other Gaga partners include **Wale** and **Beyoncé**, while her 2013 number 9 single 'Do What U Want' (*NOW 87*) saw her hook up with **R Kelly** for one of his twelve *NOW* appearances. For the 2012 single 'Perfect Illusion' (*NOW 95*) she enlisted the services of not one, but two in-demand producers, **Mark Ronson** and **BloodPop®**. We suspect her 2013 single 'The Cure' (*NOW 97*) wasn't a partnership and won't add to that particular band's current total of five appearances.

When Lady Gaga was still Stefani Germanotta she attended the Convent of the Sacred Heart in Manhattan, also a location for the TV series *Gossip Girl*. In 2009 Lady Gaga made a cameo appearance in *Gossip Girl*, performing 'Bad Romance'. The same episode marked the last of six acting displays by **Hilary Duff,** who can also boast one *NOW* appearance with 'Wake Up' (*NOW 62*). In 2011 Lady Gaga filmed her TV special *A Very Gaga Thanksgiving* at the convent, performing 'The Lady Is a Tramp' with Tony Bennett.

In 2018 Lady Gaga appeared opposite Bradley Cooper in the fourth version of Hollywood blockbuster *A Star Is Born*. The original 1937 version was re-made in 1954, starring Judy Garland and James Mason. A 1976 version with Barbra Streisand and Kris Kristofferson won an Oscar for Best Original Song. In 2006 Barbra Streisand appeared on Tony Bennett's album *Duets*; five years later Lady Gaga appeared on Tony's follow-up, *Duets II*.

10s

NOW 72 Did You Know . . .

Nelly Furtado can boast two number 1 singles – 'Maneater' (*NOW 64*) and 'Give It to Me' by **Timbaland** featuring **Justin Timberlake** and Nelly Furtado (*NOW 67*) – but her bestselling single in the UK is 'Broken Strings', a collaboration with **James Morrison** from this volume. Four of the Canadian chanteuse's seven *NOW* appearances were written by Timbaland; in addition to the two aforementioned chart toppers he also co-wrote 'Promiscuous' (*NOW 65*) and 'Say It Right' (*NOW 66*).

NOW 97 Did You Know . . .

Having racked up her first seven appearances across six consecutive volumes of *NOW*, Swedish singer **Zara Larsson** scored her first number 1 single with 'Symphony' (*NOW 97*), a collaboration with **Clean Bandit**. She made her *NOW* debut with the number 5 hit, 'Never Forget You' (*NOW 92*), a joint venture with **MNEK**, and has since chalked up two further Top 20 partnerships working with **Tinie Tempah** on 'Girls Like' (*NOW 93*), and **David Guetta** on 'This One's for You' (*NOW 94*).

10s

IN OTHER NEWS . . . *NOW 72* (APRIL 2009)

'Number 1' by **Tinchy Stryder** featuring **N-Dubz** (*NOW 73*) went to number 1. That's one better than 'You're My Number One' by **S Club 7** (*NOW 45*), which only made number 2.

Scandal rocked *University Challenge* when champions Corpus Christi College, Oxford were disqualified after it was discovered that one of their team was no longer a student. Runners-up University of Manchester were declared winners in their place.

On 11 April **Susan Boyle** appeared on the ITV programme *Britain's Got Talent*, singing 'I Dreamed a Dream' from *Les Misérables*. Although she would finish second behind dance outfit Diversity, her debut album was the bestselling album in the world in 2009.

12
NOW appearances
'Just Dance', Lady Gaga Featuring Colby O'Donis, *NOW 72*, April 2009

'The Cure', *NOW 97*, July 2017

WHO DID IT BETTER?

Bonnie Tyler
NOW 1

'Total Eclipse of the Heart'

Nicki French
NOW 30

Grandmaster Flash
NOW 3

'White Lines (Don't Do It)'

Duran Duran
NOW 31

The Weather Girls
NOW 3

'It's Raining Men'

Geri Halliwell
NOW 49

Rockwell
NOW 4

'Somebody's Watching Me'

Beatfreakz
NOW 64

Harold Faltermeyer
NOW 5

'Axel F'

Crazy Frog
NOW 61

Billy Ocean
NOW 7

'When the Going Gets Tough'

Boyzone
NOW 42

Run DMC
NOW 8

'Walk This Way'

Sugababes vs Girls Aloud
NOW 66

Tiffany
NOW 12

'I Think We're Alone Now'

Girls Aloud
NOW 66

Cameo
NOW 8

'Word Up'

Little Mix
NOW 87

Erasure
NOW 13

'A Little Respect'

Wheatus
NOW 50

Mantronix feat. Wondress
NOW 17

'Got to Have Your Love'

Liberty X
NOW 53

Salt 'N' Pepa
NOW 13

'Twist and Shout'

Chaka Demus & Pliers
NOW 27

Sam Brown
NOW 14

'Stop'

Jamelia
NOW 59

Marc Cohn
NOW 20

'Walking in Memphis'

Cher
NOW 32

Brian May
NOW 23

'Too Much Love Will Kill You'

Queen
NOW 33

The Farm
NOW 23

'Don't You Want Me'

The Human League
NOW 32

Duran Duran
NOW 24
'Ordinary World'
Aurora
NOW 47

Adamski
feat. Seal
NOW 28
'Killer'
ATB
NOW 34

Ladysmith
Black Mambazo
NOW 31
'Swing Low Sweet
Chariot'
UB40
NOW 56

4 Non Blondes
NOW 25
'What's Up?'
DJ Miko
NOW 28

The Pretenders
NOW 28
'I'll Stand By You'
Girls Aloud
NOW 60

Boyzone
NOW 33
ather and Son'
Ronan Keating &
Yusuf Islam
NOW 60

Lou Bega
NOW 44
'Mambo No. 5'
Bob the Builder
NOW 50

John Lennon
NOW 45
'Imagine'
Eva Cassidy
NOW 53

Don Henley
NOW 40
'The Boys of
Summer'
DJ Sammy
NOW 54

Nelly feat.
Dani Stevenson
NOW 52
'Hot in Herre'
Tiga feat. Jake Shears
NOW 55

Tru Faith &
Dub Conspiracy
NOW 46
'Freak like Me'
Sugababes
NOW 52

Frankie
Goes to Hollywood
NOW 46
'The Power of Love'
Gabrielle Aplin
NOW 84

Keane
NOW 57
'Somewhere Only
We Know'
Lily Allen
NOW 86

Shontelle
NOW 77
'Impossible'
James Arthur
NOW 84

Robyn
NOW 76
'Dancing on My
Own'
Calum Scott
NOW 94

The Zutons
NOW 64
'Valerie'
Mark Ronson &
Amy Winehouse
NOW 68

Avicii
NOW 86
'Wake Me Up'
Gareth Malone's
All Star Choir
NOW 89

Journey
NOW 75
'Don't Stop
Believin''
Glee Cast
NOW 75

Damien Rice
NOW 80
'Cannonball'
Little Mix
NOW 81

NOW 72 Did You Know . . .

Ke$ha made her first and most recent appearances as featured vocalist on songs built around samples. 'Right Round' with **Flo Rida** was her chart debut and the first of her three number 1 singles. It samples 'You Spin Me Round (Like a Record)' (*NOW 63*), the only number 1 for **Dead or Alive** and the first chart topper for the Stock Aitken Waterman production team. Her most recent appearance was 'Timber' (*NOW 87*) with **Pitbull**, which samples 'San Francisco Bay', a 1978 single by harmonica player Lee Oskar.

NOW 99 Did You Know . . .

Paloma Faith appeared twice on this volume with 'Guilty' and 'Lullaby', the latter an alliance with **Sigala**. Paloma's only number 1 to date is 'Changing' (*NOW 89*), a 2014 collaboration with drum-and-bass duo **Sigma**. Earlier that year Paloma had a number 6 hit with 'Only Love Can Hurt Like This' (*NOW 88*), written by Diane Warren, who also wrote the similarly titled 'Nothing Hurts Like Love' (*NOW 59*) for **Daniel Bedingfield**. In 2007 Paloma starred in the film *St Trinian's*, which included **Girls Aloud** as the school band.

N OTHER NEWS . . . *NOW 99* (MARCH 2018)

Comedian, singer and actor Ken Dodd died, aged 90. Between 1960 and 1975 he had eighteen Top 40 hits, including his only number 1, 'Tears', the bestselling single of 1965.

The Emoji Movie won in four categories at the thirty-eighth Golden Raspberry Awards, including Worst Picture. The animated film's cast includes the vocal talents of **Christina Aguilera** and Patrick Stewart.

The new *Coronation Street* set was unveiled in Salford, Greater Manchester. It includes a memorial bench to the twenty-two victims of the 2017 Manchester Arena bombing.

5
NOW appearances

'Love Story',
NOW 72, April 2009

'. . . Ready for It?',
NOW 99, March 2018

TAYLOR SWIFT

Taylor Swift made her US Top 40 debut in 2007, two years before her first UK chart and *NOW* appearance with the number 2 'Love Story'. Stuck behind Kelly Clarkson and her first number 1, 'My Life Would Suck without You' (also *NOW 72*), Taylor would have to wait eight-and-a-half years for her first chart topper. Taylor's US debut was '**Tim McGraw**', a rare example of a song named after another *NOW* artist. Tim's only *NOW* appearance is as featured vocalist on **Nelly**'s third number 1, 'Over and Over' (*NOW 60*).

We had a gap of three years before three appearances on consecutive volumes, starting with 'We Are Never Ever Getting Back Together' (*NOW 83*). All three were taken from Taylor's first number 1 album, *Red*, and all three were co-written with Swedes Max Martin (him again) and Shellback (aka Johan Schuster). 'I Knew You Were Trouble' was another for the 'stalled at number 2' collection, losing out to 'Scream & Shout' by **will.i.am** featuring **Britney Spears** (both *NOW 84*).

The third song in this little sequence is '22' (*NOW 85*). **The Vamps** included a cover of '22' on the B-side of their 2013 chart debut 'Can We Dance' (*NOW 86*). That same year Taylor's career came full circle when she recorded 'Highway Don't Care', a duet with Tim McGraw featuring Keith Urban on guitar. Keith awaits his first *NOW* appearance but can ask his wife **Nicole Kidman** what it's like, following her duet with **Robbie Williams** on the 2001 number 1 'Somethin' Stupid' (*NOW 51*).

Taylor's most recent appearance is '. . . Ready for It?' (*NOW 99*), on which the Swedish songwriting talent was augmented by Ali Payami, whose credits include 'Can't Feel My Face' (*NOW 92*) by **The Weeknd**. Taylor's 'well I never' moments include duetting with Sheffield rock band Def Leppard for a 2010 TV special. And in 'ultimate cover version' news, alt-country artist Ryan Adams recorded an entire song-by-song version of Taylor's number 1 album *1989*, and got himself a number 19 chart place in the process.

00s

NOW 73 Did You Know . . .

'Mama Do (Uh Oh, Uh Oh)' was the first of nine appearances and three number 1 singles for **Pixie Lott**. It was co-written by Norwegian songwriter Mads Hauge, as was her second chart topper 'Boys and Girls' (*NOW 74*) and 'Kiss the Stars' (*NOW 81*), a 2012 number 8. Pixie's most recent appearance is the 'sample-tastic' 'Nasty' (*NOW 87*), containing elements of 'Funky President' by **James Brown**, 'Do It ('Til You're Satisfied)' by BT Express and 'Dance Across the Floor' by Jimmy 'Bo' Horne.

NOW 95 Did You Know . . .

'Is This Love (Remix)' by **Bob Marley and the Wailers** featuring **LVNDSCAPE** and **Boiler** marked Bob's fourth appearance, though his death in 1981 at the age of just thirty-six meant he didn't live to see any of them. Bob's biggest hit was another posthumous remix, 'Sun Is Shining' (*NOW 44*), this time by Danish DJ **Funkstar De Luxe**. Bob misses out on the unenviable title of most posthumous appearances though, as **Freddie Mercury** has two 'after the event' entries and also sings on four with **Queen**.

10s

IN OTHER NEWS . . . *NOW 95* (NOVEMBER 2016)

Former *Blue Peter* presenter (and mother of **Sophie Ellis-Bextor**) Janet Ellis was shortlisted for the 2016 Bad Sex in Fiction Award for her novel *The Butcher's Hook*.

Canadian singer and songwriter Leonard Cohen died, aged 82. In December 2008 his 1984 song 'Hallelujah' was at number 1 and number 2 for **Alexandra Burke** and Jeff Buckley respectively, while his original version was at number 36.

'The Wonder of You', a collection of Elvis Presley songs with new orchestral arrangements, became his thirteenth number 1 album, four of them posthumous.

12
NOW appearances

'Diamond Rings', Chipmunk featuring Emeli Sandé, *NOW 73*, July 2009

'Hurts', *NOW 95*, November 2016

EMELI SANDÉ

Before Emeli Sandé made her first solo appearance with 'Heaven' (*NOW 80*), she was featured vocalist with **Chipmunk** and with **Naughty Boy**, both of them making the first of their six appearances to date. Naughty Boy was born Shahid Khan, and appears with Emeli on three songs – 'Never Be Your Woman' (*NOW 75*), 'Wonder' (*NOW 83*) and 'Lifted' (*NOW 86*) – while he and Emeli co-wrote three further titles, including 'Diamond Rings' (*NOW 73*) and the aforementioned 'Heaven'.

Both of Emeli's number 1 singles appear on *NOW*, beginning with the 2011 hit 'Read All About It' (*NOW 80*) with **Professor Green**. This was the second of the Prof's three appearances, following 'Just Be Good to Green' (*NOW 76*) featuring **Lily Allen**. Emeli's second number 1 came in 2012 with 'Beneath Your Beautiful' (*NOW 83*), a collaboration with and the only number 1 hit so far for **Labrinth**, just as 'Read All About It' is for Professor Green.

'Heaven', 'Next to Me' (*NOW 81*), 'My Kind of Love' (*NOW 82*) and 'Clown' (*NOW 84*) were all taken from Emeli's debut album, *Our Version of Events*, which charted at number 1 in February 2012 and has returned to the top spot six times, spending ten weeks there in total. It finished 2012 as the year's bestselling album, ahead of **Adele**'s *21*, a turn of events made a little more curious given that Emeli is in fact Ms Sandé's middle name – her first name is Adele.

Emeli chose to drop her first name after 'the other' Adele won the inaugural Critics' Choice Award at the 2008 BRITs. The award was subsequently won by **Florence and the Machine**, **Ellie Goulding**, **Jessie J** and, in 2012, by Emeli. The first ten winners have all appeared on *NOW*, and we await the arrival of 2018 winner Jorja Smith. However, it is most likely that Emeli is the only person on that illustrious list to have both a degree in neuroscience and a tattoo of Mexican artist Frida Kahlo.

10s

JUSTIN BIEBER

Justin Bieber's sixteen appearances with sixteen different collaborators include all six of his number 1 singles, marking him out as the King Canuck of *NOW* and the singles chart. His closest competitor is Toronto-born **Drake**, whose four number 1 singles still leave him some catching up to do. Justin made his chart debut at the age of fifteen with 'One Time', and has since spent more than seven years of his young life in the Top 40.

In September 2015 Justin had his first number 1 with 'What Do You Mean?' (*NOW 92*), swiftly followed by his second, 'Sorry', six weeks later, only to replace himself with his third, 'Love Yourself' (both *NOW 93*), two weeks after that. 'Love Yourself' looked all set to be the Christmas number 1 before 'A Bridge Over You' (also *NOW 93*) by **The Lewisham and Greenwich NHS Choir** pipped it at the post, though they may have been helped by Justin tweeting his support for the charity single.

In January 2016 'Love Yourself' returned to the top for a further three weeks when, with his two previous number 1s queuing up behind him, he became the first artist to hold the top three places in one week. His run was eventually halted by another Canadian, **Shawn Mendes** and his first number 1, 'Stitches' (*NOW 93*). Justin managed 'the old one-two' again in August 2016 when 'Cold Water' by **Major Lazer** featuring Justin Bieber and **MØ** sat ahead of 'Let Me Love You' (both *NOW 95*) by **DJ Snake** featuring Justin Bieber.

There are four other *NOW* artists who can boast holding the top two spots in the same week – **John Travolta**, **John Lennon**, **Frankie Goes to Hollywood** and **Ed Sheeran**. And it was Ed who stopped Justin and his chums **Luis Fonsi** and **Daddy Yankee** from having the bestselling single of 2017 when his third number 1, 'Shape of You', finished the year ahead of their number 1, 'Despacito' (*NOW 97*).

10s

NOW 75 Did You Know . . .

For the only time, two different versions of the same song appeared on one volume. When **Journey** first released 'Don't Stop Believin'' in 1982 it only made number 62, though it did reach number 9 in the US. In December 2009 a version by the **Glee Cast** entered the chart after its inclusion in the *Glee* TV series, and a performance by **Joe McElderry** in the finals of *The X Factor*. In February 2010 Journey's original version finally peaked at number 6, while the Glee Cast version made number 2.

NOW 98 Did You Know . . .

A new leader emerged in the 'Shortest Combined Artist and Title' category courtesy of '17' by **MK**, a record previously held by **Moby** with 'Go' (*NOW 20*). Since *NOW* began in 1983 the most succinct artist has been **V** (two appearances), while there have been seven 'two-character' songs. At the other end of the scale we await a challenger for **John Travolta** and **Olivia Newton-John**'s 'The Grease Megamix (You're the One that I Want/Greased Lightning/Summer Nights)' (*NOW 40*).

10s

IN OTHER NEWS . . . *NOW 75* (MARCH 2010)

On 6 March, Sandra Bullock attended the thirtieth Golden Raspberry Awards, were she collected the prize for Worst Actress for her role in *All About Steve*. The following night she won the Best Actress Oscar for her role in *The Blind Side*.

The World Health Organisation appointed **Craig David** as a goodwill ambassador on World Tuberculosis Day.

Actor Sacha Baron Cohen married actress Isla Fisher in Paris. Undoubtedly the happiest day of his life since **Ali G** featuring **Shaggy** appeared on *NOW 51* with 'Me Julie'.

16
NOW appearances

'One Time',
NOW 75, March 2010

'Friends', Justin Bieber and BloodPop®,
NOW 98, November 2017

NOW 75 Did You Know . . .

Tottenham-born R&B singer **Lemar** made his most recent appearance with 'The Way Love Goes', his eleventh Top 40 hit. He finished third on the 2002 BBC talent show *Fame Academy* and had his biggest hit with the number 2 single 'Dance (with U)' (*NOW 56*), but was blocked in his bid for the top by 'Breathe' by Blu Cantrell featuring **Sean Paul**. Lemar had actually recorded his debut single 'Got Me Saying Ooh' two years earlier, but company politics saw him dropped by his label and the record went unreleased.

NOW 97 Did You Know . . .

Los Angeles DJ trio **Cheat Codes** made their third appearance with 'Promises', featuring former *Barney & Friends* actress **Demi Lovato**. They made their chart and *NOW* debut alongside Dutch DJ trio **Kris Kross Amsterdam** on 'Sex' (*NOW 94*), a re-working of **Salt 'N' Pepa**'s 1991 number 2 'Let's Talk About Sex' (*NOW 20*). Cheat Codes' second appearance was in the company of one German and one French DJ in the form of **Robin Schulz** and **David Guetta**, and the 2016 number 24 single 'Shed a Light' (*NOW 96*).

IN OTHER NEWS . . . *NOW 97* (JULY 2017)

Chester Bennington, singer with American Rock band Linkin Park, died, aged 41. Between 2003 and 2012 Linkin Park had three number 1 albums.

The war drama *Dunkirk* premiered at the Odeon cinema in Leicester Square. The cast includes Kenneth Branagh, Mark Rylance and former **One Direction** singer **Harry Styles**.

In Derbyshire extreme weather conditions forced the cancellation of the Y Not Festival. Headliners, including The Vaccines and Two Door Cinema Club, were unable to perform.

13
NOW appearances

'Starry Eyed',
NOW 75, March 2010

'First Time', Kygo
featuring Ellie Goulding,
NOW 97, July 2017

ELLIE GOULDING

Following her Top 40 and *NOW* debut with 'Starry Eyed', Ellie's next appearance was a cover of **Elton John**'s own 1971 chart debut, 'Your Song' (*NOW 78*). This was the first instance of a song recorded for a certain department store's Christmas advert appearing on *NOW*. We skipped a year in 2011 but returned for the next four years with **Gabrielle Aplin**'s 'The Power of Love' (*NOW 84*), 'Somewhere Only We Know' by **Lily Allen** (*NOW 86*), 'Real Love' (*NOW 89*) by **Tom Odell** and 'Half the World Away' (*NOW 92*) by **Aurora**.

'Burn' (*NOW 86*) had been considered for **Leona Lewis**'s third album, *Glassheart*, but ultimately gave Ellie her first number 1 in August 2013. Her second number 1, 'Love Me Like You Do' (*NOW 91*), was taken from the soundtrack of the film *Fifty Shades of Grey* and spent four weeks at the top, ending the run of 'Uptown Funk' (*NOW 90*) by **Mark Ronson** featuring **Bruno Mars**. In 2016 another film soundtrack, *Bridget Jones's Baby*, gave Ellie her eighteenth Top 40 hit with 'Still Falling for You' (*NOW 95*).

Back on the small screen, 'How Long Will I Love You' (*NOW 87*) served as the official single of the BBC Children in Need appeal in 2013. Originally a 1990 single for The Waterboys, their version failed to chart, and while that is their only *NOW* credit, former 'Boy Karl Wallinger has one appearance as **World Party** with 'Is It Like Today?' (*NOW 24*); **Robbie Williams** had his second number 1 in 1999 with a cover of World Party's 'She's the One' (*NOW 44*).

Three of Ellie's appearances are collaborations, two of them – 'I Need Your Love' (*NOW 85*) and 'Outside' (*NOW 90*) – recorded and written with Scottish DJ **Calvin Harris**. The third is the 2017 number 34 'First Time' (*NOW 97*), a partnership with **Kygo**, or Kyrre Gørvell-Dahll as it (probably) says on his Norwegian passport. 'First Time' is one of seven appearances for Kygo, each with a different collaborator. So far his best chart showing is number 7 for 'It Ain't Me' (*NOW 96*), featuring **Selena Gomez** (who also began her career with *Barney and Friends*).

10s

207

10s

BRUNO MARS

Yet again *NOW* brought you the biggest talent and their biggest hits, offering twelve of Bruno Mars's Top 40 singles and all five of his number 1s, beginning with 'Nothin' on You', his collaboration with **B.o.B**, aka Bobby Ray Simmons Jr. It was also a first appearance for B.o.B, who was back on the following volume with the number 1 single 'Airplanes' (*NOW 77*), this time featuring the vocal talents of **Hayley Williams** of Rock combo **Paramore**.

Bruno also made a swift return with his second number 1, 'Just the Way You Are' (*NOW 77*), which was subtitled 'Amazing' in some territories, presumably to avoid confusion with Billy Joel's 1978 hit. Bruno co-wrote and produced his single with Philip Lawrence and Ari Levine, under the collective name The Smeezingtons, a title they also used for their contribution to **Sugababes**' 'Get Sexy' (*NOW 74*) and **CeeLo Green**'s 2010 number 1 'Forget You' (also *NOW 77*).

In 2011 Bruno had his third and fourth chart toppers with 'Grenade' (*NOW 78*) and 'The Lazy Song' (*NOW 79*), an impressive run of four number 1s on consecutive volumes. He waited three years for his fifth, but a song like 'Uptown Funk' (*NOW 90*) doesn't come along every day. His collaboration with **Mark Ronson** spent seven weeks at the top and was the bestselling single of 2015. Bruno may be disappointed to learn that he wasn't the first Hawaiian-born artist to have a number 1 single on *NOW* – that honour goes to **Glenn Medeiros** for 'Nothing's Gonna Change My Love for You' (*NOW 12*).

Undoubtedly many readers are wondering, 'Is Bruno Mars the only Bruno to appear on *NOW*?' Strictly speaking, yes, though French-Italian House music trio **BBE** (*NOW 35* and *36*) boasted Brunos Quartier and Sanchioni. And on the subject of *Strictly*, flamboyant talent show judge Bruno Tonioli choreographed many a pop video, including **Bananarama**'s 'Venus' (*NOW 7*) and **Paul McCartney**'s 'Hope of Deliverance' (*NOW 24*). That's the same Paul McCartney who made the 1975 album *Venus and Mars* with his band Wings.

NOW 76 Did You Know . . .

San Francisco rock band **Train** were another act that looked to Scandinavia for songwriting assistance. Their first two appearances – 'Hey, Soul Sister' and their biggest hit 'Drive By' (*NOW 82*) – were written by singer Patrick Monohan with Norwegian duo Espen Lind and Amund Bjørklund, also responsible for hits by **Beyoncé**, **Kym Marsh** and **The Vamps**. However, the inspiration for their third appearance, 'Play That Song' (*NOW 96*), came from another time, rather than another place, sampling the 1938 song 'Heart and Soul' by Hoagy Carmichael and Frank Loesser.

NOW 99 Did You Know . . .

'Tip Toe' by **Jason Derulo** featuring **French Montana** was Florida-born Jason's fifteenth appearance, a total that includes four number 1s. Conveniently, one of these, 'Don't Wanna Go Home' (*NOW 79*), also samples a more mature ditty in the form of Harry Belafonte's 1957 number 2 'Day-O (The Banana Boat Song)'. Readers who are shrugging their shoulders at all this prehistoric talk may feel more comfortable knowing that 'Don't Wanna Go Home' also samples 'Show Me Love' (*NOW 24*), a 1993 number 6 for **Robin S**.

10s

IN OTHER NEWS . . . *NOW 76* (JULY 2010)

At the cinema *Despicable Me* opened, with a soundtrack by **Pharrell Williams** and featuring additional songs by **Bee Gees**, Barry Manilow and Lynyrd Skynyrd.

Jamaican reggae singer Sugar Minott died, aged 54. His one Top 40 hit was 'Good Thing Going (We Got a Good Thing Going)', which reached number 4 in April 1981.

The BBC TV drama *Sherlock* aired for the first time, starring Benedict Cumberbatch, Martin Freeman and Una Stubbs, and with music by **David Arnold** and Michael Price.

13
NOW appearances

'Nothin' on You',
B.o.B featuring Bruno Mars,
NOW 76, July 2010

'Finesse (Remix)',
Bruno Mars featuring Cardi B,
NOW 99, March 2018

10s

NOW 77 Did You Know . . .

Two former *X Factor* contestants bowed out after two appearances and one number 1 single for each. The 2009 winner **Joe McElderry** topped the charts with 'The Climb' (*NOW 75*) and followed it with 'Ambitions', before it was back to reality TV and the joy of winning *Popstar to Operastar* in 2011. **Diana Vickers**'s aptly titled number 1 'Once' (*NOW 76*) also lasted one week at the top, and she made her second appearance with 'My Wicked Heart', after which she parted company with her record label due to that old chestnut 'musical differences'.

NOW 97 Did You Know . . .

Daddy Yankee has two chart and *NOW* appearances to his name, with a gap of thirty-five *NOW*s between them. In 2005 'Gasolina' (*NOW 62*) spent six weeks in the Top 40, peaking at number 5. In May 2017 'Despacito' by **Luis Fonsi**, Daddy Yankee and **Justin Bieber** had the first of three spells at number 1, spending a total of eleven non-consecutive weeks at the top. It did even better in the US, topping the chart for sixteen weeks, equalling a record set by **Mariah Carey** and **Boyz II Men**'s 'One Sweet Day' in 1996.

IN OTHER NEWS . . . *NOW 77* (NOVEMBER 2010)

Channel 4 launched the game show *Celebrity Coach Trip*. Among those getting on board for the first series were David Van Day of **Dollar** and Cheryl Baker of **Bucks Fizz**.

Robbie Williams re-joined **Take That**, and the five-piece line-up released a new single, 'The Flood' (*NOW 78*), and their fifth number 1 album, *Progress*.

Tony Blackburn joined Radio 2, taking over from Dale Winton as host of *Pick of the Pops*.

12
NOW appearances

'Please Don't Let Me Go', *NOW 77*, November 2010

'Unpredictable', Olly Murs and Louisa Johnson, *NOW 97*, July 2017

OLLY MURS

Olly Murs first came to our attention in 2009 when he finished runner-up to **Joe McElderry** on the sixth series of *The X Factor*. He has since gone on to have eighteen Top 40 singles, including four number 1s. And – what a surprise – all four appear on *NOW*, starting with 'Please Don't Let Me Go', which topped the chart for one week in 2010 before it was replaced by **Alexandra Burke**'s third number 1, 'Start Without You'.

His second number 1 was 'Heart Skips a Beat' (*NOW 80*), a collaboration with cheeky Brighton chappies **Rizzle Kicks**, and the first of their five appearances. The writing team for this particular ditty included Samuel Preston, formerly of indie outfit **The Ordinary Boys**, who took their name from a 1988 album track by **Morrissey**. The Ordinary Boys made three appearances of their own, including their biggest hit, 'Boys Will Be Boys' (*NOW 63*), a number 3 in February 2006.

Olly's biggest hit to date is his third number 1, 'Dance with Me Tonight' (*NOW 81*). To launch the single he returned to *The X Factor*, where he performed with the cast of *The Muppets* (insert your own pun here). Sadly, this version wasn't released as a single, and The Muppets have yet to make a *NOW* appearance or add to their three Top 40 hits, the last of which was their version of 'Bohemian Rhapsody', a 2009 collaboration with **Queen**.

Olly had his fourth and most recent number 1 with 'Troublemaker' (*NOW 84*), featuring **Flo Rida**, the second of his five *NOW* collaborations and the only one of his chart toppers to last more than one week at the peak. *The X Factor* link continued in 2017 when his fifth collaboration was 'Unpredictable' (*NOW 97*), a duet with the 2015 winner **Louisa Johnson**, another Essex-born talent and, at seventeen, the youngest winner of the contest so far.

NOW 79 Did You Know . . .

Italian DJ **Alex Gaudino** made his third and most recent appearance with the 2011 number 6 'What a Feeling', featuring former **Destiny's Child** singer **Kelly Rowland**. It was Kelly's fifth appearance and also her most recent showing. Alex first came to our attention on *NOW 67* with 'Destination Calabria', featuring **Crystal Waters**. Crystal is best remembered for her 1991 number 2 'Gypsy Woman (La Da Dee)', beaten to the top by the second of **Cher**'s four number 1s, 'The Shoop Shoop Song (It's in His Kiss)', which spent five weeks at the summit.

NOW 98 Did You Know . . .

Chris Brown maintained his pattern of one song every second volume of *NOW* when he made his fourteenth appearance with 'Questions'. Hailing from Tappahannock, Virginia (population 2,386), Chris made his debut on *NOW 70* alongside **Jordin Sparks** with their 2008 number 3 'No Air', and a second song, 'With You'. The first of Chris's two number 1 singles came in 2012 with 'Turn Up the Music' (*NOW 82*), while the second was 'Freaky Friday', a 2018 collaboration with rapper Lil Dicky.

IN OTHER NEWS . . . NOW 79 (JULY 2011)

Amy Winehouse was found dead at her flat in North London. An inquest confirmed that the 27-year-old singer died as a result of alcohol poisoning.

After 168 years the *News of the World* ceased publication, following allegations that the newspaper's journalists hacked into the mobile phones of celebrities and politicians.

BBC TV launched *Pointless Celebrities*. Those who have appeared include H and Claire from **Steps**, Vernie and Easther from **Eternal**, and Sara and

13
NOW appearances

'The A Team',
NOW 79, July 2011

'Galway Girl',
NOW 98, November 2017

ED SHEERAN

10s

Extraordinary Ed has thirteen appearances so far, spread across nineteen volumes, or six-and-a-half years. By comparison it took our 'founding father' **Phil Collins** sixty-eight volumes, or twenty-four years, to reach the same level. And while Phil could boast of his additional appearances with **Genesis**, Ed can also point to two number 1s written for **Justin Bieber** – 'Love Yourself' (*NOW 93*), and 'Cold Water' (*NOW 95*) by **Major Lazer** featuring Justin Bieber and **MØ** – plus another chart topper for **One Direction**, and Top 10 hits for **Liam Payne** and **Rita Ora**.

Ed has broken so many records that, in March 2017, he practically broke the chart. All sixteen songs from his third album entered the Top 20, occupying nine of the Top 10 – only 'Something Just Like This' (*NOW 97*) by **The Chainsmokers** featuring **Coldplay** stopped his clean sweep. The previous best was set thirty-eight years before Ed was born, way back in 1953, when Frankie Laine had four of the Top 10. The chart rules have now been changed to allow for a maximum of three songs by one artist at any one time.

Ed scored his first number 1 in June 2014 with 'Sing' (*NOW 88*), co-written with **Pharrell Williams**, who has twenty-four writing credits on *NOW*, six of them number 1s. 'Thinking Out Loud' (*NOW 90*) took nineteen weeks to get to the top, where it stayed for just one week before returning five weeks later. In January 2018, Ed joined an exclusive club of artists who have knocked themselves off the top spot when 'River' by **Eminem** featuring Ed Sheeran replaced 'Perfect' at number 1. A feat only previously achieved by The Beatles, **John Lennon**, Elvis Presley and Justin Bieber.

Ed has appeared in both *Game of Thrones* and Australian soap opera *Home and Away*, and in 2016 he pulled off the tricky task of playing himself in the film *Bridget Jones's Baby*. In 2018 he added his name to the *NOW* alumni that have voiced characters in *The Simpsons*, a list that includes **Elton John**, **Chris Martin**, **Katy Perry** and **Lady Gaga**. In December 2017, Ed made time in his diary to add an MBE to his numerous awards, including three BRITs and four Grammys.

10s

NOW 80 Did You Know . . .

Following six appearances with **N-Dubz** – including their only number 1, 'Number 1' (*NOW 73*) – **Dappy** had his only solo chart-topper with 'No Regrets', not to be confused with **Robbie Williams**'s 1998 number 4 'No Regrets' (*NOW 41*). Dappy's other two appearances were 'Spaceship' (*NOW 79*), a collaboration with **Tinchy Stryder**, and 'Rockstar' (*NOW 81*), featuring rock star **Brian May**. Cousin **Tulisa** also managed a solo number 1 with 'Young' (*NOW 82*), though we await the first solo appearance by 'third Dub' Fazer.

NOW 93 Did You Know . . .

Many a tune that has graced *NOW* could qualify as an Ibiza anthem, yet the third-largest Balearic island only gets three mentions in *NOW* history. The first mention came courtesy of Dutch popsters **Vengaboys** and 'We're Going to Ibiza' (*NOW 44*), the fourth of their six appearances. Next up was **Swedish House Mafia** vs **Tinie Tempah** with 'Miami 2 Ibiza' (*NOW 77*), and our Balearic trio is completed by Detroit-born DJ **Mike Posner** with 'I Took a Pill in Ibiza' on *NOW 93*.

IN OTHER NEWS . . . *NOW 93* (MARCH 2016)

Record producer George Martin died, aged 90. In addition to his numerous accomplishments with The Beatles, he also produced **Elton John**'s 'Candle in the Wind 1997', the biggest-selling single in chart history.

Former England rugby international Ben Cohen won the third series of celebrity talent show *The Jump*. Competitors include Tom Parker of **The Wanted** and **Brian McFadden** of **Westlife**.

In Glasgow a fan was injured at an **Adele** concert when a chain fell from the overhead rigging.

11
NOW appearances
'What Makes You Beautiful',
NOW 80, November 2011

'History',
NOW 93, March 2016

ONE DIRECTION

With eighteen Top 40 hits and four number 1s (you guessed it – all on *NOW*), it is surprising to recall that One Direction finished third in series 7 of *The X Factor*, behind **Matt Cardle** (two appearances) and runner-up Rebecca Ferguson (none so far). As is the trend with all things *X*, 1D scored a number 1 with their first attempt, 'What Makes You Beautiful', while their second, 'Little Things' (*NOW 84*), had the big advantage of being co-written by **Ed Sheeran**.

In 2013, One Direction's third number 1, 'One Way or Another (Teenage Kicks)' (*NOW 84*), was the sixteenth of seventeen Comic Relief singles to make an appearance. 'One Way or Another' was originally a track on Blondie's 1978 album *Parallel Lines*. Never officially released as a single in the UK, it did creep in at the very bottom end of the chart when 1D aroused new interest. Released the same year, The Undertones' classic debut single 'Teenage Kicks' never made it any higher than number 31.

In 2015, **Zayn Malik** 'did a Robbie' and announced that he was leaving the band, though it failed to harm their prospects, as they landed their fourth number 1 with their next single, 'Drag Me Down' (*NOW 92*), taken from their fourth-consecutive number 1 album, *Made in the A.M.* Only their debut album failed to top that chart, denied by the third of **Rihanna**'s four number 1 albums, *Talk That Talk*. Shortly after the album hit the shelves the band announced that they were history and released their final Top 40 single, 'History' (*NOW 93*).

So far all the evidence suggests that the individual members will outstrip their collective efforts, with eleven solo appearances to date. With a head start Zayn leads the way with three appearances, including his debut number 1 'Pillowtalk' (*NOW 93*). **Liam Payne** also has three, though his best showing is the number 3 'Strip That Down' (*NOW 97*), featuring **Quavo**. **Louis Tomlinson** and **Niall Horan** have both managed two, though the only other number 1 so far is **Harry Styles**'s debut 'Sign of the Times' (also *NOW 97*).

10s

SIA

Australian singer and songwriter Sia Furler had her first Top 40 hit in 2000 with the Prokofiev-sampling number 10 'Taken for Granted', and made her *NOW* debut the following year as singer with **Zero 7** on their only Top 40 hit, 'Destiny' (*NOW 49*). She made her first appearance as Sia with the 2011 number 1 'Titanium', the first of three get togethers with **David Guetta** and one of her two appearances on *NOW 81*, along with 'Wild Ones' by **Flo Rida** featuring Sia.

Sia's second Guetta link up, 'She Wolf (Falling to Pieces)' (*NOW 83*), was co-written with frequent collaborator Chris Braide. He too is an old friend of *NOW*, gaining his first credit on **S Club 7**'s fourth number 1, 'Have You Ever' (*NOW 51*). The third, 'Bang My Head' (*NOW 93*), also featured American rapper **Fetty Wap**, while the list of collaborations is completed by 'Cheap Thrills' (*NOW 94*) with **Sean Paul**, and 'Dusk Till Dawn' (*NOW 98*) with former **One Direction** singer **Zayn Malik**. Although 'Elastic Heart' (*NOW 90*) is a genuine solo project, the song was originally written for the 2013 film *The Hunger Games: Catching Fire*, when it featured **The Weeknd** and **Diplo**.

Sia's list of appearances is completed by the Top 10 hit 'Chandelier' (*NOW 88*) and 'The Greatest' (*NOW 95*), though the *NOW* solo version differs slightly from the number 5 single, which features **Kendrick Lamar**. Elsewhere on *NOW* Sia has half-a-dozen songwriting credits that include Top 40 hits for **Rita Ora**, **Jessie J**, **Katy Perry** and **Camila Cabello**, plus number 1 singles for **Ne-Yo** – 'Let Me Love You (Until You Learn to Love Yourself)' (*NOW 83*) – and **Rihanna** – 'Diamonds' (*NOW 84*).

By our reckoning 'Titanium' was the fourteenth number 1 single by an Australian artist to feature on *NOW*, though it was knocked off the top of the chart by the fifteenth with 'Somebody That I Used to Know' (also *NOW 81*) by **Gotye** featuring **Kimbra**. Our list started way back on *NOW 1* with **Men at Work**'s 'Down Under', and was added to most recently by 'Problem' (*NOW 88*) by **Ariana Grande** featuring Sydney-born **Iggy Azalea**.

10s

NOW 81 Did You Know . . .

Jennifer Lopez made her most recent appearance as one of two featured vocalists on **will.i.am**'s 'T.H.E. (The Hardest Ever)', alongside **Mick Jagger**. Sadly *NOW* has only found room for four of J-Lo's twenty-three Top 40 hits, starting with 'Ain't It Funny' (*NOW 50*), followed by the 2007 number 11 'Do It Well' (*NOW 68*), which sampled 'Keep On Truckin'', by Eddie Kendricks, previously with **The Temptations**. Her quartet is completed by 'On the Floor' (*NOW 79*), written by and featuring **Pitbull**, and the third of Jennifer's three number 1s.

NOW 98 Did You Know . . .

'Wolves' by **Selena Gomez** featuring **Marshmello** is her eighth appearance, and one of thirteen Top 40 hits. Her best chart position to date is number 7, for 'It Ain't Me' (*NOW 96*), another collaboration, this time with **Kygo**. Her 2017 hit 'Bad Liar' (*NOW 97*) sampled Talking Heads' 1977 single 'Psycho Killer', providing one of three credits for their frontman **David Byrne**. In 1999 **Tom Jones** and **The Cardigans** covered Talking Heads' 'Burning Down the House' (*NOW 44*), while David's sole artist appearance was as vocalist on the 2002 number 2 'Lazy' (*NOW 51*) by **X-Press 2**.

IN OTHER NEWS . . . *NOW 81* (APRIL 2012)

At the thirty-second Golden Raspberry Awards, *Jack and Jill*, starring Adam Sandler, won in all ten categories, including Worst Supporting Actor for Al Pacino, who appeared as himself.

American TV host Dick Clark died, aged 82. His programme *American Bandstand* ran for thirty-seven years and gave early breaks to the likes of Jackson 5, Aerosmith and **Prince**.

Marcus Mumford, singer with **Mumford & Sons**, married actress Carey Mulligan.

9
NOW appearances

'Titanium', David Guetta featuring Sia, *NOW 81*, April 2012

'Dusk Till Dawn', Zayn featuring Sia, *NOW 98*, November 2017

NOW 81 Did You Know . . .

Alexandra Burke made her fourth and most recent appearance with 'Elephant', featuring **Erick Morillo**. This was Erick's first credit since 1996, when he made his fourth appearance as **Reel 2 Real** with 'Jazz It Up' (*NOW 34*). Alexandra famously made her first appearance with 'Hallelujah' (*NOW 72*), which spent three weeks at number 1 and has sold over 1.4 million copies. However, it remains the second-bestselling *X Factor* winner's single, trailing **James Arthur**'s 'Impossible' (*NOW 84*), with sales of 1.57 million at the time of writing.

NOW 98 Did You Know . . .

'Rockstar' gave **Post Malone** (aka Austin Richard Post) his second appearance and a first number 1 on both sides of the Atlantic. His collaboration with fellow rapper **21 Savage** is the third time we've had a variation on this song title, following 'Rock Star' (*NOW 69*) by **Nickelback** and 'RockStar' (*NOW 81*) by **Dappy** featuring **Brian May**. 'Rockstar' includes a credit for producer and songwriter Louis Bell, also responsible for another number 1 on *NOW 98*, 'Havana' by **Camila Cabello** featuring **Young Thug**.

15
NOW appearances

'Cannonball',
NOW 81, April 2012

'Reggaetón Lento',
CNCO and Little Mix,
NOW 98, July 2017

IN OTHER NEWS . . . NOW 98 (NOVEMBER 2017)

Actor and singer David Cassidy died, aged 67. In the seventies he starred in the musical comedy *The Partridge Family* and had two number 1 singles as a solo artist.

The seventeenth series of *I'm a Celebrity . . . Get Me Out of Here!* launched on TV. Contestants included singer Vanessa White of **The Saturdays** and eventual winner Georgia Toffolo from *Made in Chelsea*.

Noel Gallagher's High Flying Birds performed on *Later . . . with Jools Holland* with a band member 'playing' scissor as percussion. Brother **Liam Gallagher** responded by asking for a fan to peel potatoes at his upcoming gig.

LITTLE MIX

With over 200 weeks in the Top 40, Little Mix have spent longer at the upper end of the chart than any of our other girl groups, though they are a little way off matching **Spice Girls**' nine number 1s. Par for the course, *NOW* has all four of the Little Mix chart toppers, beginning with 'Cannonball', their reward for winning *The X Factor* in 2011. Putting aside post-**One Direction** solo efforts, the girls currently have the highest tally of appearances by any act to emerge from that particular show.

Their second number 1 came in September 2012 when 'Wings' replaced 'Bom Bom' (both *NOW 83*) by one-hit wonders **Sam and the Womp** at the summit. 'The Womp' includes Aaron Horn, son of

the great Trevor Horn, whose first credit was way back on *NOW 1*, where he co-wrote and produced **Malcolm McLaren**'s 'Double Dutch'. Little Mix's fourth appearance was 'Word Up!', originally a hit for **Cameo** on *NOW 8* and a 1999 number 13 for **Melanie G** (neé B) on *NOW 43*.

'Black Magic' (*NOW 91*) was the girls' third number 1 and is their biggest hit to date. The *High School Musical*-style video was filmed at the University of California, previously a location for *The O.C.* and *The Fresh Prince of Bel Air*. **The Fresh Prince**, along with **DJ Jazzy Jeff**, made his only appearance with the 1993 number 1 'Boom! Shake the Room' (*NOW 26*). Little Mix's fourth number 1 is 'Shout Out to

My Ex' (*NOW 95*), which, like 'Black Magic', spent three weeks at the top and in 2017 won a BRIT Award for Best British Single.

Five of Little Mix's appearances have been collaborations, including two number 6 singles – 'Secret Love Song' (*NOW 96*), featuring **Jason Derulo**, and 'Power' (*NOW 97*), featuring **Stormzy**. However, their most successful partnership is 'Reggaetón Lento' (*NOW 98*), with Latin American five-piece **CNCO**, which peaked at number 5. Like Little Mix, CNCO found fame via a reality TV show, winning the first series of Spanish-language singing competition, *La Banda*, a programme produced by **Ricky Martin**.

00s

RITA ORA

Naturally, Rita's first four number 1 singles are all on *NOW*, starting with two collaborations on *NOW 82* – 'R.I.P.' with **Tinie Tempah** and 'Hot Right Now' with **DJ Fresh**. 'R.I.P' is the result of a multinational effort, as Kosovo-born Rita used Canadian **Drake**'s song 'I'm Ready for You' as a starting point, with additional songwriting and production by the Norwegian Stargate team, and a sample of **Chase & Status**' remix of Nigerian singer Nneka's 2009 number 20 single 'Heartbeat'.

'Hot Right Now' seems an apt title, as Rita had three number 1 singles in 2012 – more than any other artist. Royalties from her third number 1, 'How We Do (Party)' (*NOW 83*), were spread thin across twelve songwriters as this song sampled 'Party and Bull' by The Notorious B.I.G., which in turn sampled 'I'll Be There' by Johnny Hammond and 'The Show' by Doug E. Fresh and the Get Fresh Crew. **Calvin Harris** doesn't have to share the royalties for Rita's fourth number 1,'I Will Never Let You Down' (*NOW 88*), with anyone else.

Rita made her eighth appearance with 'Poison' (*NOW 91*), co-written by **Kate Nash**, who made the first of her own appearances on *NOW 67* with the number 2 single 'Foundations'. Meanwhile, Rita's United Nations ploy continued on two number 4 collaborations, 'Black Widow' (*NOW 89*) with Australian **Iggy Azalea** and 'Lonely Together' with Swedish DJ **Avicii** (*NOW 98*). In February 2018 the Official Charts website reported that Rita had equalled the record for the most Top 10 singles by a British female artist, joining Shirley Bassey and Petula Clark on twelve each.

At the age of thirteen Rita appeared in the ITV drama *The Brief*, and more recently had roles in the films *Fifty Shades of Grey* and *Southpaw*. Something of a *NOW* nursery, Rita is a graduate of London's Sylvia Young Theatre School. They have also gifted us **Amy Winehouse**, **Billie Piper**, **Javine**, **Leona Lewis**, 75 per cent of **All Saints** (Melanie, Natalie and Nicole), 50 per cent of **Little Mix** (Jesy and Leigh-Anne) and 25 per cent each of **McFly** (Tom) and **Rixton** (Jake).

NOW 82 Did You Know . . .

Ben Drew, better known as **Plan B**, made his most recent appearance with 'ill Manors', marking the only *NOW* credit for Russian composer Dmitri Shostakovich, as elements of his Symphony No. 7 were included in the music. Plan B made his first appearance with Chase & Status on 'End Credits' (*NOW 74*), which – as the name implies – played over the end credits of Michael Caine's 2009 film *Harry Brown*. Of course, Michael was written into *NOW* history way back in 1984 when he provided guest vocals for **Madness'** second appearance 'Michael Caine' (*NOW 2*).

NOW 98 Did You Know . . .

Charli XCX made her sixth appearance with 'Boys', whose accompanying video had cameo appearances from *NOW* boys **Charlie Puth**, **G-Eazy** and **Ty Dolla $ign**. Charli had her first number 1 in July 2017 with 'I Love It', a collaboration with **Icona Pop** that ended the four-week run at the top for 'Blurred Lines' (both *NOW 85*) by **Robin Thicke** featuring **Pharrell**. Robin can't have been too upset as he chose to cover 'I Love It' for a 2013 Radio 1 *Live Lounge* session – and anyway, 'Blurred Lines' returned to number 1 two weeks later.

10s

IN OTHER NEWS . . . *NOW 82* (JULY 2012)

The opening ceremony for the 2012 Summer Olympic Games was held in East London. The music director was Rick Smith of **Underworld**.

Keyboard player Jon Lord died, aged 71. He was a founder member of rock giants Deep Purple and played in **Whitesnake** from 1978 to 1984.

Katy Perry and comedian Russell Brand divorced due to 'irreconcilable differences'.

12
NOW appearances

'R.I.P.', Rita Ora featuring Tinie Tempah, *NOW 82*, July 2012

'Lonely Together', Avicii featuring Rita Ora, *NOW 98*, November 2017

10s

NOW 84 Did You Know . . .

East London rapper **Devlin** made his third appearance with 'Rewind', a reworking of a 2009 song by American singer **Diane Birch**, who also featured on Devlin's recording. His first appearance, 'Runaway' (*NOW 78*), also saw the introduction of Manchester-born singer **Yasmin**, who returned with her first solo appearance, 'Finish Line', on *NOW 79*. Devlin's biggest hit to date is 'Watchtower' (*NOW 83*), his 2012 collaboration with **Ed Sheeran**. It samples Bob Dylan's 1968 song 'All Along the Watchtower', and the Jimi Hendrix cover version, providing the only *NOW* credit for the American guitar great.

NOW 99 Did You Know . . .

Another London rapper, **B Young** made his debut chart and *NOW* appearance with 'Jumanji'. It was co-written by 'B' (real name Bertan Jafer) with Lewis Jankel, who under the name **Shift K3y** made his own debut on *NOW 88* with the number 3 single 'Touch'. Lewis is also co-writer of 'Not Letting Go' (*NOW 91*), the 2007 number 1 for **Tinie Tempah** featuring **Jess Glynne**. Lewis's father is the great Chas Jankel, co-writer of Ian Dury and the Blockheads' 1978 number 1 'Hit Me with Your Rhythm Stick' and Quincy Jones's 1981 number 14 'Ai No Corrida'.

IN OTHER NEWS . . . *NOW 84* (MARCH 2013)

Justin Timberlake released his third consecutive number 1 solo album *The 20/20 Experience*, the bestselling album of 2013 in the USA.

The *Guardian* newspaper published a list of their fifty best-dressed people over fifty. It included **Bryan Ferry**, **Chrissie Hynde**, **Grace Jones** and **Paul Weller**.

Channel 4 launched the reality TV programme *Gogglebox*. Celebrity editions in aid of Stand Up to Cancer have featured **Example**, **Big Narstie** and **Liam Gallagher**.

11
NOW appearances

'Latch', Disclosure featuring Sam Smith, *NOW 84*, March 2013

'One Last Song', *NOW 99*, March 2018

SAM SMITH

And so to Sam, whose eleven appearances include all six of his number 1 singles, a total only bettered by six of the two-thousand-plus artists who have appeared on *NOW*. Sam and **Disclosure** made their chart and *NOW* debuts together with the 2012 number 11 'Latch', and have since paired up again for 'Omen' (*NOW 92*). Sam had his first number 1 with 'La La La' (*NOW 85*), a collaboration with **Naughty Boy**, who was making the third of his six appearances.

Sam had his second number 1 with 'Money on My Mind' (*NOW 87*), and his third – 'Stay with Me' – just two months later when it knocked 'Rather Be' (both *NOW 88*) by **Clean Bandit** featuring Jess Glynne off the top spot. Both 'Stay with Me' and 'Rather Be' were co-written by Jimmy Napes, aka James Napier, Sam's writing partner on nine of his eleven appearances. 'Stay with Me', which spent forty-five weeks in the Top 40, also includes a credit for the late Tom Petty, as it shares elements of his 1989 number 12 'I Won't Back Down'.

'Lay Me Down' (*NOW 90*) first charted in March 2014, when it peaked at number 46. Re-recorded and re-released in early 2015, it made number 15, though in March Sam released a third version in support of Comic Relief, this time sharing vocals with **John Legend**. Beginning mid-March 2015, there was a five-week spell when versions two and three were both in the Top 40. Later the same year, 'Writing's on the Wall' (*NOW 92*) became the first James Bond theme to reach number 1 (after fifty-two years of trying), and the second to win an Oscar for Best Original Song, after **Adele**'s 'Skyfall'.

In October 2005 Sam's debut album *In the Lonely Hour* was recognised by Guinness World Records for the Most Consecutive Weeks in the UK Top 10 Albums Chart, following a whopping sixty-nine-week stay, beating the sixty-three weeks set by **Emeli Sandé**'s debut *Our Version of Events*. Obviously anticipating that he would be our hundredth featured artist, Samuel Frederick Smith, born nine years after the first volume of *NOW That's What I Call Music* was released, allows us to bow out with his sixth number 1, 'Too Good at Goodbyes' (*NOW 98*) and 'One Last Song' (*NOW 99*).

10s

INDEX

First published in Great Britain in 2018 by Trapeze
an imprint of The Orion Publishing Group Ltd
Carmelite House, 50 Victoria Embankment
London EC4Y 0DZ

An Hachette UK Company

1 3 5 7 9 10 8 6 4 2

A CIP catalogue record for this book is
available from the British Library.

ISBN (Hardback): 978 1 409 17994 8
ISBN (eBook): 978 1 409 17995 5

Printed in China

www.orionbooks.co.uk

FSC
www.fsc.org

MIX
Paper from
responsible sources
FSC® C008047

Acknowledgements

Additional material written by Pete Selby.

All statistics in this book based on the first
ninety-nine volumes of *NOW That's What I Call Music*,
November 1983 to March 2018.

All chart positions courtesy of The Official Charts Company
and their indispensible website www.officialcharts.com

With thanks to:
Pete Duckworth, Steve Pritchard and Jenny Fisher
at *NOW* Music.

Friends at Sony Music, Universal Music, Warner Music,
BMG, Absolute Label Services, Pete Waterman at PWL
and Martin Talbot at Official Charts Company.

Anna, Marleigh and Steve at Trapeze / Orion.

Thank you 'Big Time' (Number 13, May 1987)
to Pete Selby, without whom none of this would
have been possible.